THE BUTTERICK
FABRIC HANDBOOK

THE Butterick FABRIC HANDBOOK

A Consumer's Guide to Fabrics for Clothing and Home Furnishings

**Edited by
Irene Cumming Kleeberg**

Published by
BUTTERICK PUBLISHING
A Division of American Can Company
New York, New York 10013

Editor
IRENE CUMMING KLEEBERG

Associate Editor
BARBARA WEILAND

Textile Consultant
DR. IAN HARDIN
Department of Consumer Affairs
Auburn University

Cover Photos Courtesy of
COTTON INCORPORATED
1370 Avenue of the Americas
New York, New York
and
BURLINGTON INDUSTRIES
Carpet Division
Valley Forge Industrial Park
Norristown, Pennsylvania

Copyright © 1975 by
BUTTERICK PUBLISHING
161 Sixth Avenue
New York, New York 10013

A Division of American Can

Library of Congress Catalog Card Number: 74-29071

Design by Bob Antler

First Printing, March 1975
Second Printing, July 1975
Third Printing, December 1975
Fourth Printing, June 1977

Contents

Introduction

Fabrics are a fact of life—something we take for granted and use everyday in our wearing apparel and in our homes. For thousands of years fabrics remained essentially the same. The first known fibers were the natural fibers—notably, cotton, linen, wool, and silk. They were the only fibers and they were supplemented with leather and furs. As a result, once you learned the characteristics of the natural fibers—how to care for them and what to expect from them—that was all you needed to know to be a good consumer. You knew that cotton would perform one way, silk another, wool another and linen still another. Within the last fifty years, however, this situation has altered radically and dramatically.

With the development of the first commercially feasible man-made fibers, fibers and fabrics have changed tremendously. Our expectations of how the final fabric should perform have also changed as we have become accustomed to certain characteristics of the man-made fabrics. Wrinkle-resistance is one of those characteristics. Because we are accustomed to this feature in polyester, for example, we have also come to expect it from the natural fibers as well. In addition, even though one may learn the basic characteristics of the man-made fibers, there can still be occasional surprises since production techniques may be slightly altered or completely changed at any stage of the manufacturing process. These changes may result in fiber or fabric variations with performance characteristics slightly different from the original.

WHAT HAPPENS—AND WHY

This handbook was written to help keep fabric "surprises" to a minimum. It is a comprehensive treatment of fibers and fabrics for you, the consumer, who uses them everyday. It explains how fibers and fabrics are made in down-to-earth terms to help you understand how to buy and care for fabric and for articles made of textile fibers—clothing, carpeting, draperies and other articles of home furnishings.

In the following pages you will find a discussion of the production of fibers, natural and man-made. However, if you need to find the characteristics of a particular fiber, look on the Fiber Properties Chart or in the dictionary section of this book.

The trademarking system can be pretty confusing to the consumer. Even more confusing is the fact that many trademarks are often used incorrectly as generic names. In textiles, a generic name is the name of a family of fibers of a similar chemical composition. Polyester, nylon, and acrylic are some generic fiber names. The trade name or trademark is the name used by a fiber producer to identify its own fibers. For example, Dacron is the trademark for a polyester fiber which is produced by DuPont. To help clear up the confusion, trademarks are listed in the dictionary section at the back of this book and are cross-referenced to their generic names. Under the generic entry, you will find the characteristics of the particular fiber that interests you. This information is also available in the Fiber Properties Chart.

Fabric care is an important part of any fabric's life story. In fact, it's so important that most countries, including the United States, require that very specific care information be provided to the consumer. In the United

States this information must be attached to the textile item. In the case of fabric purchased by the yard, this care information must be provided by the retail clerk, but you usually won't get it unless you ask for it specifically. The care of fabrics has become much more complicated with the man-made fibers so you will find a discussion of care techniques as well as a chart of the care labels currently in use in the United States with complete explanations for their meanings.

Since stains can happen to the best of us, you will want to know how to care for them as well. Not all stains can be removed, and not all stain removal methods work all the time, but the common stains and the removal methods that are most likely to work are included in a special Stain Removal Chart.

Since home furnishing items—rugs, carpets, bedding, towels, curtains, draperies, and upholstery—are almost always made of textiles, information that will help you in purchasing and caring for these items is also available in the handbook.

THE DICTIONARY SECTION

There is a definite need for a dictionary of fabric and fiber terms as a handy, ready reference for the person faced with a new or an unfamiliar term. The last section of *The Butterick Fabric Handbook* is such a dictionary listing the terms that we think consumers might encounter in purchasing and caring for textile items as well as those that relate to the production of fabric and their relationship to performance characteristics.

The dictionary is heavily cross-referenced so that you will be able to find the information you need even if you only know, for instance, a trademark. A complete index is also included in case you need to find information very quickly.

THE APPENDIX

The information and charts in the appendix of *The Butterick Fabric Handbook* are especially designed to help the home sewer make wise fabric and notions purchases. Included is information on choosing interfacings, a fabric width conversion chart, and a stretch gauge for determining fabric stretchability. In addition, a complete group of charts in the metric measurement system appears to help make the expected transition to this measuring system a little easier for the consumer. Of special interest is the Metric Measurement Chart for determining correct pattern size.

HOW TO USE THIS BOOK

Here then, in brief, is how *The Butterick Fabric Handbook* works. General principles are grouped into the individual chapters, so that if you want to know the general principles to take into account in buying rugs and carpets you would read the chapter on rugs and carpets. Much of this same material, although without as much detail, of course, is repeated in the charts which accompany the chapter—in the case of rugs and carpets, you would look at the Chart of Rug and Carpet Fibers. If, however, you merely want to know what the term "Aubusson rug" means, you would use the dictionary section for a quick answer.

The dictionary section of the handbook caused the greatest thought. We have tried to avoid both the overly technical terms and words that are self-explanatory. Where there has been a question, however, we have tried to provide more information than you may need rather than less.

Fabrics which have been out of fashion for years have a way of returning, which is why you'll find descriptions of some fabric types which may not always be available at a given point in time. Many traditional fabric names are used for fabrics that, strictly speaking, don't meet the dictionary definition. We give the traditional definition first and then go on to present day applications.

One feature of this dictionary which is unique is a pronunciation guide. The common pronunciation in the fabric industry in the United States is given and, where this differs from the correct pronunciation (as in the case of certain French terms), the correct pronunciation is also given. The history of various terms is given only in cases where the history will help you understand the meaning.

In preparing this book for your use, Butterick has been aware that the language of fibers and fabrics is very much a living language and as such is changing constantly as new terms arrive and old words take on new meanings. Our goal has been to give you the information you'll need to buy textile products with the confidence that you're making the right choice for the intended use and that once you take them home you'll know how to use them and care for them properly. We hope you will find *The Butterick Fabric Handbook* helpful as you make your way through the often confusing maze of fiber and fabric terminology.

1

Fiber-The Start of It All

Fabric starts with fiber which, after various treatments, becomes the yarn which becomes the fabric. Fibers are hair-like substances, usually very small in diameter. They are the fundamental units used in making textile yarns and fabrics. The basic characteristics of a fiber can be slightly altered, but never totally changed, which is why it's worth knowing the generic names of fibers and understanding their properties. This information will help you every time you see a particular fiber, whether you are purchasing home furnishings, clothing, or fabric by the yard. (Information on furs and leathers can be found in Chapter Three.)

THE NATURAL FIBERS

Until fairly recently, all fibers were natural fibers. The best-known natural fibers are cotton, linen, silk, and wool. Other natural fibers include jute (used in making burlap), hemp, ramie, and those used to make true barkcloth and tapa cloth, fabrics that show up in such places as the Pacific Islands.

After centuries during which only natural fibers were

1

known, scientists have recently (within the last 100 years) developed numerous man-made fibers, each with certain characteristics in common, but different enough to qualify them for specific, individual generic names.

GENERIC NAMES

The generic name is the name used for a specific type of fiber, and all fibers with the same generic name have similar characteristics.

Things get confusing only when we come to trademarks. Trademarks are the brand names, usually owned by individual fiber producers, for the various fibers. Polyester, for instance, is a generic name. Dacron is DuPont's trademark for its polyester fiber just as Trevira is Hoechst's trademark for its polyester. Fiber producers often have more than one trademark for the same generic fiber; these varying trademarks indicate some differences in the manufacturing of the fiber, such as a change in the cross-sectional shape of it.

The Textile Fiber Products Identification Act passed in 1959 requires that all textile products be labeled with fiber content in percentages and that the labels must include the generic name for the fiber as well as the name of the manufacturer or his registered identification number (trademarks are not required but can serve as identification). Unfortunately, this law isn't always followed. One of the major purposes of this law is to protect you, the consumer, through the enforcement of ethical practices. Look for this information each time you make a textile purchase.

RAW MATERIAL INTO FIBER

Raw materials become fibers in various ways.

The raw material of linen, for instance, is flax which comes from the flax plant. It is soaked in water or chemicals and then combed to separate the fibers. The flax is then spun (the fibers are twisted around each other and drawn out) to form yarn.

Man-made fibers start out as a substance which is

either put into solution or melted to the consistency of thick syrup. The fibers are produced by forcing this "syrup" through a spinneret—a device that looks very much like a shower head.

The resulting filaments can be any length at all and are hardened into filament fibers. Quite often various substances are added to the fiber solution before it is forced into filaments. These additives might include dye substances, a solution for another fiber, or a chemical which will change one or more of the characteristics of the fiber.

Man-made fiber characteristics can also be changed by changing the shape of the holes in the spinneret. Often the terms "trilobal" (three-sided) or "pentalobal" (five-sided) are used to describe some man-made fibers. This means the hole in the spinneret has three sides or five sides so the resulting fiber does, too. Trilobal fibers are silk-like while pentalobal fibers are bulkier, less shiny fibers. The usual reason for changing the shape of a fiber is to make a fiber more or less lustrous, or to help it hide dirt.

Many of the man-made fibers have certain characteristics in common. On the plus side, they generally tend to wrinkle less than natural fibers, need relatively little ironing (if care instructions are followed), and dry quickly. On the minus side, they may feel hot or clammy in wearing since the properties that make them dry quickly also make them less able to absorb moisture than natural fibers. Since all man-made fibers except rayon are heat-sensitive to varying degrees, pressing or ironing fabrics made of these fibers should be done at a low heat setting. Heat-sensitive fibers are called thermoplastic fibers because their shape changes when heat is applied. This characteristic can be an advantage in the manufacturing process. For example, pleats can be permanently heat-set in a fabric, a definite advantage to the consumer. By the same token, if care instructions are not followed and fabrics made of thermoplastic fibers are over-dried in an electric dryer, creases or wrinkles may be "set" and become difficult to remove in ironing or in garment alteration.

The man-made fibers can often be surface cleaned with a damp sponge—a boon in home furnishings—but ground-in stains and especially oily ones are difficult to remove. For more specific details on care techniques for the man-made fibers see the special chapter on fabric care.

The chart which follows is designed to guide you through the fiber maze by giving you the basic characteristics of each of the generic fibers. Some of the fibers listed are not now being made in the United States; they are included, however, for the sake of completeness as they could conceivably be produced at some time in this country.

FIBER PROPERTIES

Fiber Name	Trade Name (Owner)	Fabric Properties
acetate	Acele (DuPont) Avicolor (FMC Corp.) Celacloud (Celanese) Celanese (Celanese) Celaperm (Celanese) Chromspun (Eastman Kodak) Estron (Eastman Kodak) Estron SLR (Eastman Kodak) FMC (FMC Corp.) Loftura (Eastman Kodak) SayFR (FMC Corp.)	• Weaker than most other fibers. • Silk-like, lustrous appearance. • Some colors, unless solution dyed, fade from atmospheric fumes. • Resists mildew and moths; weakened by sunlight. • Melts under high heat.
acrylic	A-Acrilan (Monsanto) Acrilan (Monsanto) Bi-Loft (Monsanto) Creslan (American Cyanamid) Nandel (DuPont) Orlon (DuPont) Zefran (Dow Badische)	• Is weak when wet. • Good abrasion resistance. • Resembles wool, warm for its weight. • Accumulates static electricity. • Has good affinity for dyes; holds color well. • Resists mildew, moths, chemicals, sunlight. • Tends to pill.
anidex	Anim (Rohm and Haas) (not in current production)	• Elastic fiber providing stretch and recovery properties to fabrics. • Resists gas fading, oxidation, sunlight, oils, and chlorine bleach.
aramid	Kevlar (DuPont) Nomex (DuPont)	• High strength. • Low flammability; no melting point.

FIBER PROPERTIES *(Continued)*

Fiber Name	Trade Name (Owner)	Fabric Properties
		• Used almost exclusively for military and specialized civilian uses (such as bullet-proof vests).
azlon	No current production in the United States.	• Made from regenerated proteins from such natural sources such as milk • Imparts a soft feeling to fabrics when blended with other fibers.
cotton	Cotton is a natural fiber like wool, silk, and linen and has no trademarks in the way man-made fibers do. However, Sea Island, Egyptian and Pima cottons are regarded as higher quality cottons because they have a longer staple length, resulting in stronger, more lustrous yarns.	• Strong, comfortable, absorbent. • Absorbs dye well, especially if mercerized. • No build-up of static electricity. • Wrinkles in use and requires ironing after laundering unless special wrinkle-resistant finish is used. • Fabrics shrink unless treated; shrinkage is especially serious in cotton knits. • Affected by mildew and sunlight.
glass	Fiberglas (Ownes-Corning Fiberglas)	• Strong, resistant to heat, flame, most chemicals. • Does not absorb moisture, has little stretch. • Can be cleaned by rinsing or wiping with a cloth. • Fibers may break along folds.
lastrile	Lastrile fibers have never been commercially produced.	• A non-rubber elastic fiber.
linen	Linen is a natural fiber like cotton, silk, wool and has no trademarks in the way man-made fibers do. Terms such as Irish or Belgian linen, used as indications of quality, actually refer to where the linen is produced.	• Strong, durable fiber with natural luster. • Somewhat stiff. Garments of linen may show wear at edges. • Bright, and deep colors may run in washing. • Shrinks when washed unless treated.

FIBER PROPERTIES *(Continued)*

Fiber Name	Trade Name (Owner)	Fabric Properties
		• Wrinkles in wear and requires ironing after washing unless treated. • Does not lint, is not attractive to moths.
metallic	Lurex (Dow Badische Co.)	• Used almost entirely with other fibers and as decorative accents. • Non-tarnishing when coated with plastic. • Unaffected by salt or chlorinated water.
modacrylic	A-Acrilan (Monsanto) Acrilan (Monsanto) Dynel (Union Carbide) Elura (Monsanto) Kanekalon (Kanegafuchi Chemical) Orlon (DuPont) Sef (Monsanto) Verel (Eastman Kodak)	• A non-allergenic fur substitute. • An inexpensive substitute for human hair (used in wigs). • Lustrous. • Quick drying. • Flame resistant. • Good elasticity. • Tends to accumulate static electricity. • Extremely sensitive to heat; melts at a lower temperature than most fibers.
novoloid	Produced by Carborundum Company	• Resists flame, doesn't melt, shows little shrinkage on exposure to flame. • Resists acids and most alkalies. • Used primarily in protective clothing.
nylon	Actionwear (Monsanto) Anso (Allied Chemical) Antron (DuPont) Astroturf (Monsanto) Ayrlyn (Rohm and Haas) Beaunit Nylon (Beaunit Corp.) Blue "C" (Monsanto) Bodyfree (Allied Chemical) Cadon (Monsanto) Cantrece (DuPont) Caprolan (Allied Chemical) Captiva (Allied Chemical)	• Strong and elastic; resists abrasion. • Lustrous, dyes well but fades in sunlight. • Resists wrinkles, moths, mildew. • May pill. • Melts under high heat. • May be clammy and uncomfortable in warm, humid weather.

FIBER PROPERTIES *(Continued)*

Fiber Name	Trade Name (Owner)	Fabric Properties
	Cedilla (Fiber Industries, Inc., marketed by Celanese)	
	Celanese (Fiber Industries, Inc., marketed by Celanese)	
	Cordura (DuPont)	
	Courtaulds Nylon (Courtaulds)	
	Crepeset (American Enka)	
	Cumuloft (Monsanto)	
	Enka (American Enka)	
	Enkaloft (American Enka)	
	Enkalure (American Enka)	
	Enkalure II (American Enka)	
	Enkalure III (American Enka)	
	Enkasheer (American Enka)	
	Guaranteeth (Allied Chemical)	
	Monvelle (biconstituent nylon-spandex) (Monsanto)	
	Multisheer (American Enka)	
	Phillips 66 Nylon (Phillips Fibers)	
	Phillips 66 Nylon BCF (Phillips Fibers)	
	Qiana (DuPont)	
	Random-Set (Rohm and Haas)	
	Random-Tone (Rohm and Haas)	
	Shareen (Courtaulds)	
	Source (biconstituent nylon-polyester) (Allied Chemical)	
	Stria (American Enka)	
	Stryton (Phillips Fibers)	
	Super Bulk (American Enka)	
	Tango (Allied Chemical)	
	Twix (American Enka)	
	Ultron (Monsanto)	
	Variline (American Enka)	
	Zefran (Dow Badische)	
nytril	No current production in United States.	•Soft, resilient, non-pilling. •When produced, was used in blends as a wool substitute.

FIBER PROPERTIES *(Continued)*

Fiber Name	Trade Name (Owner)	Fabric Properties

olefin	Herculon (Hercules)
	Marvess (Phillips)
	Marvess III BCF (Phillips)
		•Strong, good bulk and
		  coverage.
		• Resists abrasion.
		• Fast drying.
		• Resists chemicals, mildew,
		  weather, soil.
		•Sensitive to heat.

polyester	Avlin (FMC Corp.)
	Blue "C" (Monsanto)
	Dacron (DuPont)
	Encron (American Enka)
	Encron MCS
	  (American Enka)
	Encron 8 (American Enka)
	Enka (American Enka)
	Esterweld
	  (American Cyanamid)
	Fiber 200 (FMC Corp.)
	Fortrel (Fiber Industries,
	  marketed by Celanese)
	Fortrel 7 (Fiber Industries,
	  marketed by Celanese)
	Golden Touch
	  (American Enka)
	Guaranteeth (Allied Chemical)
	Kodel (Eastman Kodak)
	Quintess (Phillips)
	Source (biconstituent
	  nylon-polyester)
	  (Allied Chemical)
	Spectran (Monsanto)
	Strialine (American Enka)
	Textura (Rohm and Haas)
	Trevira (Hoechst)
	Vycron (Beaunit)
	Zefran (Dow Badische)
		•Strong, resists wrinkles,
		  abrasion, stretching, and
		  shrinking.
		• Versatile.
		• Resists mildew and moths.
		•May pill and attract lint.
		•May be clammy and uncom-
		  fortable in warm, humid
		  weather.

rayon	Avicolor (FMC Corp.)
	Aviloc (FMC Corp.)
	Avril (FMC Corp.)
	Avril FR (FMC Corp.)
	Beau-Grip (Beaunit)
	Briglo (American Enka)
	Coloray (Courtaulds)
	Encel (American Enka)
		•Weaker than most fabrics, with
		  weakness increased when wet.
		•Soft, comfortable.
		•Dyes well, usually.
		•May shrink or stretch unless
		  treated.
		•Affected by sunlight.
		•High wet-modulus and high

FIBER PROPERTIES *(Continued)*

Fiber Name	Trade Name (Owner)	Fabric Properties
	Englo (American Enka) Enka (American Enka) Enkrome (American Enka) Fiber 40 (FMC) Fiber 700 (American Enka) Fibro (Courtaulds) Fibro DD (Courtaulds) Fibro FR (Courtaulds) FMC (FMC) I.T. (American Enka) Jetspun (American Enka) Kolorbon (American Enka) SayFR (FMC) Skyloft (American Enka) Softglo (American Enka) Super White (American Enka) Suprenka (American Enka) Suprenka Hi Mod (American Enka) Xena (Beaunit) Zantrel (American Enka) Zantrel 700 (American Enka)	tenacity rayons are stronger and are less likely to shrink than other rayons with the above characteristics.
saran		• Strong, flame resistant. • Resists common chemicals, sunlight, stains, mildew, and weather. • Tends to be stiff; softens at comparatively low temperature.
silk	Silk is a natural fiber like cotton, linen, and wool and has no trademarks in the way man-made fibers do. The International Silk Association is responsible for encouraging the use of silk fibers and fabrics.	• Strong, absorbent. • Luxurious, lustrous fiber. • Takes dye well but colors may run or change with age, harsh soap, and high temperature. • Resists mildew and moths. • Weakened by sunlight and perspiration. • Water spots (stains).
spandex	Lycra (DuPont) Monvelle (biconstituent nylon-spandex) (Monsanto)	• Non-rubber elastic fiber, used in blends. • Strong; good stretch and recovery; light in weight for its elasticity. • Damaged by chlorine bleach, may be affected by heat.

FIBER PROPERTIES *(Continued)*

Fiber Name	Trade Name (Owner)	Fabric Properties
triacetate	Arnel (Celanese)	• A refinement of acetate (see acetate entry). • Can be ironed at higher temperature than acetate. • Resists shrinkage, wrinkles, fading.
vinal	No trademarks in use.	• May be referred to as polyvinyl alcohol fiber. • Highly resistant to chemicals. • Softens at low temperatures.
vinyon		• Occasionally referred to as polyvinyl chloride fibers or vinyl. • Softens at a fairly low temperature but resists chemicals. • Commonly used in bonding nonwovens.
wool	The Woolmark identifies 100% wool fabrics; The Woolblendmark identifies blends of wool with other fibers.	• Strong, resilient, warm. • Takes color well. • Shrinks; attracts moths unless treated.

TESTING FABRICS FOR FIBER CONTENT

The following tests are simple enough to do at home and are fairly reliable. In order to really test fabrics for fiber content, especially today when many fabrics are made of blends and mixtures of several different fibers, it would be necessary to view the fibers through a microscope and also to make tests using some chemicals which are too dangerous for home use. Blends cannot be identified by any burning test.

Therefore, we have limited this chart to the burn test for fiber content and the acetone test for acetate. Be careful with both. Snip a small piece of fabric or ravel several yarns from a place where it will not affect the item and make the test on that. These tests destroy the fiber you are testing.

Burn tests are dramatic because they involve fire. Make burn tests over the kitchen sink and hold the fiber with tongs rather than your fingers. Ignite samples with a match.

FIBERS AND THEIR REACTIONS TO FLAME

Fiber	Reaction to Flame and Results
Cellulosic Fibers (Cotton, Linen, Rayon)	Burns rapidly with a yellow flame and continues to glow after it is removed from the flame. Smells like burning paper and leaves a soft, gray ash.
Protein Fibers (Silk, Wool)	Burns slowly, sizzling and curling away from the flame. Sometimes self-extinguishing when removed from the flame. Smells like burning hair or feathers and leaves a crushable black ash.
Acetate	Burns and melts while in the flame and after removal from the flame. Leaves a hard, brittle, black bead. May smell like vinegar when burning.
Acrylic	Burns and melts while in the flame and after removal from the flame. Burning leaves a hard, brittle, black bead.
Modacrylic	Shrinks away from the flame; then, burns very slowly and melts. Self-extinguishing when removed from the flame. Burning leaves a hard, brittle, black bead.
Nylon	Shrinks away from the flame; then, burns slowly and melts. Usually self-extinguishing when removed from the flame. Smells like celery and leaves a hard gray bead.
Olefin	Shrinks away from the flame; then, burns and melts. Self-extinguishing when removed from the flame. Burning leaves a hard tan bead. May smell like a candle burning.
Polyester	Shrinks away from the flame; then, burns slowly and melts giving off black smoke. Usually self-extinguishing when removed from the flame. Smells slightly sweet and leaves a hard black bead.
Glass	Does not burn.

Test for acetate by placing a small piece of fabric or a few yarns in a dish of acetone (nail polish remover). Acetate will disintegrate leaving, at most, only dye behind.

2

From Fiber to Fabric

Fabrics are made in three ways—they are knit, woven, or nonwoven. In the fabric industry, the word knit is sometimes used to include, for instance, crochet, and the inexact term nonwoven means anything that isn't knit as well as anything that isn't woven. However, the actual making of the fabric by one of these methods is almost the end of the story. First, the fiber is made into yarn which is processed and then usually dyed before being manufactured into the actual finished fabric.

YARN PROCESSING

Yarn processing is a big business in the United States, but relatively little is known about it by the general public. One of the oldest and best known yarn processes, mercerization, is a treatment for cotton yarn or fabric. Mercerization is a way of treating cotton to make it more lustrous, easier to dye, and stronger.

Today, with man-made fibers becoming more and more important, most of the yarn-processing techniques are used on these fibers. Among the most important are those that add texture to otherwise smooth, man-made filaments. Texturizing techniques change bundles of smooth, flat filament yarns to crimped or twisted yarns by taking advantage of the thermoplastic nature of most man-made fibers (thermoplastic fibers change shape when heat is applied). Fabrics made from textured yarns have greater wrinkle resistance than those made from untextured yarns, more natural "give" (they stretch slightly), more surface interest, and slightly more porosity—they "breathe" a little better, lessening somewhat, the clamminess associated with some of the synthetics.

Although you may see references to yarn processes on hangtags occasionally, unless you've had experience with fabric made from such yarns the information won't be of much value. Fabrics can also be changed by applying certain finishes at a later stage. This means that not all fabrics made from yarns processed in the same way will have the same performance characteristics. (See the section on Fabric Finishing in this chapter.)

Different types of yarns are often used together in making fabrics. Textured and untextured yarns of the same fiber will often be used for a fashion look or to make a more economical fabric (the untextured are usually less expensive).

SPUN MAN-MADE YARNS

Although man-made fibers come in long filaments, they can be chopped into shorter lengths, called staple, so that they are very much like the natural fibers (cotton, wool, and linen, but not silk) which are also staple lengths. Once chopped, they are then spun (twisted) into yarns, just as the natural fibers are spun. The resulting fabrics often have a more natural feeling and a better resistance to snagging than fabrics made from filament yarns.

On the other hand, spun man-made yarns have a tendency to pill (form little balls of fiber on the surface); this can be prevented or at least reduced in the finishing process.

YARN DYEING

Once the yarn has been processed you're a little closer to the final fabric. A man-made yarn may have been dyed before it became fiber (this is called solution or dope dyeing) and means the coloring was added to the fiber when it was in its thick syrup state. There are definite advantages to dyeing at this stage of fiber production, primarily color retention and clarity of color.

However, many yarns are not dyed in the dope. Dyeing at the pre-fiber stage means being very sure that a color will sell. If it doesn't, it can prove an expensive mistake for the manufacturer.

Many fibers are yarn dyed. Usually, this means the fibers are dyed after being made into yarn and wound onto spools. Space dyeing, however, is a method of dyeing yarn before it is wound onto spools. Space dyeing involves dyeing the strand of yarn different colors by putting it into variously colored dyes.

Once the yarn is dyed, it is woven or knitted into fabrics. Yarn dyeing is considered, by and large, a better method of dyeing than piece dyeing (we'll talk about that in a minute) and a premium is often paid for yarn dyed fabrics. Yarn dyed is a term you may find on labels or in advertising.

PIECE DYEING

Piece dyeing is what the term implies—the fabric is made up, then dyed "in the piece" of fabric. The process is similar to that used in yarn dyeing, but because the fabric is already made the color doesn't penetrate the yarns quite as well as it does in yarn dyeing.

Cross dyeing is a form of piece dyeing. The term is used when a fabric made of two or more different fibers (or two or more different types of the same fiber) is dyed and, when dyed, each fiber takes the dye in a different way. Yarns spun from a combination of polyester, rayon, and silk fiber, for instance, can have a soft, misty, heathery appearance when dyed in the same dye bath since each fiber reacts to the dye differently. In its most sophisticated form, cross dyeing presents a number of interesting possibilities. For example, a fabric can be made using polyester yarns for the background and rayon yarns for the design. When the fabric is piece dyed, the design will appear in one color or shade and the background in another. This process is only of minor interest to the consumer, but you may see the term occasionally and should know what it means.

MAKING THE FABRIC

No one knows what the oldest method of textile production was, although someone in the knitting business once stated it was knitting, and Joseph's "Coat of Many Colors" was, indeed, knitted.

At its simplest, in knitting, one yarn is used to make a fabric or a garment which grows longer as rows of loops are formed to lock into the previous loops while in weaving, a yarn passes over and under another yarn in alternating rows. Before he starts, a weaver must decide the final length of the fabric he will make because weaving is done on a loom. In theory, knitting could continue forever.

In commercial practice, knitting machines are much more elaborate than the two needles and single yarn used by the hand knitter. These machines have many needles and many "feeds" (spools of yarn coming down to be knitted). Each needle takes a stitch as the yarn goes past it.

TYPES OF KNITS

There are several types of knits which the consumer may see in stores, each one with certain characteristics in common. These characteristics include degree of stretch and the tendency—or lack of it—to run (come unknitted).

Weft knitting is a way of knitting in which one strand of yarn runs across forming a horizontal row of interlocked loops. Weft knitting is mechanized hand knitting. Weft knitting can be made either on a circular machine (producing a tubular fabric) or a flat machine. With flat machines, the number of stitches can be increased or decreased to shape the finished fabric, as in stockings with seams. The resulting shaped product is described as being "full-fashioned."

Single knits are made on weft knitting machines; they have a right and a wrong side and may tend to stretch out of shape. Double knits, also made on a weft machine, are usually very stable fabrics. They are knitted with two needles to form a single layer of fabric. You can identify them easily because they appear the same on both front and back with rows of fine ribs in the lengthwise direction. Another type of weft knit, the interlock knit has a smooth surface on both sides and a very fine rib like the double knit. The edges of an interlock knit, however, tend to run so seams should be finished in some way to prevent this.

In contrast to weft knits, warp knits are knit on machines where interlocking loops are formed in the lengthwise direction. On weft knits the loops are formed on the width or crosswise of the fabric.

Tricot is probably one of the most familiar warp knit constructions; its most popular use is for women's underwear and it has recently moved into the fashion picture as outerwear. Tricot has vertical ribs on the front and crosswise ribs on the back. It won't run and doesn't ravel, but raw, cut edges may have a tendency to curl. In addition to underwear and shirting fabrics, such fabrics as pile and velour knits are made with tricot constructions.

Raschel knits are made on the raschel knitting machine, a tremendously versatile machine which can make all kinds of things from heavy crochet-like knits to glamorous net stockings. Curtains and laces are often made on raschel machines.

Both weft and warp knits have more stretch than woven fabrics except for fabrics woven with stretch yarns. Usually knits have more stretch in the width or crosswise directions than in the lengthwise direction of the fabric.

TYPES OF WOVENS

In weaving, two threads meet at right angles to each other and are joined by one going over and under the other. There are tremendous variations possible on this basic pattern, of course.

The threads that are put down on the loom first in weaving, the ones that determine the length of the finished fabric, are called the warp threads. The ones that go over and under the warp threads are called the filling (or weft or woof) threads. The lengthwise grain, or straight of a fabric, is parallel to the warp threads; the crosswise grain is parallel to the filling threads.

Neither the lengthwise nor the crosswise grain have any noticeable stretch in a woven garment, but the bias—the diagonal between the warp and the filling threads—does. Woven fabrics are permanently off-grain when a design is printed on the fabric so it doesn't run evenly along the threads or when the fabric has been finished (more on finishing is coming up) so the threads are not perpendicular to each other and no amount of steaming, tugging, or pulling can make them so.

There are three basic weaving patterns and an almost infinite number of variations on these patterns. The three weaves are plain weave, twill weave, and satin weave.

Plain weave, also called tabby, is the basic method of weaving. The filling yarn goes over one warp yarn and under the next repeating this pattern across the width of the fabric. Rows alternate. In the next row, the filling will pass under all warps it passed over in the previous row and over all warps it passed under in the previous row. The pattern will be one over, one under in both warp and filling directions.

In the twill weave, the finished fabric has a distinct diagonal rib on its surface. As the fabric is woven the filling yarn goes over two or more of the warp yarns then under one or more warp yarns. The pattern progresses up and to the left or up and to the right in each successive row.

Satin weave, the third basic weave, is somewhat similar to twill weave but the yarns pass over several threads before going under a yarn. Satin has a lustrous appearance because as the yarn floats over several yarns the light catches on the float yarn. This appearance is associated with the weave and this fabric name.

PATTERNS IN WEAVING AND KNITTING

Both woven and knitted fabrics would be very dull if their patterns couldn't be changed. We've already discussed the three most common patterns in wovens.

In knits, the pattern is changed by changing the placement of the smooth (the "knitted" stitch) and the bumpy ("purl") stitch. Tremendous pattern variety can be achieved with combinations of these stitches.

No discussion of fabrics, however, would be complete if we didn't mention the word "jacquard." The jacquard machine, named for its inventor, makes it possible to produce intricate patterns mechanically. At its simplest, a jacquard machine works very much like a player piano or a music box—holes are punched into a piece of paper, cardboard, or plastic. Each hole tells one part of the machine what to do—take this stitch and omit the next one, or take two stitches, or something like that—to create a pattern. The term "jacquard" is frequently used in describing fabrics to the consumer; all it really says is that the fabric has a knitted or woven pattern.

NONWOVEN FABRICS

The third category of fabrics that exists is called the "nonwovens." This is a misnomer in a sense since knits aren't woven, but it is used to refer to all fabrics which are neither knit nor woven.

Felt is a common example of a nonwoven fabric. Fibers are placed together and, through a combination of moisture, heat, and mechanical action, a matted or "felted" fabric is produced.

Some nonwovens are made with thin layers of glue between the fibers to join them together and there is talk of nonwoven textile-like fabrics which don't even begin with fiber—but these are a product of the future.

CHANGING FABRIC COLOR

So far we haven't discussed changing the color of a fabric in any depth.

In addition to the basic commercial dyeing processes we mentioned earlier, there are also various methods which were important in the past but which are today used only in hand-dyed fabrics.

One of these methods is tie dyeing. In tie dyeing, bunches of the fabric are twisted and tied tightly, usually with string, and then immersed in the dye. These bunches may be arranged at random on the fabric or may be spaced to form a pattern. The dye does not penetrate the fabric where it is tied and this forms the design on the colored fabric. Batik is an Indonesian method of dyeing in which wax is placed on parts of the fabric where the dye is not wanted. The wax cracks during the dyeing process which may produce a random veined effect in the design. Both these hand methods of dyeing are imitated commercially— but by printing, rather than dyeing, in most cases.

You may see the term "vat dye" on labels or in advertising. This refers to the dyes used rather than the dyeing method, which is piece dying. The color in vat dyes develops after they are inside the fiber. Since the developed dye is water-insoluble, vat dyes are frequently more colorfast than other dyes.

PRINTING FABRICS

Despite the many different dyeing methods and the variety of effects they produce, not all fabrics are dyed to achieve color. Fabrics are also printed to add color as well as interest and design. Printed fabrics vary tremendously in quality, probably more than dyed fabrics do.

Any printing process can be used to produce excellent printed fabrics, but some processes have come to have a reputation for rather sloppy results (roller printing, for instance) while others have a reputation for quality results (screen printing).

Roller printing and screen printing are the two methods most commonly mentioned in descriptions for the consumer. Other types of printing will be discussed under the entry for "printing" in the dictionary section.

To understand how most printing works, remember block printing—you probably learned it at some time in art class. A block, made of linoleum, wood, or other material, is cut so that the design to be printed is left raised on the block and the remainder of the block is cut away. Ink is put on the surface of the block, then the block is placed by hand on the material being printed. Block printing is rarely used commercially on fabrics since each color requires a separate block and the work is tedious and time-consuming. Block printing is more commonly used today by hand craftsmen.

Roller printing, so important that it has several names, including calender, cylinder, and direct printing, is similar in concept to block printing. A design is etched onto a roller through which the fabric, usually pre-bleached, is fed. For each color a different roller is used, and the fabric must move through each of the different rollers. This is often (not always) a high speed process and produces an economical product. It is also one where it is possible for the fabric to be printed off-grain quite easily and sometimes the color looks blurred—technically it is "out of register." These failings are not part of the process, however, and some fine roller-printed fabrics are made with more than a dozen separate rollers and colors. The quality of roller printing is determined by the skill of the engraver, who etches the design on the roller, and the care taken in feeding the fabric through the rollers. Probably the majority of printed fabrics on the market today are roller-printed.

Screen printing is considered one of the best printing methods, and fabrics are often identified as being screen printed. Like roller printing, quality in screen printing can vary enormously, but usually it tends to be of higher quality.

Usually, a nylon fabric screen is made with some design areas open and others closed. The screen is placed over the fabric to be printed and the color pigment is poured onto the screen and worked through the open sections of the screen and into the fabric. A different screen is needed for each color and the work proceeds rather slowly.

Heat transfer printing is a process which is quite new. Described simply, the desired color and patterns are placed on a special paper. The paper is placed on the fabric and, through the use of heat, the color and pattern moves from the paper to the fabric. Quite complicated designs with a good deal of depth of color can be produced more economically by using heat transfer printing than by other methods giving similar results.

FABRIC FINISHING

Coloring the fabric in one way or another is only one of the steps on the way to the final product. When the fabric has been manufactured and colored, it is quite unattractive. It usually feels rough to the touch, is wrinkled and uneven in width and length. Finishing is done to this fabric to make it more acceptable and attractive.

Among the most important of the finishing processes is that called heat setting when it's applied to synthetics, crabbing when it's applied to wools, and tentering when it's applied to other fabrics. Heat setting, however, is so explanatory that it can be used interchangeably with the other terms. During heat setting the fabric is stretched to its desired width and length. Then it is passed through high heat and, often, moisture, and then dried. This gives it its final shape.

Various things can be added to the fabric before or after heat setting. To produce a moiré pattern (watermark) on a fabric, for instance, the finishing process might include passing the fabric through rollers (called calenders) to give it this pattern. (See entry for finishing and moiré in dictionary section.)

A resin might be added to the fabric to improve, for instance, its ability to hold a press or crease. In the past, starch was often added to fabrics at the finishing stage to give them the appearance of being of a higher quality than they actually were. The starch, also called sizing, came out at the first washing. Starching is rarely used now. Almost all finishes on fabrics today are permanent. A few finishes, however, are added to some fabrics to make them easier for clothing manufacturers to handle. These include finishes added to denim used for blue jeans, which is why jeans are stiff when new.

Surfaces of fabrics can be changed in the finishing. When napped fabrics are in style, for instance, the fabric may be passed through a machine which gives it the soft, somewhat hairy appearance of a napped fabric. (See entry for nap in the dictionary section.)

Other finishing steps will control shrinkage, provide water repellency or stain repellency (important in home furnishings), increase flame resistance, or provide greater absorbency. Many finishes for man-made fabrics are designed to cut down on their plastic feeling by making them softer to the touch. For information on specific finishes, see the dictionary entries.

COMMON FABRIC TYPES AND HOW TO RECOGNIZE THEM

Fabric Name	Construction	Description
basket weave	woven	In basket weave, pairs of warp yarns pass over pairs of filling yarns in a plain weave. This gives a more open, slightly coarser looking fabric than does conventional plain weave with its single yarn.
bonded	bonded	Bonding is the term used for the joining together of layers of fiber, usually through the use of glue or the melting of some of the fibers. Nonwoven fabrics are produced this way. The term is occasionally used as a synonym for laminated. See laminate, below.
braid	braided	Braided fabrics are formed by interlacing three or more strips of fabric or yarns to form a flat or tubular, usually narrow, length of fabric. Braided rugs are made from strips of braid which are subsequently joined together.
dobby weave	woven	A dobby weave is a small geometrically patterned weave made with a special loom attachment, somewhat similar to a jacquard but less complicated and resulting in a smaller design. The pattern is usually raised. A typical dobby weave is piqué. See piqué in dictionary section.
double knit	knit	Fabric knit of two interlocking layers which cannot be separated. Except when the double knit is made with a pattern, the face and back are identical.
felt	felted	Felt is the term used to describe fabrics which are made from fibers which are joined by heat, moisture, and mechanical action. Wool is the traditional felted fabric and wool is usually required in mixtures of other fibers to form the bond that results in a felt.
herringbone	woven	Herringbone is a twill weave in which the lines of the twill change direction, forming a pattern of V's. This weave is often described as a "broken twill" weave.
jacquard	knit or woven	Jacquard is the name of an attachment for a knitting or weaving machine which enables the machine to make complicated

COMMON FABRIC TYPES AND HOW TO RECOGNIZE THEM
(Continued)

Fabric Name	Construction	Description
		and quite large patterns in the course of weaving or knitting the fabric itself. Damask is an example of a woven jacquard; many patterned double knits are made on machines with jacquard attachments.
laminate	laminated	Laminating is a method of joining two different fabrics together by use of a fusing material which melts and forms a bond between the two fabrics. Synthetic foam is often laminated to fabric in home furnishings fabrics. The permanency of a laminate depends on the quality of the manufacturing process.
leno	woven	An open, somewhat lace-like fabric made when warp yarn pairs are crossed over each other and around the filling yarn in a figure 8. The airy quality of leno weaves makes them especially popular in curtains and summer dresses. A special attachment for the loom is required for this weave.
net	netted	Net is produced on machines that imitate handwork which originally produced this fabric. Net has geometrically shaped holes outlined by yarn. It ranges from the sheerest and lightest of weights used for bridal tulle to heavy fishnet, used for decorative as well as industrial purposes. Net is often the ground on which lace is worked.
pattern knits	knit	Pattern knits are made on weft knitting machines with the dropping, adding, re-arranging, and crossing of various stitches— as in hand knitting—to create intricate designs.
pile	woven or knit	Pile is a fabric in which yarns are left on the surface of the fabric in either loops (as in the case of terry cloth) or clipped to form a hair-like surface (as in the case of velvets and many rugs). See also dictionary entry for nap.
plain knit	knit	Plain knit is a descriptive term for a flat-surfaced, even design made on a knitting machine. It is the basic pattern in both

COMMON FABRIC TYPES AND HOW TO RECOGNIZE THEM
(Continued)

Fabric Name	Construction	Description
		hand knitting (when it is called stockinette stitch) and machine knitting. The face of the fabric is smooth and the reverse has visible loops.
plain weave	woven	Plain weave is the simplest weave, in which the filling threads pass over and under the warp threads in alternating rows.
purl knit	knit	Purl knit describes alternating rows of knit and purl stitches (purl is the reverse of a plain knit fabric) forming a pattern design which has considerable stretch in the crosswise direction.
raschel knit	knit	Raschel knits are made on the raschel machine, a warp knitting machine which can use bulky yarns to form designs which imitate crochet or net.
rib knit	knit	Rib knit, a popular basic knitting pattern, is similar in appearance to one of the most important hand-knitting patterns. Rib knitting consists of alternate plain and purl stitches (the reverse of a plain knit with loops showing). Rib knit fabrics have a snugger fit than plain knit, and ribbing is frequently used at wrists, waists, and necklines of plain or patterned knitted garments.
rib weave	woven	A rib weave is a plain weave in which the yarns in either the warp or the filling direction are thicker or further apart than those in the other direction, producing a regularly furrowed bumpy surface. Grosgrain and faille are common examples of rib weave fabrics.
satin weave	woven	Satin weave is one of the basic weaves. It is characterized by warp floats, warp yarns which "float" or pass over four or more filling yarns before passing under a filling yarn. Sateen weave is similar to satin but in sateen the filling floats over warp threads. Satin and sateen weaves usually result in fabrics with a smooth lustrous surface.
sewing-knitting	sewing-knitting	Sewing-knitting is the rather inadequate term which is used to describe one of the newest developments in the manufacture of

COMMON FABRIC TYPES AND HOW TO RECOGNIZE THEM
(Continued)

Fabric Name	Construction	Description
		fabrics. On the Malimo sewing-knitting machine, probably the best-known type in America, the warp threads are placed on top of the filling threads. They are then stitched in place with a third thread.
single knit	knit	Single knit, made on a weft knitting machine, is identical to plain knit. See entry for plain knit.
stable knit	knit	Stable knit is a descriptive term referring to any knit which is unlikely to stretch excessively. Double knits are stable knits.
sweater knit	knit	Sweater knit is a loose descriptive term used for weft knit fabrics, usually single rather than double knit, which resemble hand-knit fabrics. Sweater knits are usually very stretchy.
stretchable knit	knit	Stretchable knit is a descriptive term for a knit which has a good deal of give. Most double knits would not be considered stretchable knits; most single knits are stretchable.
tabby	woven	Tabby is another term for plain weave. See the entry for plain weave.
tricot	knit	Tricot is a warp knitted fabric which can be recognized by a vertical rib on the right side and a horizontal rib on the wrong side. Traditionally, tricot was used for underwear, but recently it has been made in heavier yarns with greater opacity for outer clothing. It is usually described in such cases as simply a "warp knit." See entry for opacity in dictionary.
warp knit	knit	A warp knit is made on a machine in which parallel yarns run lengthwise and are locked into a series of loops. Warp knit fabrics have a good deal of stretch in the crosswise direction.
weft knit	knit	A weft knit is made on a machine which forms loops in a circular direction and has one continuous thread running across the fabric.

3

The Fur and Leather Story

Furs and leathers are probably man's oldest types of clothing. Fur is an animal's coat and is usually shorter and thicker than hair. Different animals produce different types of furs, from the sleekness of mink to the shagginess of fox. Furs move in and out of fashion over the years. Although some furs are still trapped, many are bred in captivity specifically for the fur industry. Recent developments in man-made fibers have enabled manufacturers to almost match real furs in appearance and warmth. Furs are also often imitated in cloth.

Leather is the hide of an animal with the fur removed. It can be finished in a variety of ways similar to some of the finishing processes used on cloth—embossing, glazing, and brushing to raise a nap, for instance. Imitations of leathers are also widely available.

Recently, public reaction against the exploitation of animals has led to laws against the hunting, sale, or importation of certain animals for their furs or hides. Charts of the best known furs and leathers follow the section on care of furs and leather.

CARE OF FUR AND LEATHER

Both fur and leather are harmed if exposed to excessive heat while wet. If either becomes wet, it should be dried away from radiators or open fires.

Suedes and leathers can be kept fairly clean by brushing with a terry towel. Gum erasers and emery boards can also remove small spots. Some smooth and grain leathers can be cleaned with a damp cloth and saddle soap (not detergent) but professional cleaning is safer.

Don't put leathers or furs in plastic storage bags—they need to breathe. Although there are methods for cleaning both furs and leathers at home, much better and surer results are usually obtained through professional cleaning.

FUR CHART

Name of Fur	Description
astrakhan	See Persian lamb.
beaver	Beaver is warm, soft, and hard-wearing. It is naturally brown, but may be dyed.
broadtail	Broadtail is a form of lamb fur, with a flat curled look. It is usually black.
caracul	See Persian lamb.
chinchilla	Chinchilla is a soft, usually bluish-white fur with dark tips. It is one of the most expensive furs.
coney	See rabbit.
ermine	Ermine is a thick, white, lustrous fur. It is usually dyed other colors except when used for trimming. Ermine is the traditional royal fur.
fox	Fox is a soft, long-haired fur, which is dyed or bred in many colors. It is made into coats and often used for trimming.
karakul	See Persian lamb.
leopard	Leopard fur has small dark irregular spots on a tan ground. This is one of the shortest haired furs.
lynx	Lynx is a soft, long-haired black fur with spots that range in color from gray to beige. It is often used for trimming.
marten	Soft, thick marten fur is available under various names including stone marten.

FUR CHART *(Continued)*

Name of Fur	Description
mink	One of the most popular furs, mink is both wild and (more usually) ranch bred. Breeding techniques have resulted in many different mink colors, resulting from genetic changes in the minks. These are called mutations from the genetic term for such changes. Mink is soft and glossy and very expensive.
monkey	Monkey fur is long, silky, and black, giving the effect of fringe.
nutria	Nutria is a soft, naturally brown fur.
otter	Otter is a dense, silky brown fur.
Persian lamb	Persian lamb is the name given to fur from young karakul lambs. It has a silky, very curly appearance. Karakul lambs are native to Bukhara, now in the Soviet Union. Persian lamb is also called astrakhan and karakul (sometimes spelled caracul).
pony	Pony is a short-haired, often curly fur, similar to broadtail. It comes in various colors from beige to black and may also be spotted.
rabbit	Rabbit is a popular inexpensive fur which may shed and become unwearable quickly. Rabbit is often dyed or otherwise changed for greater fashion appeal. It is also occasionally called "coney" or "lapin" (French for rabbit). Rabbit may be white, black, or shades between.
raccoon	Raccoon is a long-haired, very warm fur used primarily for bulky coats although occasionally as trimming. It is brown striped with darker brown.
sable	Sable is a very warm and dense fur. This usually dark brown fur is both luxurious and expensive.
seal	Seal is a shiny, thick, very warm and extremely long-lasting fur. It is naturally black or dark brown.
skunk	Skunk is a fur which, like monkey, is very much a creature of fashion. The fur, black with white stripe, is thick and wears well.
squirrel	Squirrel is usually dyed to resemble other furs. It is a soft and fluffy fur. Its color is originally brown or gray.

LEATHER CHART

Leather Term	Description
alligator	Alligator is a leather with rectangular markings, usually finished with a glaze. Much leather called crocodile is actually alligator.
buckskin	Buckskin is a strong, supple leather, usually given a suede (napped) finish and often used for shoes and gloves. It comes from deer and elk, or occasionally from domesticated animals such as cattle.
calfskin	Calfskin is supple and soft, takes a high polish, and is often the base for true patent leather.
chamois	Soft, pliable, usually yellow leather from the chamois goat, although other animal skins may be substituted. Chamois is traditionally used as a polishing cloth but has recently become popular for clothing because of its softness.
cordovan	Cordovan is a heavy but soft horsehide leather, used for quality shoes.
cowhide	Cowhide is a heavy leather which is sometimes used for clothing.
crocodile	Although much that is called crocodile is actually alligator, true crocodile has slightly different although rectangular markings. Crocodile was used extensively for accessories but is now threatened with extinction.
doeskin	Doeskin is the skin of a white sheep, mainly used for gloves.
glace or glazed	Glace or glazed leather describes leather finished to a high gloss.
grain leather	Grain leather is the term which describes any leather finished on the outside of the hide. It is used primarily to distinguish it from reversed leather. See reversed leather.
kid	Kid is the skin of a goat, commonly used for gloves and shoes.
lambskin	Lambskin comes from sheep and is used for warm, furry linings, gloves, and outerwear.
lizard	Lizard is a reptile leather, used for accessories such as shoes, handbags, and wallets.
morocco	Morocco refers to leather from sheep or goats tanned by a process which originated in Morocco.
nappa	Nappa refers to a tanning process which produces a leather popular for gloves, and occasionally for clothing.

LEATHER CHART *(Continued)*

Leather Term	Description
patent	Patent leather is leather treated with varnish to produce a glossy finish. Much of what is called patent leather today is actually synthetic.
peccary	Peccary is fine pigskin, used primarily for gloves.
pigskin	Distinctive dot-like markings appear on pigskin when the bristles are removed. This leather is popular for accessories such as gloves and luggage.
pin seal	Pin seal is a soft, glossy, strong leather used for accessories. It is made from the skin of the pin seal.
reptile	Reptile is a term used for such leathers as alligator and snake-skin—in other words, any leather from a reptile.
reversed leather	Calf which is finished on the inside is called reversed leather; it results in a napped finish which is rougher than suede.
Russian	Russian leather refers to a finish, popular for accessories. Many processes are given the name Russian but the finished leather is usually red.
seal	Seal leather is soft and strong.
shearling	Shearling is the term for sheepskin which is tanned with the wool left on. The wool is usually white and thick.
skiver	Skiver is a term which refers to a thin layer of leather, usually from sheepskin, used for linings.
snakeskin	Snakeskin is one of the reptile leathers and its appearance varies according to the species of snake used.
suede	Suede is a soft, velvety finish which gives a nap to leather, usually calfskin. Extremely popular for shoes and coats.

4

Basic Fabric Care Techniques

The care chart which follows is based on the recommendations of most fiber producers, including organizations which represent producers of natural fibers. In theory, this chart should be unnecessary since permanent care labeling of most fabrics is now required. (Refer to the section on Care Labels You'll See following the Fiber Care Chart.)

In practice, however, labels aren't always provided and aren't always accurate. And, of course, you may own items purchased before the law came into effect or purchased in other countries. You may know the fiber content of these items but you may not know how to care for them.

CAUTION

The instructions in the chart and those you'll find on care labels are perhaps slightly over-cautious, but then, it is better to be safe than sorry. Some synthetics, notably nylon and polyester, can often be washed at higher temperatures than those recommended, and often these same fibers must be pressed at a higher temperature than those recommended to remove creases and obtain crisp outlines. The problem is that you never know when you have a fabric which can take greater heat than usual and when you don't. It is a good idea to heat test a small piece of the fabric first—on a place in the garment that won't be seen (inside the cuff or hem).

If you don't have a washing machine and dryer you have to make a choice between washing items by hand or risking what may happen to them at the laundromat or at a commercial laundry. Dry cleaning is sometimes a third option, but note cautions. There are some fabrics that cannot be dry cleaned by some dry cleaning methods.

WATCH OUT FOR CHLORINE BLEACH

Chlorine bleach should be tested before being used on most fabrics. It should never be used on spandex fiber found in many girdles and brassieres and some clothing since spandex is chlorine retentive which leads to yellowing and loss of strength. On the other hand, colored fabrics made from many other fibers can often be bleached with a chlorine bleach to remove the gray film they sometimes acquire.

Again, the problem is that you don't know when it will work and when it will cause a disaster—certain fabric finishes are also chlorine retentive, and many colors are removed with chlorine bleach. Testing on a scrap of fabric (take it from a seam on ready-made garments) is the only way to judge what will happen. Oxygen bleaches can be used where chlorine bleaches can't, but they aren't nearly as effective. Read the information on the bleach container to determine whether the bleach is a chlorine or oxygen bleach.

Many fabrics today are flame retardant. The law requires that certain children's items must be flame retardant. Although the most efficient way of making a fabric flame retardant is to put the proper chemicals into a man-made fiber at the solution stage before it becomes fiber, flame retardancy is often established by a finish. These finishes can become ineffective if certain things—bleach and no-phosphate detergent in some cases—are used in washing. Follow *exactly* the instructions for washing on any flame-retardant items to retain their effectiveness.

Many general care instructions say "See the label." We're assuming you will do that automatically and that you will use this chart for supplementary information. Not all fibers listed on the Fiber Properties Chart will be found here; only those which are in general consumer use.

And a word of caution. General care instructions often suggest that in cleaning a blend you should care for it as you would care for the dominant fiber in the blend. We recommend, however, that you care for the blend as you would care for the most sensitive fiber in it. A polyester and cotton blend, for instance, should be treated as a polyester, no matter what the proportion of the blend, rather than as a cotton. Polyester is more heat sensitive than cotton and if treated as a cotton you would find the fabric melting and sticking to the sole plate of your iron.

FIBER CARE CHART

Fiber	General Care	Special Instructions
acetate	Usually dry clean. If labeled for washing, wash by hand in warm water and mild suds. Don't wring or twist, don't soak colored fabrics. Press while slightly damp on wrong side with cool iron or use a press cloth on the right side.	Keep away from acetone, nail polish remover, for example. It dissolves acetate.
acrylic	Most items should be washed in warm water by hand. Squeeze out water, don't wring. Smooth item and dry on hanger. If labeled for machine washing, use warm water, machine dry at low, and remove from dryer as soon as tumbling cycle is over.	Dry knitted items flat (they'll stretch otherwise). Static electricity build-up can be reduced by using fabric softener in every four or five washings, whether by hand or machine. (Not more often— it tends to dull clothes.)
anidex	May be washed or dry cleaned depending on fibers used with it. May be tumbled or drip dried. Use a moderate heat setting if ironing is necessary.	This elastic man-made fiber (unlike spandex) is not damaged by chlorine bleach.

FIBER CARE CHART *(Continued)*

Fiber	General Care	Special Instructions
cotton	Most 100% cottons can be washed by machine at the regular cycle with hot water, and dried at the regular setting. Use chlorine bleach only on whites and colored fabrics which you have tested for color retention. High temperature iron setting may be used. Wash cotton knits by hand to avoid excessive shrinkage.	Don't assume that all cotton fabrics are colorfast. Check the label or test a small portion; if the color runs, have the item dry cleaned.
glass fibers	Wash only by hand and hang to dry while wet.	Be careful in washing; slivers of glass can injure hands.
linen	Machine wash in hot water, dry at regular cycle. Dark colors should be washed in water of a lower temperature to keep them from fading. Dry cleaning is especially satisfactory for color and shape retention of linens.	Do not bleach colored linens.
modacrylic	Pile garments (fake furs, for instance) should be dry cleaned or cleaned commercially by the fur method. Some items are washable. Machine wash in warm water, use low setting of dryer and remove items promptly.	A fabric softener will reduce static electricity in the washable items. Use lowest possible setting when ironing is necessary; modacrylic is extremely sensitive to heat.
nylon	Most items can be machine washed in warm water and tumble dried at low setting. Remove from dryer promptly to avoid heat-set wrinkles. If ironing is desired, use only a warm iron. Nylon tends to pick up colors from other fabrics if not washed separately. Sponge upholstery and rugs or use special cleaners for these items.	Static electricity can be reduced by the use of fabric softener in every four or five washings.
olefin	Machine wash in lukewarm water, machine dry only at lowest setting. Remove from dryer as soon as tumbling stops. Do not dry in a commerical or	Notice cautions on temperature for drying and ironing.

FIBER CARE CHART *(Continued)*

Fiber	General Care	Special Instructions
	laundromat type gas-fired dryer. In blends, use lowest possible setting when ironing. Never iron 100% olefin. Stains on rugs, carpets, and upholstery can be sponged clean.	
polyester	Machine washing at a warm setting with drying at a low temperature is recommended for polyester. Remove items from the dryer promptly to avoid heat-set wrinkles. Iron with a moderately warm iron. Some white polyesters pick up color from other fabrics; wash separately if this would be objectionable. Polyester fabrics can be dry cleaned but watch prints—some color substances often used on printed polyesters are injured by dry cleaning.	Avoid over-drying of polyester and especially of polyester knits—it will give the effect of shrinkage. Notice caution on dry cleaning of polyesters.
rayon	Dry cleaning is definitely safest for rayon; however, if washing, wash by hand in lukewarm water. Do not wring or twist, and don't use chlorine bleach as some finishes on rayon are chlorine retentive which leads to yellowing and loss of strength. Smooth the item, hang on hanger to dry, press while still damp on the wrong side with a moderate iron or use a pressing cloth on the right side.	Notice caution on the use of chlorine bleach.
saran	Saran fibers are usually found domestically only on garden furniture; sponge or hose clean.	
silk	Dry cleaning is best for silk, although some silks can be hand washed (only if so labeled). Squeeze suds through fabric, do not wring or twist. Iron on the wrong side. To avoid water	Never use chlorine bleach on silk.

FIBER CARE CHART *(Continued)*

Fiber	General Care	Special Instructions
	spotting (marks made by drops of water) do not use steam when pressing silk. Iron at medium temperature.	
spandex	Wash by hand or machine in lukewarm water, drip dry or dry at low temperature by machine.	Do not use chlorine bleach as spandex is chlorine retentive causing yellowing and loss of strength. Avoid ironing. If ironing is essential, iron rapidly at the lowest possible temperature setting. Spandex slowly disintegrates from heat.
triacetate	Machine wash and dry at normal hot settings, except pleated items, which should be hand washed. A high iron temperature may be used.	Keep away from acetone—see caution for acetate.
vinyon	Sponge vinyon clean.	
wool	Woven woolens should be dry cleaned, except for those labeled "washable." Follow care instructions on such woolens exactly.	Never use chlorine bleach on wool. Dry knits flat to avoid stretching.
	Machine-made knitted woolens should also be dry cleaned, unless labeled "washable," in which case follow label instructions. The dry cleaner should be told these fabrics are woolens to ensure the proper technique is used in cleaning and drying.	
	Hand wash socks, mittens, and hand-knitted items in lukewarm or cold water using special soap for wool.	

CARE LABELS YOU'LL SEE AND WHAT THEY MEAN

Under a rule passed by the Federal Trade Commission which took effect for all merchandise manufactured on or after July 3, 1972, most wearing apparel and fabric sold by the yard to be made into wearing apparel must have a care label. The only exceptions are items which would be ruined by having a care label attached (very small, sheer scarves, for instance) and items selling for $3 or less which are completely washable by any method. In the case of fabrics by the yard, only remnants up to 10 yards are exempt.

The labels for ready-made items must be sewn in by the manufacturer; those for fabric by the yard are to be provided when the fabric is purchased, to be sewn in later. These labels must be given to the customer—the fabric store or department has no choice, but you'll probably need to make it a point to ask for them.

Charts which show the most common labels follow. The American Apparel Manufacturers Association designed the ones for ready-made clothing and the Textile Distributors Association designed the ones for fabric by the yard.

There are a few things which you should know about the labels.

- □ If a fabric sold by the yard will shrink, there is no requirement that you be told this when you purchase it.
- □ If an article is not white, there is no requirement to say "do not use bleach" when it should not be used. All white articles are considered bleachable; if they are not, they will be labeled "Do Not Bleach."
- □ "Low labeling" is prohibited—which means it's forbidden to say "Dry Clean" on an item which can be washed successfully.
- □ Furthermore, if a label says "hand wash" you are expected to know this means that the water should be lukewarm and you should not machine wash the item.

Remember that a manufacturer can label any way he wants—with more specific instructions, for instance—provided he includes the required information.

If you follow label instructions and your garment is ruined, complain to the store, to the manufacturer, and to the Federal Trade Commission. Although the labeling law is a good beginning, the labels often leave much to be desired. Check the Fiber Care Chart for more specifics.

CARE LABELS FOUND IN READY-MADE CLOTHING*

When label reads:	It means:
Machine wash	Wash, bleach, dry and press by any customary method including commercial laundering and dry cleaning.
Home launder only	Same as above but do not use commercial laundering.
No bleach	Do not use bleach.
No starch	Do not use starch.
Cold wash Cold rinse	Use cold water from tap or cold washing machine setting.
Warm wash Warm rinse	Use warm water from tap or warm washing machine setting.
Hot wash	Use hot water or hot washing machine setting.
No spin	Remove item before final machine spin cycle.
Delicate cycle Gentle cycle	Use appropriate machine setting; otherwise, wash by hand.
Durable press cycle Permanent press cycle	Use appropriate machine setting; otherwise, use medium wash, cold rinse and short spin cycle.
Wash separately	Wash alone or with similar colors.
Hand wash	Launder only by hand in lukewarm (hand-comfortable) water. May be bleached. May be dry cleaned.
Hand wash only	Same as above, but do not dry clean.
Hand wash separately	Hand wash alone or with similar colors.
No bleach	Do not use bleach.
Damp wipe	Surface clean with damp cloth or sponge.
Tumble dry	Dry in tumble dryer at specified setting—high, medium, low or no heat.
Tumble dry Remove promptly	Same as above, but in absence of cool-down cycle remove at once when tumbling stops.
Drip dry	Hang wet and allow to dry with hand-shaping only.
Line dry	Hang damp and allow to dry.
No wring No twist	Hang to dry, drip dry or dry flat only. Handle carefully to prevent wrinkles and distortion.

*Courtesy of the American Apparel Manufacturers Association.

CARE LABELS FOUND IN READY-MADE CLOTHING* (Continued)

When label reads:	It means:
Dry flat	Lay garment on flat surface to dry.
Block to dry	Maintain original size and shape while drying.
Cool iron	Set iron at lowest setting.
Warm iron	Set iron at medium setting.
Hot iron	Set iron at hot setting.
Do not iron	Do not iron or press with heat.
Steam iron	Iron or press with steam.
Iron damp	Dampen garment before ironing.
Dry clean only	Garment should be dry cleaned only at professional or self-service cleaners.
Professionally dry clean only	Do not use self-service dry cleaning.
No dry clean	Use recommended care instructions. Do not use dry cleaning solvents.

*Courtesy of the American Apparel Manufacturers Association.

LABELS FOR FABRIC SOLD BY THE YARD*

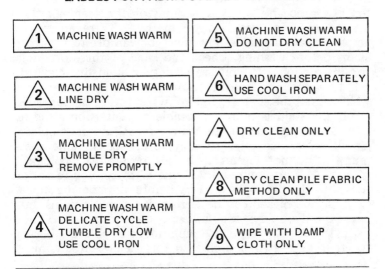

1. MACHINE WASH WARM

2. MACHINE WASH WARM
LINE DRY

3. MACHINE WASH WARM
TUMBLE DRY
REMOVE PROMPTLY

4. MACHINE WASH WARM
DELICATE CYCLE
TUMBLE DRY LOW
USE COOL IRON

5. MACHINE WASH WARM
DO NOT DRY CLEAN

6. HAND WASH SEPARATELY
USE COOL IRON

7. DRY CLEAN ONLY

8. DRY CLEAN PILE FABRIC
METHOD ONLY

9. WIPE WITH DAMP
CLOTH ONLY

*Courtesy of the Textile Distributors Association.

5

Stain Removal

Stains happen to all of us, and then we are faced with the problem of removing them. One of the most important principles to remember in removing stains is to use the mildest possible stain remover first in an attempt to avoid making matters worse.

Many stains will come out with washing or dry cleaning. A rough rule is that if the stain is a light, faint, not terribly noticeable one, try washing or dry cleaning rather than a specific stain removal method. There are many aerosol sprays available now that you can use to pre-treat stains before washing. Check the label of these products for instructions. If you are having an item dry cleaned, point out the location of the stain and tell the cleaner both what caused the stain (if you know) and what the fabric is.

If the stain is more noticeable or if it is on a rug or upholstery, try one of the stain removal methods below. You'll notice we refer to enzyme pre-soaks; some communities do not permit their sale or use for ecological reasons. If your community is one of these, you're out of luck, but the pre-soaks are very helpful in removing stains.

Chlorine bleach can be terrific in removing stains, but never use it on any fabric unless you are certain it will not harm the fabric. Never use ammonia and chlorine bleach together. The two combine to form a poison gas. Most non-flammable cleaning fluids include some form of carbon tetrachloride. Be careful using it; breathing carbon tetrachloride in an enclosed area can kill you. And, of course, keep fire and open flame away from the flammable dry cleaning fluids.

Always wash washable fabrics after removing a stain. Some stains, unfortunately, are impossible to remove. The longer stains stay in most items, the harder they are to get out.

There are several stain and spot removers available commercially. Test these, and the stain removal methods included here, on an inconspicuous section of the item before trying it on the stain.

See the Stain Removal Chart following for specific stains and removal methods.

STAIN REMOVAL CHART

Stain	Removal method
ballpoint pen ink	Ballpoint pen ink comes out quite easily when sponged with rubbing alcohol. On a washable fabric, any stain which remains should be rubbed with soap or a detergent and then the fabric should be washed. The same method should be used on non-washable items, followed by sponging with a mild detergent solution of 1 teaspoon detergent to 1 cup of water.
blood	Washable fabrics should be soaked in cold water immediately. If they do not respond to cold water, an enzyme pre-soak (when available) should be used. The fabrics should then be washed in the usual way. Non-washable items should be sponged with cold water followed by a mild detergent solution (1 teaspoon detergent to 1 cup of water). If the detergent solution doesn't work, try a solution of 1 tablespoon ammonia in a cup of water—and if that changes the color of the item, follow it up by sponging with ¼ cup white vinegar in 1 cup of water to bring back the original color. Test both the ammonia solution and the vinegar solution in some inconspicuous spot before using on the stain.
candle wax	Follow instructions for chewing gum, below.
chewing gum	Chewing gum can be removed from most fabrics if it is first hardened by rubbing it with an ice cube and then scraped off with a blunt knife or your fingernail.

STAIN REMOVAL CHART *(Continued)*

Stain	Removal method
	This takes time and patience but it does work. In desperate cases, you can try sponging the gum with a nonflammable cleaning fluid, but this can spread the stain.
coffee, tea	Simple washing will usually remove coffee and tea stains on washable fabrics. On non-washable fabrics, sponge with cold water first, then try mild detergent solution of 1 teaspoon detergent to 1 cup of water.
cream, milk	Washing will remove cream and milk from washable fabrics. On non-washable fabrics, start by wiping with a damp sponge. If that fails, shake cornstarch or white talcum powder onto the stain, allow to dry thoroughly, then use a brush or vacuum to remove the residue.
greasy stains, including lipstick, tar	Start by following the ice-cube method given for chewing gum, then use lighter fluid to remove remaining stain on both washable and non-washable fabrics.
nail polish	Nail polish remover will remove nail polish from most fabrics, but NEVER use it on acetate or triacetate. On these fabrics, try to scrape the polish off with a blunt knife or fingernail.
paint (oil based)	See instructions for nail polish, above.
paint (water based)	If the paint is still wet, sponge with water trying not to spread the stain further. If the paint is dry, nothing (including dry cleaning) will get it out, but you may be able to scrape some off the surface with a blunt knife or your fingernail.
perspiration	Certain man-made fibers seem to hold perspiration odors longer than other fabrics; although a stain will come out with washing, the odor may not. Rub the area of the odor with a deodorant soap before washing.
urine, vomit, mucous	On washable fabrics, soak in an enzyme pre-soak (if possible) then wash using a suitable bleach (chlorine or oxygen type). On non-washable items, such as rugs, sponge first with mild detergent solution (1 teaspoon detergent to a cup of water) and rinse. If that doesn't work, try white vinegar solution—¼ cup white vinegar to 1 cup water. If this solution changes the color, try to neutralize it with an ammonia solution of 1 tablespoon ammonia to 1 cup water. Test both the ammonia solution and the vinegar solution in an inconspicuous spot before using on the stain.

6

A Guide to Rugs and Carpets

Although the words "rug" and "carpet" can correctly be used interchangeably, they have come in recent years to refer to two quite distinct types of floor coverings.

Carpet usually describes a fabric floor covering which fastens to and covers the entire floor; rug is the term usually used to describe a fabric floor covering which neither covers the entire floor nor is fastened to it.

Area rug is an inexact term which describes a rug, usually colorful or dramatic in pattern or texture (rya rugs, for instance) which is used either on a bare floor or over carpeting. Area rugs may be used to set off a dining area from the rest of a living room, or to dramatize a seating section of the room.

Rugs and carpets are probably the most expensive single fabric purchase most people make, which is why it is a good idea to find out as much as you can before you buy one or the other.

To quickly settle the question of carpet versus rugs, here are the considerations you should take into account.

□ Wall-to-wall carpeting is more expensive than rugs, but gives a look of space and luxury to a room and a home.

▢ Traffic patterns may show up on a wall-to-wall carpeting, which can't be turned as a rug can to distribute wear.

▢ Wall-to-wall carpeting must be cleaned professionally at home; rugs can be sent out.

▢ And wall-to-wall carpeting is usually difficult to reuse if you move to another house or apartment.

On the other hand, wall-to-wall carpeting is comfortable to walk on, absorbs noise as a rug on a bare floor can't do, and when one color of wall-to-wall carpeting is used throughout a floor of a home it unites the various rooms dramatically.

Different fibers have different characteristics in carpeting, but the fibers used in rugs and carpets are the same ones used in apparel fabrics. The yarns are, of course, specifically developed for carpets. Synthetic fibers have become increasingly important in carpets and rugs in recent years as they have, indeed, in all areas of fabrics. The advantages they have in common are that they absorb moisture slowly, are non-allergenic, moth and mildew proof, and they resist insects.

On the other hand, they do tend to build up static electricity quickly, causing you to get a shock when you touch metal after walking on them. This tendency can be reduced by the addition of certain finishes to the yarns or the carpeting; there are also commercial anti-static products which can be applied to rugs when this becomes a problem. See the chart on rug and carpet fibers which follows this section for a description of each fiber's characteristics when used in a rug.

CHOOSING RUGS OR CARPET

The color of a rug or carpet is entirely up to you. Bear in mind, however, that generally speaking medium shades of any color show dirt more slowly than either light or dark shades. If you don't care, pick the color you like. Again, just be sure you know what you're getting into. Patterned carpets, like any patterned fabric, also look clean longer than plain carpets.

Texture is another important consideration in choosing

a rug, as important as fiber. Texture, of course, is as much a fashion question as color, but in a rug or carpet it also affects the wearing qualities you can expect from your purchase. Pile is a general term used to describe the nap of a carpet, usually much more apparent in carpeting than in most apparel fabrics. The pile is the surface of the carpet. It creates the texture, and accounts for many of the properties of carpets such as absorbing sound. Judge carpet quality by bending the carpet back; the backing shouldn't show through the pile.

□ Plush is a thick pile. It's one of the most luxurious looking of rugs but shows foot marks, not a serious problem in a little used room but one which makes it unsuitable for other areas.

□ A sculptured rug is one in which the pile has been cut to different levels to form a design.

□ Loop is the term used to describe a rug where the loops that form the pile are uncut. They can be all the same height, different heights, or combined with plush. Loops which are all the same height are the least likely to show foot marks.

□ Twist is made of a corkscrew-like cut pile (hence the name twist); it gives something of a pebbled effect. Twist also resists foot marks.

□ Shags are the newest type of floor covering as far as rugs are concerned; they have an unusually long pile and need to be vacuumed with a special attachment or actually raked with a special tool to keep the pile from becoming overly flattened.

□ Rya rugs have become very popular recently and are usually imported from Scandinavia. They are shag rugs with very long pile and vivid colorings.

□ "Civilized" shag is the name given to rugs with a longer-than-plush pile which is shorter than a true shag. These also flatten easily but are a little bit easier to maintain.

□ Random-sheared is the term used for a rug on which some of the pile has been cut and some left uncut. This has a pattern which can become flattened.

A specialty area in rugs is the Oriental or Persian rug area. One of these rugs is more than a floor covering—it's an investment. In fact, there are families who at one time or another have put much of their money into Oriental rugs and lived for years on the proceeds, selling one or two when they needed money.

Because of its expense, an Oriental rug is a special purchase and no one should buy one without good, unbiased advice and without doing research on these rugs. There are excellent books available in most libraries on Oriental rugs which would give you a beginning. Don't expect to strike a good bargain buying an Oriental rug from a rug peddler—even if he's set himself up in a hotel. He spent his life learning the business and you are only a novice. An inexpensive area rug, however, made to resemble an Oriental rug, can be as satisfactory as any other rug, provided you don't think it has value in and of itself. For further information on specific carpet and rug names, see the dictionary section of this book.

THE PADDING UNDERNEATH

Don't stop when you've chosen the rug. The padding (also called cushion or underlay) you put under your rugs is quite inexpensive for what it does. It prolongs the life of your carpet (its primary function) as well as giving it a more luxurious feeling.

Padding is made from rubberized hair, jute, rubber (with or without a waffle texture), cattle hair, and jute-and-cattle hair. Some carpets have a bonded man-made or rubber sponge backing which eliminates the need for padding. Never try to save money by not using padding.

RUG CONSTRUCTION

Rugs are made either by knitting, weaving, or tufting. Knitting is rarely used today and you are unlikely to find a knitted rug unless you knit one yourself. In knitted rugs, the surface and backing yarns are looped together very much like any knit.

Weaving was probably the original rugmaking method;

today, relatively few rugs are woven. Those that are include Axminster and Wilton (named for the looms on which they are made), chenille (named for the yarn of which it is made), and velvet (named for its appearance). Woven rugs are more expensive than tufted rugs because they take longer to make.

Tufting is the most common method of rugmaking today. A machine is used which puts tufts of yarn into the backing (usually jute or olefin). Good carpets have a second backing joined to this first one. Machine tufting goes very fast. The more tufts to the inch the higher the quality.

Certain accent or area rugs are made by other methods. These include braided rugs which are made from strips of braided fabric (often rags) which are then sewn together.

CLEANING RUGS AND CARPETS

Rugs should be cleaned with a vacuum cleaner, preferably an upright. A carpet sweeper or broom can be used between vacuumings for cleaning the surface. There are several rug cleaning compounds on the market which can be used at home for deeper cleaning; none of these really equal a professional rug cleaning, however.

Wipe up anything spilled on a rug promptly. Blot or scrape any excess, then treat with either a detergent solution or a non-flammable dry cleaning solvent. Don't use soap.

Certain things happen to rugs and carpets like balls of fluff appearing on the surface that may seem to be defects but actually aren't. These are listed on the Rug and Carpet "Problems" Chart.

HOW TO MEASURE FOR RUGS AND CARPETS

Rugs and carpets are an expensive investment and it's important that they should fit properly into your home. To determine the size of a rug or the amount of wall-to-wall carpeting you will require, start by measuring the width and length of the rooms.

If you are measuring for wall-to-wall carpeting, measure each room as squarely as possible, figuring door openings and alcoves separately. Multiply the length and the width of each area to determine the square feet.

For rugs, the square foot measurement will give you the size of rug you can fit into the room. However, most rugs look best with at least a foot of floor surrounding them. If you want that effect, subtract two feet from your length and two feet from your width measurement before mutiplying them to arrive at a square foot amount.

Wall-to-wall carpeting is usually sold by the square yard. To determine square yards, divide your total number of square feet (individual rooms plus alcoves, hallways, and so forth) by nine. This will give you square yardage.

RUG AND CARPET "PROBLEMS"

There are certain things which you may discover with new carpets and rugs which you may consider defects but which actually aren't. Check this list before calling the store to complain.

Problem	Description	Solution
fluffing	Bits of carpet come off, forming fluffy balls of carpet fiber and lint on the surface.	Time will correct this problem—theoretically a few months, but occasionally a year or so. These fluffy balls are formed by bits of the pile which were cut off and not entirely removed from the rug after manufacture.
graying	Carpet changes color slightly; additions to carpet do not match.	This is caused by the settling of fine dust but often looks as if the carpet has faded. Carpet added later won't match but will gradually gray to the same tone. Cleaning will not correct this.
matting	Pile flattens.	Matting is caused by foot traffic or the weight of furniture. The pile should be brushed (a broom works fine), the furniture rearranged occasionally and, if possible, the rug should be shifted occasionally to even out the wear.

Problem	Description	Solution
static electricity	People receive a shock when touching metal after being in contact with the rug.	This can occur with any carpet when new or when the humidity is low (in the winter, for instance, in a centrally heated house). A home humidifier may help the problem or it can be minimized by using one of the special products which can be applied to rugs for just this purpose. Some rugs now have an anti-static finish or fiber used to eliminate or reduce this problem.
wrinkling	Carpet, apparently smoothly installed, suddenly shows wrinkles.	This is caused by changes in humidity and should correct itself when the air becomes drier. However, if it does not, contact the firm which sold and installed the carpet to have it corrected.
shading	Carpet appears to be lighter or darker in certain spots.	This is caused by the bending of cut pile fibers so that light is reflected from the side. When the carpet is fairly new, a professional cleaning or vacuuming in the natural direction of the pile may help. Those in the know, however, do not consider it a fault or even a disadvantage.

CHART OF RUG AND CARPET FIBERS

Following is a chart of the rug and carpet fibers most generally in use today and their characteristics.

Fiber	Description
cotton	• Soft, easy to clean, wears well. • Tends to mat quickly.
acrylic	• Resilient. • Dyes well, making vivid colors possible. • Soils quickly but can be cleaned at home using special commercial rug cleaners.
nylon	• Resilient and abrasion resistant.

Fiber	Description
	• Dyes well.
	• Easy to clean.
	• May crush and fuzz excessively. Today's nylon carpets are greatly improved over the earlier ones.
polyester	• Soft.
	• Resists dirt, but oil-based stain may be difficult to remove.
	• May pill and shed.
	• Extremely popular in shag rugs and carpets.
rayon	• Probably the least expensive of rug fibers, rayon dyes well but does not wear as well as other fibers.
	• Crushes easily except in dense loop piles.
	• Professional dry cleaning is recommended.
olefin	• May be incorrectly called polypropylene.
	• Stain resistant; cleans easily.
	• Crushes easily but lasts in high traffic areas.
	• Relatively inexpensive.
	• Do not vacuum an olefin rug which may have become wet— there is too much chance of shock from the vacuum.
wool	• Traditional, luxury carpet fiber; most expensive.
	• Resilient, durable, and soil resistant.
	• Should be moth-proofed.
	• Soft and warm.

7

Bedding and Towels

Bedding and towels are important textile purchases. They represent a fairly large investment, they are usually expected to last for several years and, of course, they play a role in both comfort and decorating.

The word "linens" is often used as an overall description for bedding and towels, tablecloths and napkins, and other items of this type. Department stores usually place them in a linens and domestics department.

BED LINENS

Although there were more choices years ago, today's bed linens are usually made of a blend of polyester and cotton. Linen sheets and pillowcases are virtually unavailable today so "linens" is a misnomer, but it lingers on.

Sheets and pillowcases of 100% cotton are also hard to find since sheets of polyester and cotton blends are easier to care for. However, they're worth looking for if you or someone in your family objects to the slightly clammy feeling of even the best polyester and cotton blends. Bed linens of 100% cotton may not wear quite as well as those made of polyester and cotton, but they have a reputation for luxury because of their comfort. Bed linens of 100% cotton are a good choice too if you send your laundry out rather than doing it at home. A disadvantage of cotton sheets and pillowcases is that they should be ironed, not a problem when the laundry is done commercially.

PERCALES AND MUSLINS

Sheets of 100% cotton and sheets of polyester and cotton come in two traditional weaves. Both weaves are plain weaves (that is, each yarn is passed over and under every other yarn). Refer to plain weave in the chart of Common Fabric Types in Chapter Two.

Percale, the more luxurious of these two weaves, has a thread count of 180 or more threads to the square inch. Percale is made of combed yarns. Muslin sheets are coarser; they have a thread count of between 128 and 140 threads to the square inch (the higher the thread count, the higher the quality of the sheet). Muslin sheets are made of yarns which are carded but not combed. See below for an explanation of carding and combing.

The addition of polyester to these fabrics means that today's muslin sheets tend to become soft with washing in a way in which they never did when they were 100% cotton.

Polyester and cotton percale comes in thread counts as high as 200 threads to the square inch; the addition of the polyester gives the strength needed in a fabric with such a fine thread count. The chief difference, in addition to the thread count, between percale and muslin sheets is the degree of refinement of the cotton yarn. Carded yarns are used in muslin sheets; they've had most impurities taken out but consist of both long and short fibers. Combed yarns are used in percale sheets. Combing removes dirt and the short fibers, leaving only the longest and best to be spun into yarn. This makes a much smoother, higher quality final fabric.

THE COLORFUL WORLD OF SHEETS

Sheets and pillowcases were once white, and white only. Plain white sheets can still look very elegant, especially if they are accented with something such as a large dramatic monogram. However, although the name "White Sale" is still used for the twice yearly sales of sheets and pillowcases most stores have, today's sheets are every color and pattern under the sun. If you can wait, the "White Sales" are the best times to stock your linen closets. Genuine bargains are available during these sales which usually take place in January and June or July.

The dyes used on sheets and the colors used for printing them sometimes crock, fade, or run. Therefore, it's a good idea to wash deeply colored sheets separately before using them for the first time.

Chlorine bleach is safe for most colors (it won't turn them white) used for sheets, but will cause the colors to fade very quickly. Test a small part of the sheet first before using chlorine bleach. Oxygen bleaches, while not as satisfactory in some respects as the chlorine bleaches, will prove kinder to colors.

Wash sheets with hot but not the hottest water. Dry cotton sheets at medium heat or hang to dry before ironing. Cotton and polyester sheets should be tumble dried at high heat, with the heat lowered before the end of the cycle. The sheets should be removed from the dryer before completely dry, folded at once, and hung on a rack to finish drying. This procedure will prevent heat-set wrinkles from forming.

If you own linen sheets (or linen tablecloths) they have an intrinsic value because of their rarity today. Avoid folding them. Instead, use a long roller onto which the sheets and cloths can be rolled. Otherwise, they will eventually crack and fray along the crease lines.

OTHER TYPES OF SHEETS

There are other types of sheets in addition to the ones we've just discussed. Sheets made of 100% nylon tricot, for instance, are occasionally available; they dry quickly and need no ironing. They are, however, slippery—a feeling some people like and others don't—so if you're tempted by them, try a pair before buying a household supply. Static electricity can be a problem with these nylon sheets; an anti-static rinse used in washing them can help reduce this. Sheets made with a satin weave, usually in acetate or other man-made fibers, are another specialty sheet. They too are not always widely available. Again, there's a slippery quality to these sheets that people either love or hate. Satin sheets will last longer if they are washed by hand in lukewarm water, especially the dark colored sheets. Satin sheets made of polyester, however, can be machine washed successfully.

Cotton or a blend of cotton and polyester is used for knitted sheets for babies' cribs. These sheets come with fitted corners and since they dry more quickly than woven crib sheets, can prove a real blessing.

FITTED AND FLAT SHEETS

Sheets are available in either fitted or flat types. Fitted sheets have corners which are shaped to fit around the corners of the mattress. Those sheets on which the fitted corners are edged with elastic are considered more satisfactory and less likely to tear than those where the corners are entirely cut and stitched.

Fitted bottom sheets have four fitted corners. Fitted top sheets have only the two bottom corners fitted so that the top hem can be turned back over the blankets. Fitted sheets save time in bed making but are difficult to find for mattresses which are either thicker or thinner than average sizes. It is best to buy one fitted sheet and test it on the bed before stocking up on an entire supply.

SHEET SIZES

Buying sheets and pillowcases can be confusing since sheets are measured by cut sizes, the amount of fabric the manufacturer starts out with before the sheets are hemmed. To add to the confusion, there are certain allowable shrinkage standards for certain sheets set by manufacturers' organizations. High quality sheets will often have less than 1% residual shrinkage, a definite advantage.

The normal shrinkage allowed is 7% in 100% cotton flat sheets (that's a lot). Polyester and cotton blends usually have a shrinkage allowance of about 2% (you'd rather they didn't shrink at all, but you probably won't notice the 2%). Fitted sheets, both cotton and blends, are pre-shrunk and will shrink no more than 1% which means almost not at all. The shrinkage is "allowed" in the sizes of the cut sheets by the manufacturers but usually only in the length as it is considered this is more noticeable. You'll notice the width is the same. Included here are the cut sizes, the ones you'll find on the package or label, for different types of beds. Remember that cut size means before hemming.

Bed Type	No-Iron Fitted	All Cotton Flat	No-Iron Flat
cot	rarely available	63" x 108"	63" x 104"
twin	39" x 75"	72" x 108"	72" x 104"
double (also called full)	54" x 75"	81" x 108"	81" x 104"
queen	60" x 75"	90" x 120"	90" x 110" or 115"
king	78" x 75"	108" x 120"	108" x 115"

When you buy sheets for the largest bed sizes, such as queen and king, measure the bed and allow for a good tuck-in. These beds vary considerably in size and you want to be sure you get the right size for your bed.

Pillowcases are figured as the measurement of all the fabric used to cover both sides of the pillow. Pillowcases measuring 42" x 36" fit "standard" pillows which measure 20" x 26"

MATTRESS COVERS

Mattress pads or mattress covers should be used on top of the mattress. They make the bed more comfortable, prevent the sheets from wearing out as quickly, and pro-tect the mattress. They are usually made from quilted cotton or a blend of cotton and man-made fibers. Occa-sionally, they are made of some other substance such as flannel. Mattress covers usually have elastic at the corners to hold them on the mattress snugly.

Buy only quality pre-shrunk mattress pads (they'll be more expensive than others); the ones that aren't pre-shrunk end up as useless shadows of their former selves. Mattress covers are sold by bed name (king, queen, double, twin) with the actual size in inches usually given, too. Measure your mattress before buying a mattress pad to be sure it will be large enough.

KEEPING WARM

Most Americans use blankets with their sheets for warmth. Traditionally, blankets were made of wool, usually with a napped finish for extra softness, but in recent years more and more blankets have been made of acrylic fiber, partly because of the high cost and scarcity of wool and partly because of the advantages of acrylic. Acrylic blankets wash easily by machine and dry quickly, are very warm for their weight (you may find you need only one acrylic blanket when you've been using two wool blankets), and dye to beautiful, glowing colors.

A disadvantage is that they tend to both shed and pill (little balls of fiber appear on the surface) and to build up static electricity.

Cellular blankets, made of cotton, wool, or acrylic in a weave designed to trap air and give greater warmth with less thickness, have recently become popular. In winter, a cover of some kind (an extra sheet is fine) should be placed on top of a cellular blanket to hold in body heat.

Electric blankets should be viewed more as a small appliance than a textile item. The way in which these blankets heat and how well the heat can be controlled are the most important considerations in buying electric blankets. The controls should be easily accessible when the bed is made and should have some provision for telling by sight or feel in the dark what the heat setting is. The cord on an electric blanket should, of course, be long enough to reach the electric outlet which will be used in your bedroom.

QUILTS

Quilts and eiderdowns (also called comforters) are also

used like blankets for additional warmth. An eiderdown should, at least in theory, be stuffed with down while a quilt may be filled with cotton batting, polyester batting (more likely these days), or even an old blanket. Quilts and eiderdowns are usually both warm and decorative and can substitute as a bedspread.

A continental quilt or duvet is little known in the United States but very popular in other countries and could conceivably be adopted here, too. It is usually a large, puffy quilt which is placed inside a slip cover which is washed once a week when the bottom sheet is washed. To make a bed with a duvet, all that is necessary is to pull the duvet over the bed—the bedspread, blanket, and top sheet are all considered part of the continental quilt.

BED PILLOWS

Bed pillows come in tremendous variety. Their main purpose is for comfort and to support the body when a person is sitting up or lying down in bed, but they can be decorative, too.

A pillow cover should be made of tightly woven ticking fabric. This is firmer and thicker than many other fabrics and will keep feathers in feather pillows from sifting out through it. Some feathers will sift through in any case.

Foam rubber and polyester filled pillows have become increasingly popular over the years because of their special advantages—they tend to remain resilient longer than feather and down pillows and they're non-allergenic (people who get asthma or hay fever from feather pillows find this a blessing), and some can be washed easily at home.

Sizes of pillows vary just as do sizes of beds, and pillowcase sizes vary to match. Pillows also vary in softness and the descriptive terms on their labels can be misleading —one man's soft is another man's medium and another man's firm. Pillows are very personal items and members of a family should be allowed to select their own pillow when they are purchased. The most common pillow size is 20″ x 26″; there are also queen sizes measuring 20″ x 30″

and king sizes which are 20" x 36". Pillow cases labeled as measuring 42" x 36" should fit a standard size pillow.

BEDSPREADS

Some stores stock bedspreads in the same department as bedding and towels; others have them in a separate department. Bedspreads can be as simple (and inexpensive) as a length of fabric hemmed around the edges or as elaborate (and expensive) as a hand-woven, shaped and fitted, one-of-a-kind spread. Two of the most popular bedspread styles are the throw or coverlet and the box spread.

A coverlet is a simple piece of fabric, usually extending from the top of the mattress to the top of the box spring. Coverlets are usually completely flat (when they are shaped they are considered box spreads) and are used with a dust ruffle which fits onto the box spring, hangs to the floor, and remains on the bed when the coverlet is removed for sleeping.

Coverlets are also used for beds—such as bunk beds— which have no box spring. In such a case the coverlet is either short enough to only cover the mattress or is tucked in under the mattress to keep the clean lines of bunk beds.

Box spreads are shaped and fitted to the bed size. They are in the shape of a rectangular box. Sometimes the sides are tight with square corners; more often, however, a godet (a pie slice-shaped piece of fabric) or a pleat is inserted in the corners.

Bedspreads are often decorated, too. They may be trimmed with lace or fringe, accented with ruffles, or edged with pleats.

GUIDE TO BEDSPREAD SIZES

The following chart is designed to give you a guide to the size of bedspread you will need for each type of bed named below.

The chart is based on beds on which the top of the mattress measures 21" from the floor.

See instructions following for figuring yardage for made-to-order or made-at-home bedspreads.

Name of Bed	Mattress Size	Spread Size
Day Bed	33" x 75"	75" x 109"
Twin Bed	39" x 76"	81" x 110"
Full Bed (Double)	54" x 76"	96" x 110"
Queen Size	60" x 80" (may be larger or smaller—measure)	102" x 120"
King Size	72" x 80" (may be larger or smaller—measure)	114" x 120"

FIGURING YARDAGE FOR BEDSPREADS

A bedspread, even a box spread, is basically a flat piece of fabric. Begin to figure the yardage requirements by measuring (use inches to start) the bed according to the instructions below or by following the chart on bedspread sizes.

Measuring should be done on a bed which is already made up with sheets and blankets. Take the following measurements for the finished width of your bedspread.

1. The width of the mattress.
2. The drop—the amount that will hang over the sides of the bed. Measure from the top of the mattress to the floor or to any other spot where you wish the finished spread to hang. Double this figure.

Add the drop measurement (doubled) to the width measurement. This will give you the width your finished bedspread must be.

To calculate the finished length of the bedspread:

1. Measure the length of the mattress.
2. Add the drop measurement you took for the width (do not double the drop as instructed for the width calculations).
3. Add 6 extra inches for tuck-in under the pillows.

To find the total yardage you need in square inches, multiply the finished width figure by the total length figure.

Now that you have the yardage in square inches, you'll

need to know how many yards of fabric to buy. So divide the total number of square inches by 144 (there are 144 square inches in one square foot). Then divide that number by 9 (there are 9 square feet in one square yard). If you are making the bedspread from 36" wide fabric, this figure tells you how many yards to buy. If you are using 45" fabric there may be some waste in this yardage which you could use to advantage for matching decorator pillows or ruffles on pillow coverings (pillow shams). If you do not want to have this waste, the easiest way to figure the yardage is to make a sketch.

Plan to use the full width of your fabric for the top of the bedspread and to split the full width in half for the sides. This means you will need double the amount of yardage that the mattress top measures, plus the height of the mattress from the floor, plus 6 inches for the tuck-in. Be sure to add seam allowances and additional inches for hems to your measurements before cutting.

Ruffles or box pleats around the bottom edges of the bedspread will require extra fabric. They should be full (at least twice as much fabric as the straight part of the spread) to be most effective.

DECORATIVE PILLOWS

One of the biggest changes in home furnishings in recent years has been the tremendous boom in the use of decorative or decorator pillows. Bed pillows are covered with ruffled shams so they can appear on top of the bed during the day (a sham is an envelope-like covering without a closure into which a pillow can be slipped, and very often it has a ruffle all the way around it). Square pillows, round pillows, and long skinny pillows are piled on sofas and beds.

Decorator pillows are covered with satin or patchwork, with tucking or quilting, with needlepoint or stitchery. Pillows, like bedspreads, have no limitations except those of imagination. These pillows are most satisfactory when the covering can be removed for dry cleaning or washing. A chart for figuring fabric requirements for making decorative pillows is included here.

PILLOW YARDAGE CHART

Decorator pillows have become more and more important in homes recently. If you are making a special type of pillow cover—one you are needlepointing or embroidering yourself—you will probably buy a pillow shape to fit your finished cover.

The following chart is designed to give you an idea of the yardage you will need to cover older pillows you may have to which you would like to give a new look.

The following sizes apply whether the pillows are round or rectangular.

If the size of your pillow is not on the chart, measure the top (across the diameter if it is a round pillow), the entire outside edge, and the width of the boxing. Add an additional 1" to every edge as a seam allowance. A pillow without a boxing is measured from side to side, has an additional 1" for seam allowance. Bolsters, whether round or wedge-shaped, are measured by their length, width, and circumference, plus seam allowance at all edges.

Size of Pillow	Fabric Needed to Cover
14"	½ yard
16"	¾ yard
18"	¾ yard

SLIPCOVER YARDAGE CHART

Following is a chart of yardage requirements for some of the most common pieces of furniture. The requirements are estimates, although we've tried to be on the generous side; if your furniture is either larger or smaller than average the yardage requirements will change accordingly.

The type of fabric you select will also affect the yardage you need. Small, all over prints, solid fabric, and small checks will not require extra yardage; large, splashy prints such as those on which a printed bouquet of flowers would cover an entire sofa cushion, will require more because the design should be carefully centered and/or matched. Welting, which is cord covered with matching or contrasting fabric, requires at least one yard for a sofa. Extra fabric will be needed for full, gathered or pleated skirts.

Measurements are given for fabric at least 48" wide; 36" fabric will require about 6 yards more for larger pieces, about 2 yards more for a small boudoir chair. Even if you plan to have slipcovers made for you, this chart will help you estimate the cost of slipcovering the following items.

Piece of Furniture	Number of Cushions	Yardage Needed
6 to 7 Foot Sofa	3	16
	1	15
	0	12
Love Seat	1	11
	0	10
Upholstered Arm Chair	1	8½
	0	7½
Boudoir Chair	1	7
	0	6

BATH TOWELS

Once, towels were basic and functional; today they are also important as a decorative accent in bathrooms. Towels are most widely available in two constructions—terry cloth and velour, also called terry velour. Most terry cloth towels will shrink during the first washing. Manufacturers claim this is an advantage because it means the weave ends up tighter, giving longer wear than a looser, more open weave would give.

Terry cloth is a pile loop fabric with the loops uncut. The closer the loops are together, the higher the quality and the better the terry cloth will dry.

Velour is a softer towel on which the loops have been cut; it has a depth of color similar to velvet but it tends not to dry as well since it doesn't absorb water as well.

Towels are usually still made of 100% cotton; most

man-made fibers simply don't absorb water well enough to succeed as towels.

Towels should be washed at home by machine or at a launderette; when dried in a dryer they come out softer and fluffier than when dried naturally on a clothesline. Loops which appear on towels should be cut off with a pair of scissors so they won't snag and cause the towel to rip.

Towel sizes are much less standardized than sheet sizes. A bath towel, for instance, can be 22″ x 44″, 24″ x 45″, or 25″ x 50″; a hand towel will usually measure about 16″ wide but may be anything from 26″ to 30″ long. Washcloths are squares, usually 12″ x 12″, but they may be larger or smaller. Fingertip towels are usually both longer and narrower than hand towels, measuring something like 11″ x 18″ and are often used as guest towels.

Bath sheets are larger than ordinary towels. They are designed for people who really like to wrap themselves from head-to-toe in a towel. Bath sheet sizes are not standardized, but a typical bath sheet measures 36″ x 70″.

BEACH TOWELS

Beach towels are another special towel area. They are towels used by the ocean or at a lake or swimming pool and receive a great deal of wear. Beach towels are most satisfactory when they are fairly large—the 25″ x 50″ size, for instance—so that they can also be used for spreading on the ground to be used as a mat.

Most beach towels are comparatively inexpensive. The weave is often not as tight as on quality bath towels. Beach towels come in patterns (including some amusing prints) which are usually more brightly colored than those of bath towels. Although many people use their bath towels as beach towels, because of the effects of sunlight, salt and chlorine water, and sand and dirt on the colors and fabric, it is probably best to have a supply of inexpensive towels specifically for the beach.

8

Curtains, Draperies, and Wall Coverings

Curtains and draperies are both functional and decorative. They provide a degree of insulation as well as lending color and design to the window area. They should not cut out more light than necessary and should enhance, rather than conceal, views. Some curtains and draperies are designed to hide an ugly view or correct a fault in a room (such as very peculiarly shaped windows).

Curtains and draperies are words used to describe two different types of window coverings. Curtains usually hang in front of the window, often above the sill and inside the frame. They are more likely to be of a sheer fabric than an opaque one, so that light can filter through them. A typical curtain is an organdy tie-back.

Draperies are usually more formal and more elaborate than curtains. They may extend outside the molding of the window frame, often close and open, and may extend all the way from the ceiling to the floor or even (in very formal rooms) lie on the floor itself. Draperies often have decorative headings (the top part of the drapery is called the heading) such as valances. Draperies are almost always opaque (but are sometimes combined with sheers) and serve to control light and provide privacy.

FABRICS

Almost all fabrics found in apparel are also found in curtains and draperies, with the addition of glass fiber, which is very popular for window coverings.

The big advantage of using easy care fabrics for curtains and draperies—polyester, glass fiber, nylon—is that it eliminates the time-consuming task of ironing them.

CLEANING

It's a good idea to vacuum curtains and draperies now and then to get rid of dust; they should also be vacuumed before they are washed if they are very dirty. Most curtains can be washed by machine; some draperies require dry cleaning. Curtain and drapery hooks should always be removed before washing or cleaning.

Fragile curtains and sheer curtains may survive washing by machine better if they are put into the machine in a mesh bag. Glass fiber curtains should be washed by hand so that no slivers of glass will remain in the washing machine.

White and colorfast cottons should be machine-washed for about six minutes in hot water; wash non-colorfast cottons and rayon in the machine in warm water for the same length of time. Polyester, nylon, and blends of natural and man-made fibers should be washed following machine instructions for permanent press fabrics. All machine washable curtains and draperies can, of course, also be washed by hand.

Most trimmings used on washable curtains and draperies are also washable, but it is best to test deep or dark colors first to see if the trimming runs. If it does, remove the trimming and sew it on again when the curtains or draperies are washed, or replace it with a washable trimming. Another option is to have these items dry cleaned.

Some draperies made of man-made fibers are washable, others are not. Check the label to be sure. These draperies seem to look best, if washable, when they are hung to dry or air dried rather than dried at a high temperature. Many curtains and draperies can be removed wet from the washing machine and hung to dry at the window. Put something under them to catch any drips to avoid harming the rug or floor.

For further information on specific fibers and how to care for them, see fiber and care charts in this book.

MEASURING WINDOWS FOR CURTAINS, DRAPERIES, AND SHADES

Taking the correct measurements is more than half the battle in buying or making curtains, draperies, and shades or Venetian blinds that are right for your windows and your house.

Following are instructions for the best ways to measure different windows for different types of window coverings.

DRAPERIES AND CURTAINS

Don't start measuring until you have decided on and installed the hardware you will be using with your draperies or curtains. The thickness and placement of the hardware determine subsequent measurements.

Remember when measuring for draperies and conventional curtains that the type of hooks you choose for the top will make the drapery or curtain extend one-half inch or more above the top of the rod. (To measure for café curtains, see the next section of this chapter.) Measure length from where the top of the hooks will be to where you want the draperies or curtains to end. Add 8 inches for hems if you are figuring yardage to make them yourself.

To determine drapery or curtain width, measure the width of the rod, and double (triple for sheer and lightweight curtains and draperies) the amount. Add on an extra three inches if the rod is of the type that allows the draperies to cross each other. Add at least 1½" to 2" for each side hem.

CAFÉ CURTAINS

With café curtains there are many possible options in terms of arrangement of tiers and placement of curtains, as well as treatment at the top of the curtains. Determine what you want, keeping in mind that café curtains can be double tiered (with one tier going from the top of the window to the middle and another tier going from the middle to the sill or apron of the window), single tier (covering only half of the window), or extended as far as the floor.

Measure for café curtains from the bottom of the rings on the hardware which you plan to use on these curtains. Measure from this point to where you want the tier to fall and add on 8 inches for top and bottom hems for greatest luxury; less is adequate but wider hems help the curtains to hang better. To determine the width, measure the part of the window you want covered and double (triple for sheer and lightweight fabrics) for fullness. Add about 6 inches for hems on the sides of the curtains.

MEASURING FOR SHADES AND BLINDS

Venetian blinds and shades require exact measurements. Decide where the shade or blind is to be placed (usually inside the window) and measure across exactly— from side of window to side of window, inside the frame, for a conventional positioning. You can take the measurements outside the frame for an unconventional positioning to cover a window frame you don't like.

Measure each window individually, even if you are certain they are all the same size. Measure the bottom of the window also, and make a note if it differs from the top. If the bottom is narrower than the top measurement use the bottom measurement or your shades will be too wide for the bottom of the window. Length is determined by measuring from the top frame of the window to the sill.

SPECIAL WINDOW SHAPES

Special window shapes require special measurements. French doors and casement windows are probably best treated with curtains hung on the window so they just cover the glass and attached to rods at both the top of the window and the bottom. Include hem allowances in measurements.

Sliding glass doors should have draperies or curtains which completely uncover the doors when desired. The hardware should be placed so that it extends onto the wall well beyond the frame of the glass doors. After that, measure as for any conventional window.

FIGURING YARDAGE FOR COVERING WALLS WITH FABRIC

More and more people are realizing the exciting decorating possibilities in covering the walls of a room with fabric. Fabric covers irregularities in walls if it is hung from a molding. Fabric patterns are enormously varied, and can be mixed and matched to other fabrics and color schemes in the house including curtains and draperies.

Fabric can be applied to the walls using wallpaper paste. Put the paste directly on the wall itself rather than on the fabric (wallpaper instructions tell you to apply the paste to the paper). Fabric can also be attached to walls by stapling it directly to the wall or to a molding with a staple gun designed for this purpose. (This staple gun can be purchased at many hardware stores.) If the staples are unattractive, cover them when the walls are finished with a strip of wood molding or with a trimming.

Velcro (a burr-like fastening) can also be used to attach fabric to walls. It can be glued at the top and the bottom of the walls, with the fabric attached to it by means of the opposite strip of Velcro stitched to the top and bottom of the fabric. This has the advantage of making fabric walls removable for washing. If you plan to wash your fabric wall covering, be sure to wash and dry the fabric the same way you plan to wash and dry it after covering the wall. This will prevent shrinkage once the pieces have been cut.

To determine the amount of fabric you will need, measure the length around all four walls of the room in feet. Multiply this amount by the height in feet of the room from the baseboard to the ceiling plus four to six inches for hems. This will give you the total square footage you will need. Subtract 20 square feet for every door, window, and other place which won't be covered, less if you have extremely small windows and doors. Add

30 square feet "to be safe" and another 30 to match a large pattern.

Divide the total number of square feet by 9 to get the yardage you require. This will give you more than enough fabric to cover the walls of the room and should leave extra for covering accent pillows.

Begin to cover the walls by cutting the fabric into lengths equal to the height of the room plus about four to six inches extra at top and bottom. Cut so that the pattern will match around the room. Begin hanging the fabric in a corner, preferably the darkest corner. The fabric will end at the same corner and it is unlikely the pattern will match properly, so you will want it to be as inconspicuous as possible.

Dictionary

In this section of this book are listed in alphabetical order all the words which properly belong in a dictionary of fibers and fabrics intended primarily for the consumer.

We've tried to avoid making the definitions more complicated than necessary, and we've included pronunciations. Quite often the pronunciation used in the fabric industry itself is not the "correct" pronunciation; when such is the case, we give both and indicate which is which.

PRONUNCIATION GUIDE

Our pronunciation guide contains absolutely no confusing signs and symbols. Each word is respelled phonetically in the characters of the alphabet, so that the correct pronunciation is *immediately* apparent. Here the words almost pronounce themselves!

For example, the word **acrylic** is respelled in parentheses as (uh-*krill*-ik). Say it aloud to yourself, emphasizing the *italicized* syllable.

Or take another somewhat unusual word like **ajour**. You will find the pronunciation given as (*ah*-zhur). Note how you can get the precise pronunciation by placing full stress on the syllable in italics while reading aloud.

71

abrasion (uh-*bray*-zhun) Rubbing or scraping off of the surface of a fabric. The word is only important to the consumer when you have a phrase such as "abrasion resistance." Some permanent press finishes lessen abrasion resistance so that, for instance, the knees and cuffs of slacks wear out more quickly than they would otherwise. Draperies that will be opened and closed frequently should be made of abrasion resistant fabrics.

accordion pleats (uh-*kor*-dee-un pleetz) See pleats.

accordion shades (uh-*kor*-dee-un shaydz) See shades.

Acele (uh-*seel*) Trademark of E.I. DuPont de Nemours & Co. Inc. (commonly known as DuPont) for acetate fiber. See acetate and sections on fibers and care.

acetate (*ass*-uh-tayt) A synthetic fiber made from cellulose acetate. Solution and spun-dyed acetates are colorfast to sunlight, perspiration, and air pollution; others may not be. Acetate is often used for very luxurious fabrics as it resembles silk; it is also occasionally mixed with other fibers to give additional sheen or to lower the cost. Acetone (which is part of most nail polish removers and some perfumes) destroys acetate. See also triacetate and sections on fibers and care. See also cellulose.

Acrilan (*ak*-rill-on) Trademark of Monsanto Textiles Co. for acrylic fiber.

acrylic (uh-*krill*-ik) A synthetic fiber made from acrylonitrile, which comes from coal, air, water, petroleum and limestone. Acrylic is lighter in weight for the warmth it gives than other fibers and is extremely popular for blankets as a substitute for wool. See chart of fiber properties.

afghan (*af*-gan) A knitted or crocheted blanket or throw, an afghan is usually made in sections which are subsequently joined together,

although it may be made in one piece. Traditionally, afghans were
made from wool, but in recent years, with the increasing avail-
ability of acrylic knitting yarns, they are more likely to be made of
acrylic. Patterns range from ones with intricate designs inspired by
fisherman's sweaters to the simplest of plain knitting or crochet.
Afghan stitch in crochet forms a simple raised design.

Agilon (*ah*-ji-lon) Trademark of Derring Milliken Inc. for textured
nylon. Agilon is often used in hosiery and was one of the first
stretch yarns for panty hose.

aigrette (*ay*-gret) Feathers from the egret, a heron. This bird has
been protected for some years and true aigrette feathers are no
longer available. The word is also occasionally used for any spray
of feathers or jewels. See feathers.

ajour (*ah*-zhur) An openwork design used in lace or embroidery. See
also entry for lace and entry for embroidery.

Alencon (ah-*len*-sun) See entry for lace.

all over or **allover** (awl-*oh*-ver) A word used to describe the arrangement of lace designs; distinguishes patterns or laces of this type
from others where the designs might be arranged in stripes or along
an edge or set off by large plain areas.

alligator (*al*-uh-gay-ter) See leathers.

aloe lace (*al*-oh layss) See lace.

alpaca (al-*pak*-uh) A type of llama which has very long hair which is
considered a wool. Alpaca fabric is one of the luxury fabrics—soft,
silky, and fairly lightweight. It resembles mohair. Today, the term
"alpaca" is also used for fabrics, usually made from a blend
including some wool, which have a similar appearance to true
alpaca. See also llama.

angora (ang-*gor*-uh) One of those terms about which there is some
difference of opinion. Strictly speaking, angora is the wool of the
Angora goat—long and soft—which is called "mohair" when made
into fabric or yarn. It is usually blended with other fibers. The
angora rabbit has soft, silky hair which is also made into fabrics.
The Wool Labeling Law requires that this be referred to as "angora
rabbit hair" rather than "angora" or "angora wool."

anidex (*ann*-ih-dex) A synthetic fiber made from a monohydric
alcohol and acrylic acid which gives permanent stretch and recovery to fabrics, resists gas, oxygen, sunlight, chlorine bleaches,
and oils. See sections on fibers and care.

Anim (*ann*-im) Trademark of Rohm and Haas Company for anidex
fiber.

antique lace (ann-*teek* layss) See lace.

antique satin (ann-*teek* sat-'n) See satin.

anti-static (*ann*-tee sta-tik) The buildup of static electricity is a
problem with many of the synthetic fibers. This causes typical

static electricity situations—shocks when touching metal while wearing something which has built up static electricity, clinging of clothing, crackling when removing clothing. Anti-static finishes are used on fabrics of this type to cut down on or eliminate the problems—one of which, not widely recognized, is that static electricity attracts dirt. At home, the use of a fabric softener in every four or five washings can cut down on, if not entirely eliminate, the problem of static electricity.

Antron (*ann*-tron) Trademark of DuPont for a type of nylon. See nylon, sections on fiber and care.

appenzell (*ap*-pen-zel) A type of embroidery, named for the section of Switzerland where it originated.

application printing (ap-lih-*kay*-shun *print*-ing) Another term for direct or roller printing. See printing.

appliqué (ap-lih-*kay*) A decoration. Appliqué refers to a piece of fabric cut out and added to another fabric (appliqué is the French for applied) by sewing, embroidering, glueing, or fusing. Appliqués are especially popular on children's clothes, where they often represent scenes or objects from nature such as animals or pieces of fruit. They move in and out of adult fashions and home furnishings.

area rugs (*air*-ee-ah rug) A small, usually quite decorative rug, often placed on a carpet as an accent in a room. See rugs and carpets.

Argentan lace (*ahr*-jen-ten layss) See layss.

argyle (*ahr*-gyle) See plaid, also see argyle knit, below.

argyle knit (*ahr*-gyle nit) A knitting pattern in which diamonds are crossed by narrow stripes. Popular at various times for socks and sweaters and said to be of Scottish origin.

Arnel (*ahr*-nell) Trademark of Celanese Corp. for triacetate fiber. See triacetate, also sections on fibers and care.

arrowhead (*air*-o-hed) Arrowheads are often used to reinforce and accent points of potential wear on clothing, such as the top of pleats. Arrowheads are made with satin stitch and are triangular in shape.

art linen (art *lin*-'n) See linen.

artifical silk (art-ih-*fish*-ul silk) One of the early names for rayon. See rayon.

asbestos (ass-*bess*-tus) A mineral fiber which is non-metallic. Its greatest virtue is that it is nonflammable. It is used in combination with other fibers for theater curtains and in industrial clothing where flameproofing is essential. Asbestos is often used in ironing board covers and potholders.

astrakhan (*ass*-truh-kan) Originally the word for the wool from karakul lambs, the term is also used today to describe fabric woven or knitted to look like this wool—curly and fairly heavy. See also karakul.

Astroturf (*ass*-troh-turf) Trademark of Monsanto Company for their nylon product designed to imitate grass.

Aubusson (*oh*-boo-sohn) Originally, Aubusson referred to tapestries made in Aubusson, France, and designed for use as wall hangings. With time, the word came to be applied to patterned rugs with little or slight rib and no pile. See rugs and carpets.

Austrian shade (*aws*-tree-uhn shayd) See shades.

Avlin (*av*-lin) Trademark of FMC Corporation for polyester. See polyester.

Avril (*av*-ril) Trademark of FMC Corporation for high wet modulus rayon. See rayon.

awning stripes (*awn*-ing strypz) See stripes.

Axminster (*aks*-min-ster) Name for a carpet with a cut pile made on the Axminster loom which makes complicated designs possible. The process is designed to resemble hand-knotted rugs. See rugs and carpets.

azlon (*az*-lon) A synthetic fiber made from regenerated, naturally occurring proteins. It gives a soft feeling when blended with other fibers. Not made in the United States at present.

ℬ

backed fabric (bakt *fab*-rik) A fabric with an extra warp or filling—or both—to make it heavier and thicker and to provide additional warmth.

backing (*back*-ing) Carpet yarns are tufted into a backing which is made of something such as olefin or jute. The backing is usually latex-coated; good backings will have a second layer of latex, forming what is called a double backing. See jute, olefin, and latex.

bagheera (bahg-*eer*-uh) Name for an uncut pile velvet clothing fabric which is crease resistant because the surface is not smooth. See also pile; see velvet.

baize (bayz) Loosely woven fabric originally made from cotton or wool but now made of other fibers. Traditionally used for school bags and to cover the doors leading to English servants' quarters, baize also has industrial uses. Traditionally dyed green, although it is made in other colors.

baku straw (bah-*koo* straw) See straw.

balanced plaid (*bal*-'nst plad) See plaid.

balanced stripe (*bal*-'nst stryp) See stripe.

balibuntal straw (*bal*-ih-*bun*-t'l straw) See straw.

ball fringe (bawl frinj) See trimming.

bandanna (ban-*dan*-uh) An evenly woven fabric usually about 24″ square and hemmed on all sides used for a handkerchief, neckerchief, or head-scarf. Traditionally, bandannas were printed in stylized geometric patterns on bright blue or red fabric with black and white contrast. A bandanna print is a print which imitates this look and often is made of individual bandanna squares. The traditional red and blue colorings are not always used today.

banding (*band*-ing) See trimming.

Bangkok straw (*bang*-kock straw) See straw.

Ban-Lon (*ban*-lon) Trademark of Bancroft Licensing for a texturizing process that uses heat setting to add bulk and a small amount of stretch to the filament yarns of thermoplastic fibers. See heat setting, thermoplastic, and filament.

bar tack (bar tak) A bar tack is a satin stitched rectangle used like an arrowhead to reinforce potential points of wear in clothing. See arrowhead.

barathea (bayr-uh-*thee*-uh) A fine cloth, originally made of silk or wool, with a broken rib pattern. Today, barathea is made in many fibers.

bargello (bar-*jeh*-loh) Bargello is a type of needlepoint design which creates repetitive geometric designs, diamonds and peaks and valleys (flames) among the most common. Unlike traditional needlepoint in which the stitches slant as the canvas mesh is filled, bargello is composed of stitches which run parallel to the threads of the needlepoint canvas. Bargello stitches usually cover two or more meshes with each stitch, so the work goes very quickly. See also needlepoint.

barkcloth (bark-kloth) Originally, the term barkcloth referred to a fabric found throughout the South Pacific. It is made from the inner bark of certain trees. The bark is beaten into a paper-like fabric, and is then dyed or otherwise colored. Tapa cloth is one of the best known types of true barkcloth. Barkcloth is a term which also refers to a fabric, often cotton or rayon, with a somewhat crepe-like feeling which is designed to resemble true barkcloth. This fabric is used extensively for draperies, slipcovers and other home furnishings. See also crepe and tapa cloth.

bark crepe (bark crayp) This is another fabric which is designed to resemble bark, but the effect is more exaggerated than in the case of barkcloth. Usually, one fiber is used for the warp and another for the filling to help create the textured look of bark. See barkcloth, above.

barre (bah-*ray*) A fabric—either knit or woven—in which stripes run in the crosswise direction. Barre also refers to a flaw in fabric which appears as unwanted crosswise stripes of texture or color.

basket weave (*bas*-kit weev) One of the most important patterns in weaving. See weaving.

batik (bah-*teek*) A form of resist dyeing of Indonesian origin. Wax is spread on fabric before dyeing and the unwaxed areas take the color while the wax-covered fabric remains its original color. Often several waxings and dyeings are used to get a final pattern. The wax usually cracks during dyeing giving a characteristic veined effect to the design. Batik is extensively copied by machine printing today. See resist dyeing under entry for dyeing.

batiste (bah-*teest*) A sheer, fine fabric, light in weight, which may be made of almost any fiber. Its degree of sheerness depends on the fiber. Cotton and synthetic batiste are probably the lightest and sheerest, wool batiste the heaviest.

Battenberg lace (*bat*-en-berg layss) See lace.

batting (*bat*-ing) See batting under linens and domestics.

bayardere (bye-ar-*dare*) Stripes which run in the crosswise direction of a fabric. This term is usually used only to describe very brightly colored stripes. See also, barre.

beaded velvet (*beed*-id *vel*-vit) Also called cut velvet. See velvet.

beading (*beed*-ing) See lace; see embroidery.

beaver (*bee*-vur) A fur-bearing animal. See furs. Also a glossy, coating weight fabric made with a long nap which somewhat resembles the fur of the beaver.

bed head (bed hed) See headboard.

bed pad (bed pad) See mattress cover under linens and domestics.

Bedford cloth (*bed*-ford kloth) A strong woven fabric with lengthwise ribs used extensively for upholstery and riding breeches. It may be made from any fiber.

bedspreads (*bed*-spredz) See spread.

beetling (*beet*-ling) A finishing process in which linen is pounded to produce a hard, flat surface with a sheen.

Belgian lace (*bel*-jin layss) See lace.

belting (*belt*-ing) Any heavyweight, fairly stiff fabric which can be used to support the top of a skirt or a pair of pants or to line a belt to give it additional support. Beltings come in various widths.

Bemberg (*bem*-burg) Trademark of Beaunit for cuprammonium rayon. See rayon.

Benares (beh-*nahr*-eez) Lightweight fabric from India, usually woven with metallic threads.

bengaline (*beng*-uh-leen) Strong fabric with clearly defined crosswise ribs.

bias (*by*-us) The diagonal of a woven fabric between the warp and the filling threads. This part of a woven fabric has the greatest amount of stretch. See also Chapter Two, From Fiber to Fabric.

bias plaid (*by*-us plad) See plaid.

bias tape (*by*-us tayp) See trimming.

biconstituent fiber (by-kon-*stit*-you-ent fy-ber) A fiber made by mixing two different man-made fiber materials together in their syrupy stage before forcing it through a spinneret. See Chapter One, Fiber—The Start of It All.

billiard cloth (*bill*-yard kloth) The cloth used on billiard tables, always dyed green. This is traditionally a very fine twilled fabric made from quality wool. Today, billiard cloth may be made from other fibers.

binche lace (beench layss) See lace.

binding (*bynd*-ing) See trimming.

birdseye (*berdz*-eye) Fabric woven with a pattern which has a center dot and somewhat resembles the eye of a bird. Birdseye is a popular pique weave. See also pique.

blanket (*blang*-ket) Any loose covering and especially those used on beds for warmth. Most blankets were formerly made of wool, but today many are made of acrylic and other man-made fibers. Blanket cloth is a heavyweight fabric, often vividly patterned in plaid designs, and usually used for coats. It often has a napped surface. Blanket is also a technical term referring to an experimental piece of fabric which shows a designer how the final cloth will look. Blankets of this kind often have several designs and colorings woven or knitted on one piece.

blanket plaid (*blang*-ket plad) See plaid.

blazer cloth (*blayz*-er kloth) Fabric traditionally used for loosely fitting tailored jackets worn by men and women. The fabric was formerly almost always made of wool with a satin weave; today it is of any fiber. Blazers may be striped, plaid, or solid colored and are especially popular for students in their school colors.

blazer stripe (*blayz*-er stryp) See stripe.

bleach (bleech) A chemical which removes color from an item. Fabrics are often bleached after manufacture and before dyeing to make sure the dyed colors are "true." Household bleaching is used to disinfect clothing and remove soil from whites and colorfast colors. Chlorine bleaches are the most common household bleaches, but are too strong for some colors and fabrics. See chart on Fabric Care.

bleed (bleed) An elegant term for running—the way in which non-fast dyes merge into each other and "run" into the water when they are immersed. The term bleed is often used in a positive sense, applied to fabrics such as bleeding Madras where the bleeding process is considered desirable. When the bleeding is undesirable, it's more likely to be referred to as running.

blend (blehnd) A combination of fibers that produces a fabric which has the good qualities of both fibers. The development of blends of polyester and cotton, producing fabrics which require a minimum of ironing, has been one of the most significant developments in fabrics during the past twenty-five years. Correctly, the term blend refers only to fabrics made from yarns which have been spun to combine the two fibers in one yarn. The term "mixture" should be used to describe fabrics in which, for instance, the warp thread is polyester and the filling thread is cotton. See also mixture and biconstituent fiber.

blending (*blehnd*-ing) The most common use of the word blending is to describe the process of combining different fibers (see blend, above). Occasionally, blending is done for reasons of economy (as when an expensive fiber is blended with a cheaper one) more than as an attempt to mix two desirable qualities. Traditionally, blending is a process used in the production of natural fiber yarns. Fibers from several lots of a single natural fiber are mixed together to provide a yarn of greater uniformity than would result from the use of any single lot.

blinds (blyndz) See shades.

blister (*blis*-ter) A bump on a fabric. Blisters are often used to give additional depth to a design—flowers, for instance, may be blistered to make them stand out from the rest of a fabric. Blister crepe is technically a fabric produced chemically by shrinking some of the yarns and leaving others unshrunk in a crepe pattern after the fabric is manufactured. (See crepe.) In practice, many crepe fabrics with well-defined patterns are referred to as blister crepes whether they are actually made in this way or not.

block printing (blok *print*-ing) A hand-printing process in which a design is carved on a block of wood or linoleum. Dye is placed on the surface and the block is then placed on the fabric, transferring the dye. Every color requires a different block, making this type of printing both tedious and expensive. It is now almost entirely limited to the craft field. See printing.

Blue "C" (*bloo* see) Trademark used by Monsanto to identify some of their fibers. It must be used with the fiber's name as in "Blue 'C' nylon."

bluing (*bloo*-ing) A mild blue dye traditionally added to white clothes in the final rinse water after washing to make them look whiter—the blue tinge offsets the yellow cast some white fabrics tend to acquire with age. With changes in laundering techniques, bluing of clothes as a separate step in washing has almost disappeared. A form of bluing is, however, added to some washing detergents. Bluing is occasionally used in a similar way and for a similar purpose in fabric finishing. See also optical brighteners and optical dyes.

board (bord) A flat piece of cardboard or plastic foam around which fabric to be sold by the yard is wrapped.

board ends (bord endz) The ends of the board (see board, above) around which fabric is wrapped. Board ends are often marked with fiber content and care information.

boarding (*bord*-ing) A process similar to heat setting (see heat setting) used in the manufacture of hosiery which is not full-fashioned, such as seamless stockings and panty hose. Because of nylon's thermoplastic nature (it changes shape under heat) these stockings can be knitted with the same number of stitches throughout the leg. Shaping for ankle and calf is then created by placing the hosiery on forms in the desired shape and submitting the hosiery to high temperature. With the development of stretch yarns for hosiery, this step has become unnecessary since the stocking easily conforms to the shape of the leg. It is still used, however, to improve the appearance of the finished product made of stretch yarns. See full-fashioned and heat setting.

bobbin (*bob*-in) A spool, usually hollow, which holds thread on a sewing machine or yarn on a loom.

bobbin lace (*bob*-in layss) See lace.

bobbinet lace (bob-in-*et* layss) See lace.

bolster (*bohl*-ster) See pillow.

bolt (bolt) A rather loose term referring to a quantity of fabric. Most fabric sold in fabric stores and departments is folded in half lengthwise and then wrapped around a flat piece of cardboard or plastic (see board, above). The fabric and board together are called a bolt. A bolt usually has between 15 and 20 yards of fabric, but may have more or less. The term is also used to mean "a great deal of" fabric, as in "I used bolts of fabric to decorate the living room."

bombazine (bom-buh-*zeen*) A black twilled fabric, used for mourning clothing in the past.

bonding (*bond*-ing) Bonding is a method of joining two layers of fabric with glue or a web of fibers which melts when heat is applied. Nonwoven fabrics are made in this way. The term is also occasionally used as a synonym for laminating, but this is technically incorrect. See laminating.

border (*bor*-der) Any type of distinct edging, such as a decorative edging on a fabric or a pillow.

border design (*bor*-der deh-*zyne*) A printed, woven, or knitted design which runs along the selvage of a fabric. Border designs are often made so they taper from small to large across the width of the fabric. To utilize the design properly, border fabrics usually must be used with the length of the goods running horizontally around the body, in contrast to the usual practice.

Botany (*bot*-uh-nee) A name for Australian wool (from Botany Bay, a section of Australia). Because this wool has a reputation for high quality the term is also used in trade and store names.

boucle (boo-*klay*) A rough, fairly thick, quite slubby yarn. Fabric made from boucle yarn, also called boucle, has a textured nubby surface which is usually dull unless shiny yarns are used. This look moves in and out of fashion. Boucle fabrics may be woven or knitted by hand or machine.

bourdon lace (*boor*-dohn layss) See lace.

box pleat (boks pleet) See pleat.

box spread (boks spred) See spread.

box-edged pillow (boks-edjd *pill*-oh) See pillow. See boxing, below.

boxing (*boks*-ing) Term describing the straight strip of fabric which covers the sides of a three-dimensional round or square pillow. The boxing is joined to the rest of the cover with seams which occasionally include a decorative trimming such as welting.

braid (brayd) Also known as plaiting. A method of making fabric by interlacing three or more yarns or strips of fabric. See braid rug, below, and trimming.

braid rug (brayd rug) A braid rug is made by joining strips of braid together with stitches. Braid rugs may be either rectangular, oval or round. See rugs and carpets.

Breton lace (*bret-*'n layss) See lace.

broadcloth (*brawd*-kloth) Although the term broadcloth originally meant any fabric made on a loom of a certain width, it now means a fine, tightly woven fabric with a faint rib. Originally, it was made of mercerized cotton but today is made of any fiber. Wool broadcloth (also imitated in man-made fibers) usually has a soft, slightly napped surface and is of medium weight.

broadloom (*brawd*-loom) A carpet term referring to any carpeting woven on a loom which is 9, 12, or 15 feet or wider. The term is frequently used incorrectly in advertising to imply a high quality product. See rugs and carpets.

brocade (broh-*kayd*) In clothing fabrics, brocade refers to a heavy, luxurious fabric made on a jacquard loom. Patterns often include flowers and leaves. Metallic threads are often used in brocades. Although true brocades are woven, today the term is also used for knits with a similar luxurious look. In carpeting, a brocade rug is one in which different yarns of the same color create a subtle pattern.

brocatel (broh-kuh-*tel*) A fabric similar to brocade made on a jacquard loom. The design has a distinct blistered or puffed appearance. See blister; see also, brocade, above.

broderie anglaise (brohd-ur-*ee* on-glayz) Another name for eyelet embroidery. See embroidery. See also eyelet.

brushing (*brush*-ing) A finishing process in which the fabric is swept by bristles to raise the nap. Blankets are often brushed; recently, brushed denim has been popular. Hand-knitting yarns,when made into garments, can be brushed for a soft, fluffy effect. Brushing is also used to remove threads and lint from the surface of a fabric. See also finishing.

Brussels (*bruss*-lz) See curtains, lace, and rugs and carpets.

buckram (*buck*-rum) A stiff open-weave fabric made from coarse yarns used primarily for stiffening as in interfacings and hat shaping. Originally, buckram was sized with starch which was not permanent, but today most buckrams have a permanent stiff finish.

buckskin (*buhk*-skin) A fairly inexpensive leather from deer and elk skins. See leather. Also, a fabric made in a form of satin weave with a napped finish. Originally wool, the term buckskin is now applied to various synthetic fabrics with smooth surfaces with or without the napped finish.

bugle beads (*byou*-gl beedz) Tube shaped beads, originally made of glass although often man-made today. They are used for jewelry and sewn to dresses as decoration.

bulking (*buhlk*-ing) A yarn finishing process in which the yarn is made thicker or "bulkier" by heat setting crimp into the filaments or by looping individual fibers with an air jet. Bulking gives the yarn and fabrics made from it a less shiny, fluffier appearance. Bulking is often used in making sweater yarns. See crimp; see heat setting.

bullion (*bul*-yun) See trimming.

bunting (*bunt*-ing) A loosely woven fabric used primarily for flags and draping. Usually, bunting used in public places must be flameproof. Bunting is also a term used to describe a simple rectangular square of material in which a baby is wrapped for warmth.

burlap (*burr*-lap) Coarse, heavy fabric made of jute and used for upholstery, wall coverings, commercial items (such as sacks), and occasionally fashion items. Burlap dyes well but may have a disagreeable odor unless treated.

burn-out printing (bern-out *print*-ing) See printing.

butcher's linen (*butch*-erz *lin*-'n) Strong, heavy, plain weave fabric, originally of linen (and originally worn by butchers) now made of any fiber.

butcher rayon (*butch*-er *ray*-on) A medium-weight fabric woven in a plain weave and originally intended as a substitute for butcher linen. See butcher linen, above.

buttonhole twists (*but*-'n-hole twist) See thread.

C

café curtains (ka-*fay kur*-tenz) See curtains and draperies.

calender printing (*kal*-en-der *print*-ing) See printing.

calendering (*kal*-en-der-ing) See finishing.

calf (kaf) See leather.

calico (*kal*-ih-ko) A smooth-surfaced plain weave cloth. Now the term is almost always applied to fabric with bright, sharply contrasting, usually small print designs. Calico is usually woven although calico prints may appear on knits. Calico is a traditionally popular fabric for patchwork.

cambric (*kaym*-brik) A plain weave fabric which is finished with a slightly glossy surface. The fabric is traditionally made from cotton or linen but can be made from any fiber. It was formerly used in underwear and handkerchiefs but today its major uses are for reinforcing book bindings and in upholstering, where it is used on the underside of chairs and sofas.

cambric finish (*kaym*-brik *fin*-ish) A glossy finish applied to fabrics. See finishing; see also, cambric, above.

camel hair or **camel's hair** (*kam*-'l hair) True camel hair, a luxury fiber, is considered a wool and comes from the camel. Today, camel hair is almost always blended with another fiber—sometimes sheep's wool, sometimes man-made fibers. Camel hair or camel's hair is also a color term, used to describe a rather yellowish tan.

candlewick (*kan*-d'l-wik) A thick, soft yarn used to form tufts by pulling it through a base fabric and then cutting it. The term also describes the fabric made by this method—a traditionally popular bedspread fabric.

Cantrece (kan-*treess*) DuPont trademark for a biconstituent nylon yarn which is given a crimp through a heat treatment resulting in a stretchable yarn. Often used for "one size fits all" hosiery. See nylon.

canvas (*kan*-vus) A heavy, strong, usually plain weave fabric which historically was made of flax, hemp, or cotton. Today it is usually made of cotton but some fabrics made of man-made fibers or blends are also called "canvas." Canvas is, roughly speaking, heavier than duck or sailcloth although the three names are often used interchangeably. See also duck and sailcloth.

Caprolan (*kap*-roh-lan) Trademark of Allied Chemical for nylon. See nylon.

caracul (*kair*-uh-kool) See astrakhan.

carding (*kard*-ing) Carding is a process in the conversion of cotton, wool, some silks, and man-made staple fibers into yarn. Carding separates the fibers and causes them to lie parallel to each other. It also removes dirt and impurities. See combing.

carpet (*kar*-pit) Originally a term which was interchangeable with rug, today the word carpet usually refers to a heavy fabric floor covering which covers the entire floor and is most often fastened to it in a somewhat permanent fashion. See rugs and carpets.

cartridge pleats (*kar*-trij pleetz) See pleats.

casement cloth (*kays*-ment kloth) A general term for fabrics, usually sheer, which can be used for curtains, draperies, or shades, although in practice the term is usually limited to open weave curtain fabrics.

cashmere (kash-*meer*) Cashmere is the wool of the cashmere (or Kashmir) goat, noted for its softness. Cashmere is one of the luxury fibers and today is usually blended with sheep's wool or man-made fiber to lower the cost of the finished fabric and to improve its wearing ability.

cavalry twill (*kav*-'l-ree twill) A strong twilled fabric, traditionally used for riding breeches and uniforms.

Celanese (*sel*-ah-neez) Celanese Corporation is a fiber producer.

cellular cloth (*sel*-you-lar kloth) A fabric woven so that it traps air, reproducing the effects of layers of clothing or blankets. A cellular blanket should be used with another, non-cellular covering on top of it to hold in the warm air produced by body heat.

cellulose (*sel*-you-lohs) The naturally occuring polymer (giant molecule) that forms the solid framework of plants. Cellulose from wood pulp is the base for rayon and acetate, both of which are man-made fibers. Cotton is more than 90% cellulose before it is cleaned (scoured). See cotton, rayon, and acetate.

cellulosic fibers (*sel*-you-loh-sik *fy*-bers) Fibers made from cellulose. See cellulose, above.

chainette fringe (*chayn*-et frinj) See trimming.

chalk stripe (chawk stryp) See entry under stripe.

challis (*shal*-ee) Soft, lightweight fabric made of wool, cotton, or man-made fibers. Challis is traditionally printed with vivid floral patterns on dark grounds or with Paisley designs. See Paisley.

chambray (*sham*-bray) A lightweight cloth with a colored warp and a white filling thread, originally made of cotton but today made of any fiber. Although chambray is traditionally woven, the look itself is so popular it is imitated in knitting. It is similar in appearance to denim but much lighter in weight. Chambray is usually solid with the white filling threads giving it a pastel look, but it can also be woven in patterns. See denim.

chamois (*sham*-wa [correct pronunciation] *sham*-ee [customary pronunciation]) Soft, pliable leather from the skin of the chamois goat, although other animal skins may be substituted. Chamois cloth is woven to imitate the leather, usually has a slightly napped surface and is usually yellow, as is the goat skin.

Chanel (sha-*nel*) Gabrielle ("Coco") Chanel (1884?-1971) was a French fashion designer whose influence has lasted beyond her lifetime. A Chanel tweed is a colorful tweed woven from bulky yarns which are usually thick and thin with many slubs. The term "Chanel tweed" is used loosely for any large-patterned tweed of this kind and comes from the tweeds used by this designer for suits. A Chanel chain is a metal linked chain sewn into the bottom edge of suit jackets to help them keep their shape.

changeable fabric (*chayn*-juh-b'l *fab*-rik) Fabric woven with yarns of one color in the warp and another color in the filling so that the fabric seems to change color as the light strikes it. Other names for this type of fabric are iridescent and shot.

Chantilly (shan-*til*-ee) See lace.

check (chek) A check is any small, regular pattern of squares which is woven or knitted into or printed on a fabric. See types of checks below.

    broken check (*broh*-ken chek) A check pattern in which the checks are irregular rather than forming perfect squares.

    district check (*dis*-trikt chek) District check is the name given to several quite different woven check patterns which originated in Scotland. The term applies to designs ranging from glen checks to shepherd checks.

    gingham check (*ging*-um chek) Regular check in which the design is woven so that, in a red and white checked gingham, for instance, there are squares of solid red, squares of solid white, and squares with white warp and red filling as well as squares with red warp and white filling. Gingham checks are also printed on woven and knitted fabrics and are knitted into some fabrics by means of a jacquard attachment.

    glen check (glen chek) Glen patterns usually consist of checks in varying colors with overlines or overchecks of other colors. Glen checks and glen plaids are the same.

    gun club check (gun klub chek) A double check design in which a large check is superimposed on a smaller one. The name is rarely used in the United States but the design is a popular one.

houndstooth check (*howndz*-tooth chek) A broken check, regular in pattern. This check is extremely popular. It shows up periodically on everything from woolens to shower curtains.

overcheck (*oh*-ver chek) A design in which one check is woven or printed over another of a different size. Glen checks are overchecks.

pin check (pin chek) A checked pattern in which the squares are extremely small.

shepherd check (*shep*-erd chek) A pattern of small, regular checks which is usually brown and white or black and white. It is called a shepherd check because as one theory states, the wool for it could be taken from white and black sheep and woven without further dyeing. It is made in many fabrics. This is a district check and is rarely out of fashion.

Tattersall check (*tat*-er-sol chek) Tattersall checks are an overcheck pattern in two colors, usually on a white or other colored ground. An example would be a pattern of brown lines going in one direction crossed by green lines in the opposite direction forming the checks on a yellow background. These checks were named for Richard Tattersall who used the pattern on horse blankets. See overcheck, above.

cheese cloth (*cheez* kloth) Loosely woven, plain weave fabric originally used in making cheese. Today, cheese cloth is popular for polishing cloths because of its softness and economy. From time to time, cheese cloth becomes fashionable for curtains.

chenille (shuh-*neel*) A pile yarn originally made by weaving a pile fabric and subsequently cutting it into strips. Chenille is popular in rugs, bedspreads, and bathroom accessories. See pile.

cheviot (*shev*-ee-ut) A rough-surfaced fabric, usually with a heavy nap, popular at various times primarily for coatings. Originally, a woolen fabric made from the wool of cheviot sheep which originated in the Cheviot hills of Great Britain.

chevron (*shev*-run) A design which forms horizontal rows of joined V's. Also called flame stitch. In effect, chevron fabrics are almost identical to bargello or Florentine embroidery. See embroidery.

chiffon (shif-*ahn*) Sheer, lightweight, drapeable woven fabric, originally made of silk but usually made from man-made fibers today. Chiffon is usually available in a wide color range from soft pastels to bright bold colors. It is often used for dresses of colored layers to form a rainbow effect.

China silk (*chy*-nuh silk) Traditionally an inexpensive, lightweight lining fabric. China silk has almost disappeared today and has been replaced with lining fabrics of man-made fibers.

chinchilla (chin-*chil*-uh) Chinchilla cloth has a short, more or less curly surface design made to mock chinchilla fur. It is used primarily as a fabric for coats. See also chinchilla under dictionary entry for furs.

chine (*shee*-nay) This French word, meaning speckled, is used for fabrics in which the warp threads are printed before weaving while the filling threads are left plain, giving a shadowy effect to the finished fabric. See warp printing under printing.

chino (*chee*-no) Originally, chino was a slightly twilled fabric used for summer military uniforms. Today, the name is given to any medium-weight, sturdy fabric with a slight sheen. Khaki green and military tan are still common chino colors, but the fabric is also made in other colors.

chintz (chintz) Any closely woven, plain weave fabric printed in bright designs which are most often floral. Today, most chintz has a glazed finish. It is used extensively for draperies and upholstery and is one of the few fabrics still made almost exclusively of 100% cotton; however, it will probably soon be made in man-made fibers as well.

chip straw (chip straw) See straw.

chlorine retentive (*klor*-een ree-*ten*-tiv) Term used to describe fibers and fabrics which yellow and lose strength when chlorine bleach is used on them. Spandex is a chlorine retentive fiber. Chlorine also renders some finishes ineffective.

circular (*sir*-kyou-lar) Circular is a term used to describe both weaving and knitting machines and their finished products. A circular loom or knitting machine produces a tubular fabric which is often slit as one of the manufacturing steps, to make it more like flat fabrics.

cire (*seer*-ay) An extremely shiny, glossy surface given to fabrics as part of the finishing process. Cire fabrics have a much higher shine than glazed fabrics and are usually somewhat slippery.

cisele velvet (*sis*-eh-lay *vel*-vit) See velvet.

classic (*klass*-ik) A term applied, quite loosely, to any traditional print, pattern, design, weave, or style which has been considered excellent over a period of years.

cleaning (*kleen*-ing) See section on care.

clock (klok) A small decorative design usually knitted or flocked in a vertical line on the outer ankle of stockings and socks.

cloque (*kloh*-kay) Term used to describe a fabric with a raised design, often used interchangeably with matelasse and blister. Cotton cloque is frequently popular for summer dress and jacket or coat costumes. See blister, matellasse.

cloth (kloth) Another term for fabric or material. Implicit in the word cloth and not in fabric or material is the use of fibers to produce the resulting product.

cluny lace (*kloo*-nee layss) See lace.

coating (*koht*-ing) A term used to describe a fabric suitable for outerwear, such as coats, as in "coating fabric." Also, something applied to a finished fiber or fabric, such as a rubber coating to make a fabric impervious to water. Coating suggests a thicker layer of the substance than does the word finish. In other words, a rubber-coated fabric is probably more resistant to water than one that has been treated with a water-resistant finish.

coin dot (koyn dot) See dots.

Coloray (*kul*-ur-ray) Trademark of Courtaulds for rayon.

colorfast (*kul*-er-fast) A term which implies that the color in a fabric will not wash out or fade upon exposure to sunlight or other atmospheric elements. There are no standards for the use of this term, so it may be relatively meaningless to the consumer.

combing (*kohm*-ing) A process in the manufacture of cotton and man-made yarns in which the fibers are combed to remove short lengths of fiber leaving only longer ones. Combed fibers are finer than ones which are not combed. A similar process called hackling is used on flax in the course of manufacturing linen. Carding, a similar process, is a first step in refining yarns; combing produces even finer yarns.

comforter (*kum*-fer-ter) See quilt.

coney (*koh*-nee) See rabbit, under fur.

continuous filament (kon-*tin*-you-us *fil*-ah-mint) A term which emphasizes the long, uncut nature of a filament of fiber, always man-made except in the case of silk. Nylon made in continuous filament form for carpeting wears better than other fiber forms.

coq (kohk) See feathers.

cord (kord) See trimming, see corded fabric, below.

corded fabric (*kor*-did *fab*-rik) The term corded fabric (often shortened to cord) refers to fabrics with a lengthwise rib, often woven in stripes. Any fabric with a lengthwise rib is a corded fabric.

cord gimp (kord gimp) See trimming.

cording (*kord*-ing) See trimming.

cordovan (*kor*-de-van) See leather.

corduroy (*kor*-duh-roy) A corded fabric in which the rib has been sheared or woven to produce a smooth, velvet-like nap. Traditionally made of cotton, corduroy can be made of many different fibers today.

cornice (*kor*-niss) A decorative heading for window draperies, often covered with fabric to match. It has corners and usually juts out into the room. A cornice is often made of wood.

cotton (*kot-*'n) Cotton is the name of the fiber from the cotton plant and also the fabric made from this fiber. Different types of cotton plants produce cotton of higher or lower quality usually associated with staple length and fineness of the fiber. Certain names for these plants are occasionally seen in advertising—Sea Island, Egyptian, Pima, for instance—to indicate quality of the fiber. See Chapter One, Fibers—The Start of It All; and Chapter Two, From Fiber to Fabric.

cotton gin (*kot*'n jin) The machine which revolutionized cotton production by enabling the removal of seeds from cotton by machine rather than by hand.

cotton knits (*kot*'n nits) Cotton knits are made by the same methods as other knits, although they often are of finer gauge than wool and man-made fiber knits. They are the traditional underwear fabric but have become popular for shirts, dresses, and sportswear recently. Many cotton knits today include some man-made fiber to reduce shrinkage and give the knit somewhat greater stability.

coverlet (*kuhv*-er-let) See throw.

covert cloth (*koh*-vert kloth) A twill weave, medium or heavyweight cloth, originally made from woolen or worsted yarns but now also made from man-made fibers. Popular for coats, sportswear, riding clothing.

cowhide (*kow*-hyd) See leather.

crabbing (*krab*-ing) One of the final finishing processes in the manufacture of woolens, similar to heat setting. This finish gives woolens their final appearance. See finishing.

crash (krash) Coarse woven fabric with a rough surface, used in binding books and, occasionally, as a fashion and curtain fabric.

crease resistant (*krees* ree-*zis*-tant) The term crease resistant means that a fabric has been treated so that it will wrinkle less than it would normally. Fabrics are usually made crease resistant as part of the finishing process. See finishing.

crepe (krayp) A dull-surfaced fabric with an all over crinkled surface. This surface may be obtained through the use of crepe yarns (yarns which have such a high twist that the yarn kinks), chemical treatment with caustic soda, embossing, or weaving (usually with thicker warp yarns and thinner filling yarns). Although crepe is traditionally woven, crepe yarns are used now to produce knit crepes. See finishing.

crepe-backed satin (*krayp*-bakt *sat*'-n) A two-faced fabric which can be used on either side. One side is satin while the reverse, made of twisted yarns, is crepe.

crepe de Chine (*krayp* duh *sheen*) Traditionally, a very sheer silk fabric. Today, any lightweight crepe, usually made of man-made fibers, is likely to be given this name.

crepe georgette (*krayp* jor-*jet*) See georgette.

Creslan (*kres*-lan) Trademark of American Cyanamid for acrylic fiber.

cretonne (kreh-*tahn*) A printed drapery and home furnishings fabric, similar to unglazed chintz. It is traditionally made of cotton.

crewel (*kroo*-'l) A type of embroidery which utilizes almost every embroidery stitch and is worked with a fairly thick wool yarn called crewel yarn. The designs are often quite large and often extremely stylized.

crimp (krimp) The waviness of a fiber which affects the final performance. Wool has a natural crimp. Man-made yarns are often crimped during yarn processing. Crimp is desirable because it increases resiliency, absorbency, and resistance to abrasion. It also adds bulk and warmth to the final fabric.

crinkle crepe (*krink*-'l krayp) A fabric with an uneven surface created by the use of caustic soda which causes it to shrink unevenly. Plisse is an example of a crinkle crepe fabric. Crinkle crepe and plisse usually have a larger pattern to the surface irregularities than crepe. See plisse and seersucker.

crinoline (*krin*-uh-lin) Although crinoline is used as a term for a stiff, bouffant petticoat designed to support a very full skirt, strictly speaking it refers to the fabric from which these petticoats are made—a stiff open fabric which has been heavily sized in the finishing process. Originally crinoline was made of linen and horsehair but today any fiber like nylon may be used.

crisp fabric (krisp *fab*-rik) A comparative, descriptive term used as the opposite to soft fabrics. Organdy is a typical crisp fabric. Crisp fabrics stand away from the figure and have more body than soft fabrics.

crochet (kroh-*shay*) A method of making fabric in which one yarn and one needle are used to form loops into which other loops are inserted. True crochet is a handcraft. Machine made crochets are usually knitted on raschel machines.

crock (krok) Technical term which describes the way in which dye on the surface of a fabric rubs off onto other fabrics or onto the skin. In some fabrics, such as colored suede leathers, crocking is unavoidable.

crocodile (*krok*-uh-dy'l) See leather.

cross-dyeing (krawss *dy*-ing) A method for coloring fabrics made from more than one kind of fiber, for example a wool and cotton blend. Each fiber in a fabric designed for cross-dyeing will take a specific dye in a different color or in variations of one color. Therefore, a fabric that is cross-dyed is more than one color. Cross-dyeing is often used to create heather effects (soft, misty colorings), but strongly patterned fabrics can also be achieved depending on the fibers used in the fabric.

cross stitch (krawss stich) See embroidery.

Cupioni (koo-pee-*oh*-nee) Trademark of Beaunit for a slubbed cuprammonium rayon fiber. See rayon.

cuprammonium rayon (koo-pree-*moh*-nee-um *ray*-on) See rayon.

cure (kyoor) See durable press.

curtains and **draperies** (*kur*-tenz and *dray*-per-eez) Curtains are a window covering, usually unlined, which hang within the framework of the window, ending at the windowsill. They are decorative and functional at the same time. Draperies are almost always lined and are usually made of fairly heavy fabrics which are often quite luxurious such as satin or velvet. They normally hang to the floor, but in very formal rooms they may even lie on the floor.

Curtains and draperies can be made of almost any fabric. Fabrics made of glass fiber are extremely popular for window coverings as curtains or draperies. "Drapes" is an abbreviation for draperies, commonly used instead of the longer word. Following are specific types of curtains and draperies.

> **Brussels curtains** (*bruhs*-selz *kur*-tenz) Curtains made of net with an embroidered design done either by hand or machine, over the net. The net may be one layer or two.

> **café curtains** (ka-*fay kur*-tenz) Curtains which are hung in tiers, so that one row covers the top half of a window, a second row the bottom. They are hung on a wood or metal pole which is placed across the top and across the center of the window. Café curtains are often finished with scalloped edges through which the pole slides or there are also café curtain rings available for hanging them. These curtains are usually hung only in two tiers, but may be hung in any number of tiers.

> **glass fibers** (glass *fy*-berz) Curtains made of glass fiber yarns. Sheer glass fiber curtains are often used behind draperies, but glass fiber curtains are also available in heavier, opaque fabric constructions. Glass fiber curtains should be washed carefully by hand and hung to dry while they are still wet. See Fiberglas. See also charts on fabric care.

> **tie-backs** (*ty*-baks) A full length (either to the windowsill or to the floor) curtain or drapery which is looped back at the side of the window with a band of trimming or self-fabric. The curtain or drapery is closed at the top of the window, and almost entirely open at the point of the tie-back. The look is popular in informal houses in such fabrics as organdy and batiste and in formal houses in luxurious fabrics.

cushion (*kuhsh*-'n) See pillow. See also padding (for rugs and carpets).

cut pile (kut py'l) Many fabrics are formed with loops on the surface. When these are cut, they form a cut pile. Some velvets and many pile rugs are made in this manner. See pile.

cut-and-sewn (kut-and-sohn) A description of how certain knit garments are made. A cut-and-sewn knit garment is made by cutting the garment pieces from a piece of knit fabric and then stitching the pieces together. The other method of making knit garments is full-fashioned. See full-fashioned.

cut velvet (kut *vel*-vit) See velvet.

cylinder printing (*sil*-en-der *print*-ing) See printing.

𝕯

Dacron (*day*-kron) Trademark of DuPont for polyester fiber.

damask (*dam*-usk) a heavy jacquard weave fabric used for tablecloths, home furnishings, and occasionally clothing. Linen damask is the traditional fabric for fine tablecloths.

darn (darn) A form of embroidery normally used to repair worn spots in fabric, the darn is occasionally used for the sake of novelty. A darn is formed by making a series of long stitches in one direction covering the area to be darned. Another thread is woven over and under these long stitches to form the finished darn.

decorative fabric (*dec*-kra-tiv *fab*-riks) A term used to describe fabrics used in home decorating for upholstery, slipcovers, and curtains and draperies. These fabrics are usually of heavier weights than the fashion fabrics used in clothing. Also called decorator fabrics and home furnishings fabrics.

decorator fabrics (*dek*-er-ay-tor *fab*-riks) See decorative fabrics.

delavé (*day*-lah-vay) French word for "washed out" and applied to jeans. When jeans became popular all over the world, the bleached jeans became popular too. American buyers importing jeans from France into America picked up the word delavé and used it in preference to the word bleached. See also jeans.

delustering (dee-*luhst*-er-ing) A process which dulls the characteristic shine of man-made fibers. Particles of a chemical are added to the fiber mixture before it is "spun." This results in fibers with softer, muted color tones.

denier (*den*-year) A technical term referring to the weight of silk and man-made yarns; used in hosiery as a description of sheerness. The lower the denier number, the sheerer the stocking, panty hose, or garment. For instance, 40 denier hose are much finer and more sheer than 60 denier hose.

denim (*den*-'m) Officially, denim is a twill weave fabric with a colored warp and a white filling thread. However, when the fabric and the look became popular the name was given to many other types of fabric, including cross-dyed fabrics and brushed fabrics, both knit and woven, that resemble true denim. Most jeans are made of denim; the most popular and traditional denim color is blue.

detergent (dih-*tur*-jent) Detergent is the overall term for a cleansing agent, either soap or synthetic, but it has come to be applied only to synthetic (non-soap) detergents.

diamante (dee-ah-*mahn*-tay) Another word for rhinestone. See rhinestone.

dimity (*dim*-uh-tee) A lightweight, moderately sheer fabric which often has fine woven stripes or other patterns such as small flowers. This fabric was traditionally made of cotton but now is often made of man-made fibers. It is used primarily for dresses and curtains.

direct printing (duh-*rekt print*-ing) See printing.

discharge printing (*dis*-charj *print*-ing) See printing.

dish towels (dish towlz) See towels.

dobby (*dahb*-ee) A dobby fabric is one with small geometric figures incorporated in the weave. It is made with a dobby attachment on the loom. Less elaborate than a jacquard attachment, which also produces geometric designs, the dobby is used to produce geometric designs such as those found in pique fabrics. See pique.

doeskin (*doh*-skin) Today, usually the skin of a white sheep, although originally it was the skin of a deer, hare, or rabbit. See leather. Also used for any fabric made of wool or man-made fibers with a soft, often napped, finish.

domestics (doh-*mes*-tiks) Domestics, primarily a term used by stores, refers to such household items as sheets and towels. Domestics are also items made domestically, that is, in the United States. See linens and domestics.

Donegal (*dohn*-eh-gahl) Originally a fabric woven by hand in County Donegal, Ireland. Today the term is used to refer to any tweed made with thick, usually colored, slubs as part of the fabric. The term tweed is usually used with Donegal. See tweed.

dope dyeing (dohp-*dy*-ing) The process of coloring a man-made fiber before it is solidified or spun while it is at the syrupy or melted stage. Also called solution dyeing, spun dyeing. See Chapter Two, From Fiber To Fabric.

dots (dahtz) A popular circular design usually positioned in a regular pattern on the fabric although the placing may appear random. Dots may be woven, knitted, or printed. Sizes usually determine the name of the dots. Aspirin dots, for instance, are the size of an aspirin tablet and are also called polka dots. Coin dots are around the size of a 5¢ or 25¢ piece. Swiss dots are ones which look like those on dotted Swiss, white pin dots are extremely small dots.

dotted Swiss (*daht*-ted Swiss) Swiss is a fine sheer fabric of almost any fiber whose name has been almost forgotten except in the form of dotted Swiss. Dotted Swiss fabric is this fabric with very small dots on it, often woven in. The dots, however, may be flocked (see flock) or even printed. Some knitted fabrics, made with a thread on the surface which forms a dot, are also called dotted Swiss, although they are not the traditional Swiss fabric.

double backing (*duh*-b'l *bak*-ing) See backing.

double cloth (*duh*-b'l kloth) A double cloth fabric is made of two fabrics woven one above the other and joined at the center with threads. A true double cloth can be split into two distinct layers of fabric by cutting the threads between the layers. Velvet is often made as a double cloth and then cut to form the pile.

double damask (*duh*-b'l *dam*-usk) A rich traditional tablecloth, made in a heavier weight than ordinary damask.

double face (*duh*-b'l fayss) A double cloth which can be used on either side. Also used to describe any fabric with two right sides.

double faced satin (*duh*-b'l fayst *sat*-'n) See satin.

double knit (*duh*-b'l nit) A fabric made on a weft knitting machine. Both sides are usually identical unless the fabric has a pattern. See chart of fabrics. See also, "Types of Knits" in Chapter Two.

doupion (*doo*-pee-ahn) Silk which comes from the fiber formed by two silk worms who spun their cocoons together. Also called douppioni, dupion, and dupioni.

down (down) See feathers.

drapeable fabric (*drayp*-uh-b'l *fab*-rik) A descriptive term for fabrics which are soft and flowing, tend to cling somewhat to the body, and can be arranged in soft gathers. Drapeable fabrics are made from a variety of yarns and in a variety of ways, including both knitting and weaving. They must be fairly lightweight to drape properly.

draperies (*dray*-per-eez) See curtains and draperies.

drill (dril) A strong twilled fabric of cotton or man-made fibers used when strength of fabric is essential, such as for workclothes and pockets. See twill.

drip-dry (drip dry) A method for drying a garment. The term drip-dry was used at one time almost as a synonym for durable press. Drip-dry garments should not be wrung, but rather hung carefully to dry while still dripping wet and when dry they should need little, if any, ironing.

drugget (*drug*-it) See rugs and carpets.

dry cleaning (dry *kleen*-ing) A method of cleaning certain fabrics which is done with organic solvents instead of water.

drying (*dry*-ing) Drying is one of the finishing processes in the manufacture of fabrics. A great deal of water is used in the course of making fabrics and drying is important to remove this water. Fabrics which are dried at too high a temperature for too long a time become harsh, so this drying is carefully watched. See also finishing and section on care.

duchesse satin (du-*shess sat*-'n) See satin.

duck (duk) Originally, a fabric lighter in weight than canvas. Today, the terms are synonymous. See canvas.

duffel cloth (*duf*-f'l kloth) A thick, heavy, napped coating fabric, usually used for duffel coats—hooded coats with wooden buttons which fasten through rope or leather thongs. Duffel cloth is traditionally tan or green, but can be any color.

dungaree (*duhn*-guh-ree) A heavy, blue denim fabric used in work clothes. The term dungaree is occasionally used as a synonym for denim and the term dungarees as a synonym for the pants also known as blue jeans. See also jean.

dupion, dupioni (*doo*-pee-ahn, doo-pee-*oh*-nee) See doupion.

duplex printing (*doo*-plex *print*-ing) See printing.

durable finish (*door*-uh-bul *fin*-ish) A rather loose term for a finish added to fabric as one of the final steps to improve the wearability of the fabric.

durable press (*door*-uh-bul press) Durable press describes a fabric or garment treated so that it should not require ironing. There are two methods of creating true durable press garments, pre-curing and post-curing. In pre-curing, a chemical resin is applied to the fabric which is dried and then cured (baked at a high temperature). In post-curing, the resin is added to the fabric, the fabric is made into the garment, and the garment is then pressed and cured.

dust ruffle (dust *ruf*-'l) Dust ruffles were originally detachable, wide ruffles at the bottom of women's floor-length skirts which could be removed for washing before the rest of the garment required washing. Dust ruffles are now found almost exclusively as part of bedpsreads or as separate ruffles placed over the box spring. They can be removed for cleaning separate from the bedspread. See spread.

dyeing (*dy*-ing) A method of giving color to a garment, fabric, yarn, or to the solution from which the fiber is made. Common dyeing methods include:

　batik (bah-*teek*) A form of resist dyeing using wax. See resist dyeing, below.

　cross-dyeing (krawss *dy*-ing) Refers to a method of coloring fabric made of more than one fiber. The different fibers or types of fiber take the dye in different ways, producing special effects such as heathers or patterns.

dope dyeing (dohp *dy*-ing) In dope dyeing, the solution for man-made fiber is colored before making it into fiber. Also called solution dyeing and spun dyeing.

piece dyeing (peess *dy*-ing) The dyeing of a finished fabric. Cross-dyeing is a type of piece dyeing. See cross-dyeing, above.

resist dyeing (ree-*zist* *dy*-ing) In resist dyeing, areas which are to be colored are left to be exposed to the dye, while other areas, not to be colored, are covered with something impervious to dye. Batik is a form of resist dyeing in which wax is used to cover the area where dye is not wanted.

solution dyeing (suh-*loo*-shun *dy*-ing) See dope dyeing, above.

spun dyeing (spun *dy*-ing) See dope dyeing, above.

tie dyeing (ty *dy*-ing) A form of resist dyeing. Items to be dyed are tied or knotted so that the folds of the fabric form barriers to the dye to create patterns or designs on the fabric.

vat dyeing (vat *dy*-ing) Vat dyeing refers to the type of dye rather than to the way in which the dyeing is done. Vat dyes are oxidized after they combine with the fibers to form the color and are considered more wash-fast than most other dyes.

yarn dyeing (yarn *dy*-ing) In yarn dyeing, fiber already made into yarn which will be used for the manufacture of fabric is dyed, usually on a spool, under heat and pressure. Yarn dyed fabrics are considered more colorfast than piece dyed fabrics or fabrics which are printed.

Dynel (dy-*nel*) Trademark of Union Carbide for modacrylic fiber.

E

easy care (*ee*-zee kehr) An extremely loose term which implies that a limited amount of ironing will be necessary after the item is washed. Easy care fabrics seem to be most successful when they are made of at least 65% polyester or have had a special finish applied to them. Durable press is a more reliable indication that garments or other items require little or no ironing.

Egyptian cotton (ee-*jip*-shun *kot*-'n) A fine, long, staple cotton generally grown in Egypt. Egyptian cotton fibers produce a strong, lustrous yarn. See cotton. See also staple.

eiderdown (*eye*-der-down) See linens and domestics. See also, feathers and quilt.

elastic (ih-*las*-tik) The word elastic implies stretch, recovery, and spring (a certain amount of bounce). For years, the word was limited to items made of rubber, but in recent years man-made elastics (anidex, spandex) have been developed. Woven elastic and braided elastic in fairly narrow widths are used in clothing on edges where it is desirable to have a certain degree of stretch and recovery. Woven elastic remains the same width when it is stretched; braided elastic becomes narrower when it is stretched.

embossing (im-*bawss*-ing) A method of producing an indented design on a fabric. Embossing is done usually with a heated roller with a raised section which forms the design. It is done as part of the finishing process. Today, most embossing is permanent. See finishing.

embroidery (im-*broyd*-er-ee) The term for a group of decorative, usually nonfunctional stitches done with thread or yarn on fabric. Most machine embroidery is done by the Schiffli machine which can imitate many different hand embroidery stitches. Although embroidery is usually thought of as being done in several colors, white work (white embroidery on white fabric) and black work (black embroidery on white fabric) are fairly common.

Embroidery terms are tremendously variable, with different words being given to the same stitches in different countries and even in different sections of the same countries. Some of the most common embroidery stitches are: beading, buttonhole stitch, chain stitch, chevron stitch, cross stitch, feather stitch, French knot, lazy daisy stitch, satin stitch, stem stitch, back stitch, and straight stitch.

embroidery floss (im-*broyd*-er-ee flawss) A fine, low twist yarn made of silk, rayon, cotton, or man-made fibers used for embroidery. See also thread.

embroidery thread (im-*broyd*-er-ee thred) A fairly loose term for a thread which can be used in embroidery. Buttonhole twist is often referred to as embroidery thread. See thread.

Encron (*en*-kron) Trademark of American Enka Company for polyester fiber.

even plaid (*ee*-vin plad) See plaid.

Everglaze (*eh*-ver-glayz) Trademark of Bancroft Licensing for certain finishes, most notably a permanent glazed finish applied to chintz.

extract printing (*eks*-trakt *print*-ing) See printing.

eyelash (*eye*-lash) Term used to describe clipped yarns which lie on the surface of a fabric, giving an effect of eyelashes.

eyelet (*eye*-lit) Fabrics embroidered with openwork patterns created with holes which are reinforced with buttonhole stitches. The entire fabric is called eyelet and it comes in various widths, from narrow widths for use as trimming to wide widths for use as entire garments. White eyelet embroidery on a white ground is also called Broderie Anglaise, but other color combinations for eyelet embroidery are also used. The term eyelet is also used to refer to the holes in very open knitted fabrics.

F

fabric (*fab*-rik) Any braided, felted, woven, knitted, or nonwoven material, including not only cloth but also hosiery and lace. Fabric is also referred to as cloth, goods, material, and stuff.

face (fayss) The "right" side of the fabric, the side of the fabric which is meant to be seen.

face cloth (fayss kloth) See towels.

face finished fabric (fayss *fin*-isht *fab*-rik) A fabric which is finished (napped or brushed, for instance) only on the right side. See finishing.

faconne velvet (*fass*-oh-nay *vel*-vit) See velvet.

faille (fyle) A silk or man-made fiber fabric which has a very narrow crosswise rib. Ottoman is similar to faille but has a wider rib. Faille is considered a dressy fabric and is used usually for evening clothes, handbags, and shoes. See ottoman.

fake fur (fayk fur) Slang term for pile fabrics and garments made from them which imitate animal pelts. The most popular fake furs are probably those made from modacrylic fiber. See also modacrylic and pile.

false furs (fawls furz) Another term for fake fur. See fake fur.

fashion fabric (*fash*-un *fab*-rik) A general term describing any fabric which is made into apparel. The term is also used as a name for material which is sold to the consumer by the yard. Fabrics used in home furnishings are not fashion fabrics but decorative fabrics. See decorative fabrics.

feathers (*feth*-ers) The plumage of birds, feathers were once an important fashion accessory and ornamentation used profusely on hats and as trimming. With time, however, an awakened social conscience resulted in the passage of laws protecting the birds. Today, although the names of the original birds are still used,

101

almost all feathers come from domesticated fowl (chickens, turkeys) and are treated to resemble the feathers of the most exotic, protected birds. Among the most important feather names are:

aigrette (*ay*-gret) A spray of feathers. See individual entry for aigrette.

coq (kohk) A term used to describe feathers, usually fairly short ones, which are used in trimming.

down (down) The softest, shortest feathers are called down. Types of down include eiderdown, originally only from ducks but used to refer to any very soft feathers and also to describe a feather-filled bed covering, and goose down.

marabou (*mayr*-uh-boo) Short fluffy feathers now taken from domesticated fowl, usually dyed to match the garments on which they are used as trimming. They were originally taken from the stork.

osprey (*oss*-pree) Osprey feathers are, like marabou feathers, usually from domesticated fowl today. The term is used for feathers which form a plume.

ostrich (*oss*-trich) Ostrich feathers are long, usually coiled feathers, often dyed to match a garment.

peacock (*pee*-kahk) Peacock feathers are extremely long and can be recognized by the eye-like design at the end of the feather. They are rarely used in fashion but occasionally become popular as a room accent.

felt (fehlt) A fabric made from wool, fur, and hair fibers which mesh together when heat, moisture, and mechanical action are applied. Some percentage of wool is necessary in the manufacture of true felt to achieve the felted effect.

festoon (fess-*toon*) See trimming.

fiber (*fy*-ber) The basic material from which fabrics are made is called fiber. Fibers are much longer than they are wide. The term at one time was limited to materials which could be spun into yarn but now is used to include filaments which do not require spinning, such as, silk and man-made fibers.

Fiber Products Indentification Act (*fy*-ber *prahd*-ukts eye-dent-ih-fih-*kay*-shun akt) This act is a ruling by the Federal Trade Commission requiring that certain textile items, including garments and fabric sold to the consumer by the yard, be labeled to show fiber content by generic name, proportions of each fiber by weight, the manufacturer of the item and, if the fabric was not made in the United States, the country where it was made. The requirement of the manufacturer's name is modified so that instead of a name, the manufacturer can use an anonymous number, called an RN number.

fiberfill (*fy*-ber-fil) A man-made fluffy material used, among other things, to pad brassieres, stuff pillows, and make quilts. Most fiberfill is polyester.

Fiberglas (*fy*-ber-glass) Trademark of Owens-Corning for glass fiber.

Fibro (*fy*-broh) Trademark of Courtaulds for rayon fiber.

filament (*fil*-ah-ment) Extremely long fibers which, therefore, do not require spinning to form yarn. Silk is the only natural filament; man-made fibers can be filament or staple (short, to be spun into yarn). Filaments usually produce a fabric which is smooth and shiny; this can be changed in various ways, including crimping the yarn or changing the shape of the filament itself. Man-made filaments are often grouped into a filament bundle for a more effective final yarn. See Chapter One, Fiber—The Start of It All.

filling (*fill*-ing) The crosswise thread which interlaces with the warp threads on a woven fabric is called filling. Also called weft, woof, shoot, and shute. Filling, however, is the most common term used in the textile industry in the United States, partly because it describes the function of the yarn so well.

findings (*fynd*-ings) Findings is a term for such items as buttons, interfacings, pockets, belts, snap fasteners, and zippers used in making garments. Findings is a term used in the fabric and fashion industry primarily. Notions is the consumer term for these items. They are normally purchased in a notions department but sometimes you'll find them in smallwares or haberdashery.

fingering yarn (*fing*-er-ing yarn) A two-ply or three-ply yarn, usually made of wool or acrylic. Fingering yarn has an even thickness, is light or medium in weight, and is popular for hand knitting of such items as baby sweaters. See ply.

finishing (*fin*-ish-ing) An over-all term which usually refers to all processes, with the exception of coloring, which make fabric more acceptable. (Some experts also include coloring.) To the consumer, the most important finishing steps are those which have an obvious impact on final performance. Terms referring to finishes of that nature are defined in this dictionary individually. Much of the look, feel, and behavior of a fabric is determined by the finishing steps taken.

Finishing can be mechanical (as in calendering, see below) or chemical, or both. Special treatments are applied to fabrics during finishing to make them perform better—shrink less, resist flames, and repel water, for instance.

Calendering refers to a process in which the fabric is passed through heated cylinders. This gives the fabric a lustrous surface and can also emboss it. Another important step in finishing and usually the final process is tentering; it gives the fabric its final shape by passing it through heat while it is in a stretched position.

fireproof (*fyr*-proof) Fireproof means that a fabric literally will not burn. To be labeled fireproof, the Federal Trade Commission requires that a fabric must be 100% fireproof. If the fiber or fabric has been treated to prevent flames from spreading, it must be labeled as fire resistant. See fire resistant, below. See flame retardant fabric.

fire resistant (*fyr* ree-*zis*-tant) Fire resistant refers to a fabric or fiber which has been treated to discourage the spreading of flames. See flame retardant fabric, below.

fisheye (fish-eye) A large woven geometric pattern, similar to birdseye. See birdseye.

fishnet (fish-net) A coarse fabric which has knots in each corner of a geometrically shaped hole. It is sometimes used for curtains and hosiery as well as for fishing. See net.

flameproof (*flaym*-proof) Flameproof is a synonym for fireproof. See fireproof.

flame retardant fabric (*flaym* ree-*tar*-dent *fa*brik) A fabric which resists or retards the spreading of flames. A flame retardant fabric can be made by using fibers which are in themselves flame retardant or by using special finishes on fabrics. Below is a listing of some of the names of flame retardant fabrics. Many companies produce similar items but have not given them names referring specifically to their flame retardant nature.

>   **Cordelan** (*kohr*-deh-lan) Kohjin Company's biconstituent, flame retardant fiber of 50% vinyl and 50% vinyon. See biconstituent fiber.
>
>   **Fire Stop** (fyr stop) Name given by Cotton Incorporated to 100% cotton or cotton blend fabrics treated to meet government or industry flammability standards.
>
>   **Fire Foe** (fyr *foh*) Spring Mills' name for their flame retardant fabrics.
>
>   **Kevlar** (*kehv*-lar) DuPont's flame resistant aramid fiber. See also, chart of fiber properties.
>
>   **Nomex** (*no*-meks) A flame resistant aramid fiber made by DuPont.
>
>   **SayFR** (*say*-fer) Name for flame retardant rayon and acetate made by the FMC Corporation.
>
>   **Sef** (sayf) Monsanto's modacrylic flame retardant fiber.

flange (flanj) A flat border. In fabrics, the term usually applies to a flat border on a pillow. See pillow.

flannel (*flan*-il) A soft fabric, usually with a brushed surface. Flannel may be made of just about any fiber although the traditional fibers used for flannel are wool and cotton. The brushing of the fabric weakens it to a certain degree but this is not considered undesirable in most applications.

flannelette (flan-el-*et*) Theoretically, a fairly lightweight fabric, traditionally cotton, with nap on only one side. In practice, the terms flannel and flannelette are used interchangeably, with flannelette more commonly used for cotton or man-made flannels intended for use in children's garments, especially in shirts and nightwear.

flat (flat) A description both of a loom or knitting machine and the finished product. A flat machine weaves or knits a fabric which is all in one plane as opposed to circular looms and machines which produce tubular fabrics.

flax (flax) The fiber from which linen yarn and fabric is produced. It is a product of the flax plant. The word linen is derived from "linum," part of the scientific name for the flax plant. See linen.

fleck (flek) A spot, usually of color, included in a fabric to add visual and textural interest to it. Flecks are often made by the addition of small pieces of colored fiber to the base fiber during the process of spinning it into yarn.

fleece (fleess) The wool of any animal, most usually a sheep. Fleece is also used to describe certain coating fabrics which have a deep, thick pile that imitates this wool. See pile.

fleece-lined (fleess-lynd) A term used to describe items in which the leather of a sheep and its wool make a naturally lined garment, and also items lined with an artificial fleece, such as sweat shirt fabrics.

flimsy (*flim*-zee) Description for a fabric which lacks body and wearing ability. The term flimsy is almost always used in a derogatory sense.

flock (flok) A method of adding design with texture to a fabric. Flocking involves the use of glue (either on its own or as part of a printing dye) which is printed onto a finished fabric in a pattern. Small pieces of fluffy material are then sprinkled over the fabric which stick to the glue in the desired pattern. Flocked fabrics are often intended to imitate more expensive fabrics such as cut velvets. Dotted Swiss today is often made with the dots flocked rather than woven. Flocking is traditional for college seals on pennants and some floor coverings. Hosiery often has flocked clocks. The flock should be cleanable in the same way as the fabric itself, but occasionally it wears off with time. See clock.

fluorescent fabric (floor-*ess*-ent *fab*-rik) A fabric which glows with a more vivid color than usual under daylight, headlights, and ultraviolet light. Fluorescent fabrics are important, especially in colors such as orange, where high visibility is essential for safety as in hunting clothes, clothes for crossing guards, and outfits for school children. Occasionally, fluorescent fabrics become fashionable for other items of clothing.

foam (fohm) Materials with bubbles as part of their basic structure. Foam rubber and foam polyurethane are two of the most common. The foam structure gives a springy, bouncy effect to the basic material making foam items suitable for pillows, floor padding, backings, and upholstery. See polyurethane.

foam-back (fohm bak) A layer of foam (usually polyurethane) which is laminated to another fabric. See laminating; see also polyurethane.

foam rubber (fohm *rub*-ber) Rubber made in foam form (see above) and used for pillows, floor padding, backings, and upholstery.

Ford (ford) The term Ford, a holdover from the days when the best-selling car in the United States was the Model T Ford, is used to describe an item which sells so well that everyone has one. It is used to describe best-selling fashions, accessories, and fabrics.

Fortrel (for-*trel*) Trademark of Fiber Industries Incorporated for polyester fiber marketed by Celanese Fibers Marketing Company.

foulard (foo-*lard*) A lightweight, soft fabric of twill or plain weave popular for neckties and scarves. A foulard print refers to small all over patterns like those used traditionally on men's neckties.

frieze (freez) A fabric used primarily for upholstery and slipcovers. Frieze is looped and the loops are often sheared to varying heights to form the pattern. Originally made of cotton (and still often referred to as cotton frieze) the fabric is now usually made in blends of cotton and man-made fibers. Also called frise.

frise (free-*zay*) See frieze above.

fringe (frinj) In the true sense, fringe is a border, but when it refers to fabrics for clothing and home furnishings it means a shaggy edging. See trimming.

frog (frog) A form of garment closure. See trimming.

full-fashioned (full-*fash*-und) A method of knitting in which stitches are increased and decreased as necessary to fit the item to the shape desired. Full-fashioned is used for sweaters, dresses, and stockings. The opposite of full-fashioned is cut-and-sewn. See cut-and-sewn.

functional finish (*funk*-shun-'l *fin*-ish) A finish added to a fabric as one of the final steps in its manufacture which alters the performance of the fabric in some way. A water-repellent finish, for instance, is a functional finish because it prevents water from penetrating the fabric, thereby changing the function of the fabric. See finishing.

fun fur (fun fur) A term used in the sale of furs, originally designed to overcome an image of "rich ladies only" that furs had. The term is applied to highly styled, comparatively inexpensive furs such as raccoon and rabbit. Fun fur is sometimes used as a synonym for fake furs. See fur and fake fur.

fur (fur) Fur is the coat of an animal, usually shorter and thicker than hair. The following are some of the most common furs; a more complete listing will be found in the special Fur Chart.

beaver (*bee*-ver) The fur of the beaver is naturally brown but is occasionally dyed other colors.

broadtail (*brawd*-tayl) Broadtail is a form of lamb fur. It is usually black and has a flat curly appearance.

chinchilla (chin-*chil*-ah) Chinchilla, a soft bluish-white fur with dark tips, is one of the most expensive furs.

coney (*koh*-nee) See rabbit, below.

ermine (*ur*-min) Ermine is lustrous, thick, and white with dark tips. It is the traditional royal fur and is often dyed other colors, except when used as trimming.

fox (foks) Fox is a soft, long-haired fur, dyed or bred in various colors and used for both coats and trimming.

leopard (*lep*-erd) Leopard, with its small, dark, irregular spots on a tan ground, is one of the shortest haired of furs.

mink (mingk) Mink is soft and glossy and one of the most popular of all furs available in many colorings. Mink is raised for its fur on mink ranches.

rabbit (*rab*-it) Rabbit is an inexpensive fur which is often dyed to resemble other furs or for fashion impact. It is also called coney and lapin.

raccoon (rack-*koon*) Raccoon, the traditional bulky coat fur, is long, warm, and striped. It is also used for trimming.

sable (*say*-b'l) Sable is usually dark brown. It is a warm, dense fur, and is extremely expensive.

seal (seel) Seal is thick, warm, long-lasting, and shiny. It is naturally black or dark brown.

fusible fabric (*fyou*-zi-b'l *fab*-rik) A fabric which can be joined to another fabric in a fairly permanent bond through the application of heat, moisture and pressure, accomplished with an iron. A fusible fabric has dots of polyamide resins (polyamids are the bases of many synthetic fibers) on the wrong side. The wrong side is placed against the wrong side of the outer fabric and the fusing agent melts and fuses to the other fabric when the iron is applied.

G

gabardine (*gab*-er-deen) A strong, medium to heavyweight fabric with a twill weave. Gabardine goes in and out of fashion; when it is in fashion it is made from almost every fiber and fiber blend. See twill.

galloon (ga-*loon*) A narrow edging or braid, or a narrow lace made with scallops on both edges. See trimming, see lace.

gas fading (gass *fayd*-ing) The loss of color some fabrics suffer due to the atmosphere rather than to, for instance, exposure to sunlight. Certain dyes (blues and greens, for example) are often more susceptible to gas fading than others, as are certain fibers, among them acetate. Special dyes can be used on these fabrics and for these colors to reduce or eliminate this problem. Also called atmospheric and pollution fading.

gauge (gayj) A measure of fineness or coarseness in knitting, gauge refers to the number of needles per unit length on the machine used in making a fabric. The higher the gauge, the greater the number of needles used and the finer the fabric. Gauge is usually used in describing hosiery while the term cut, which means much the same, is more common in describing other knit fabrics.

gauze (gawz) A thin sheer, woven fabric which is quite open. It can be made in many fibers and used for many purposes including bandages, costumes and curtains.

generic name (jih-*nair*-ik naym) A name which describes a class of items, such as soap or polyester. Ivory is a trade name for a type of soap just as Dacron is a trade name for a type of polyester. In textiles, a generic name is the name of a family of fibers of similar chemical composition. See trademark.

georgette (jor-*jet*) A sheer fabric, very similar to chiffon, made with a crepe yarn which gives the fabric a crepe appearance. See chiffon; see crepe.

108

Germantown yarn (*jur*-men-town yarn) A four-ply medium-weight yarn usually made of wool or acrylic. It is soft and thick and used for hand-knitting items such as afghans, sweaters, and socks.

gimp (gimp) See trimming.

gingham (*ging*-um) A plain weave fabric with a pattern made from dyed yarns. Traditionally made of cotton (although other natural fibers have been used in ginghams and given that name), today gingham is usually made of a blend or a man-made fiber. When the pattern is checked it is called checked gingham, when plaid it is called plaid gingham. Plain weave fabrics are sometimes printed with gingham patterns, such as checks, and are also called ginghams. When the gingham look is in fashion, even knits knitted in checked patterns are called ginghams. Gingham patterns are available in a wide range of colors and checked ginghams are the most popular. See gingham checks under entry for check.

glacé or **glazed** (glah-*say* or glayzd) Both the terms glacé and glazed are used to refer to a very shiny finish applied to leather or fabric. At one time the glaze was often not permanent and came out in the first washing or cleaning; today, however, most glazes are permanent. See also finishing.

glass fiber (glass *fy*-ber) Fiber made from glass. It is used extensively for curtains and draperies. Glass fiber fabrics are very strong and wash well, but care should be taken to avoid getting small splinters of the glass yarns in the hands. Glass fiber is stiff and has poor resistance to wear and abrasion. It is also fireproof. See fireproof.

glass curtains (glass *kur*-tenz) Sheer window coverings which hang in front of a window affording a degree of privacy without cutting off an excessive amount of light. Glass curtains are often used behind draperies. See curtains and draperies.

glass towel (glass towls) See towels.

glazed (glayzd) See glacé.

glitter (*glit*-er) See lamé.

godet (go-*day*) A godet is a piece of fabric, tapering from wide to very narrow, inserted into another fabric section, often at a seam, for additional fullness either for function or appearance. Godets move in and out of fashion and are often used in home decorating at corners of beds, chairs, sofas, and slipcovers.

goods (goodz) See fabric.

goose down (gooss down) See feathers.

gossamer (*gahs*-uh-mer) Any very sheer, fine fabric may be given the name gossamer, although the term was traditionally used to describe silk fabrics.

grain (grayn) The direction in which the yarns run in weaving. The straight grain is the direction of the warp yarns; the crosswise grain is the direction of the filling yarns. Off-grain is a term used to describe a fabric in which these yarns are not at right angles to each other. Off-grain fabrics can be corrected by wetting them with water and then pulling the fabric until the two grains are at right angles. This straightening of the grain, however, is only successful if a pattern has not been printed off-grain on the fabric and if the fabric has not been given a permanent press finish.

grain leather (grayn *leth*-er) See leather.

grass cloth (grass kloth) A plain weave, loosely woven fabric made from such fibers as hemp, ramie, and even nettle. Today, true grass cloth is relatively rare but the appearance of grass cloth is copied in wallpaper and fabrics of man-made fibers. See hemp, ramie, nettle.

gray goods (gray goodz) A textile industry term referring to fabric after it has been manufactured but before it has been colored or finished. It is also spelled grey and greige.

greige (grehj [correct pronunciation]; gray [common pronunciation] See gray goods, above.

grey (gray) See gray goods above.

grosgrain (*grow*-grayn) A fairly heavy ribbed fabric, often made in narrow widths for use as trimming. The most common use of grosgrain is for ribbons in which the ribs are usually quite narrow, but it can be made with larger ribs for such uses as academic gowns.

gros point (grow pwanh [correct pronunciation]; grow poynt [common pronunciation]) See needlepoint.

ground (grownd) The background of a fabric design or print, as when red flowers are printed on a black ground.

guimp (gihmp) See gimp under trimmings.

gun club checks (gun klub cheks) See checks.

H

hackling (*hak*-ling) See combing.

haircloth (*hair*-kloth) A stiff fabric made from a combination of natural or man-made fibers and animal hair, usually either goat or horse hair. It is used in upholstery and as interfacing for its strength.

hairpin lace (*hair*-pin layss) See lace.

hand or **handle** (hand or hand-'l) The way a fabric feels. One of the important elements in fabric selection is the subjective judgement on the feel of a fabric and whether or not it will work well for its intended purpose. To make this judgement, the fabric must be felt, and the resulting decision is based on the hand or handle. Fabrics may be described as having a crisp hand or a soft, drapeable hand. See crisp; see also, drapeable fabrics.

hand knotted rug (hand *not*-'d rug) See rugs and carpets.

hand loomed (hand loom-'d) See hand woven.

hand-rolled hem (hand rold hem) A hand-rolled hem is an extremely narrow hem made by turning under a small edge of fabric and securing it with small hemming stitches. It is most often used on scarves and on full skirts of sheer fabrics such as chiffon and georgette. See stitches.

hand-woven (hand-*woh*-vin) A self-explanatory term, referring as it does to a woven fabric which has been made by hand on a loom rather than on a power loom.

handkerchief (*han*-ker-chif) A small rectangular piece of fabric which traditionally has a hand-rolled hem. Handkerchiefs are made of plain weave fabric and were usually made of linen in the past. Today, either a combed cotton or blend of cotton and a man-made fiber is used. Handkerchiefs are available in many colors but the most popular are all white or a woven design of plaids or checks surrounding a white center. See also bandanna.

111

handkerchief linen (*han*-ker-chif *lin*-'n) Traditionally, a very lightweight, fine linen used for handerchiefs and clothing where a batiste-like fabric is considered desirable. Today, the term is rarely used, but when it is, it usually refers to a woven fabric made of a blend of polyester and linen. See linen; see also, batiste.

hank (hangk) A measure of yarn which is loosely coiled upon itself rather than wound onto a spool or into a ball.

harlequin (*hahr*-luh-kwin) A diamond design. The name comes from the traditional costume, which is diamond-patterned, of the Harlequin, a character in the Harlequinade, the 16th century "Commedia dell 'arte" dramatic presentation.

Harris tweed (*hair*-iss tweed) A tweed which is hand-woven from yarns spun on the islands of the Outer Hebrides off the coast of Scotland. Harris is one of these islands. The yarns may be spun by hand or machine. See also tweed.

headboard (*hed*-bord) A board or frame at the pillow end of a bed. The headboard stands perpendicular to the floor. Headboards may be made of wood or slipcovered or upholstered to match a bedspread or other decorative areas of a room. The term bed head is a synonym.

heading (*hed*-ing) The top portion of a curtain or drapery. Headings are usually decorative and are often made from trimmings such as braid. See trimmings.

heat setting (heet *set*-ing) Although practices similar to heat setting are used in the finishing of almost all fabrics, the term heat setting, strictly speaking, refers only to thermoplastic man-made fibers. Because of the thermoplastic nature of most man-made fibers (they change their shape when heat is applied), certain features such as pleats can be made permanent by treating them under very high heat. Heat setting usually gives a smooth appearance to a fabric and sets its final measurements. Boarding, a process in the manufacture of stockings, is a type of heat setting.

heat transfer (heet *trans*-fer) See printing.

heather (*heh*-ther) A misty coloration in a fabric achieved by crossdyeing or by using one color for the warp yarns and another color for the filling yarns. It can also be achieved by the addition of certain soft fibers like rabbit hair to the basic yarn, which, because of their fluffy nature, give a misty appearance to the fabric. See cross-dyeing.

Herculon (*her*-kyu-lon) Trademark of Hercules Incorporated for olefin fiber.

hem (hem) A finish on the edge of a fabric or garment designed to prevent it from running or ravelling. A hem is made by turning the fabric up to the inside and stitching it in place. A hem may be finished by adding a decorative trimming of some kind to protect the edge.

herringbone (*hair*-ing-bohn) A twill weave in which the weave reverses so the twill pattern forms a "V" pattern. Herringbone weave is also called broken twill. See twill under entry for weaving.

hessian (*hesh*-un) The word hessian is occasionally used as a synonym for burlap. See burlap.

high-bulk yarn (hy-bulk yarn) Although the term high-bulk yarn is definitely a technical one, it is used occasionally in advertising to the consumer. High-bulk yarns are processed so that, through a form of shrinkage in the processing, they are thicker and bulkier than they would be otherwise.

holland (*hol*-und) A plain weave fabric which is used in the home primarily for window shades.

homespun (*hohm*-spun) Originally, fabrics made from yarns which were spun by hand. Today, homespun is used for fabrics which imitate this look. Homespun has a fairly rough surface and is made from nubby, uneven yarns.

Honan (*hoh*-nan) Originally, a pongee-type of silk fabric made from wild silk. Today, the term Honan is used interchangeably with the term pongee for man-made fiber fabrics that resemble the original silk fabric. See pongee and wild silk under entry for silk.

honeycomb (*hun*-ee-kohm) A weave which results in fabrics which have diamonds or other geometric shapes resembling a honeycomb. Waffle weaves are identical to honeycomb weaves, and many weaves called thermal are honeycomb weaves. See thermal.

hooked rug (hukt rug) See entry for rugs and carpets.

hopsacking (*hop*-sak-ing) Originally, a word for certain types of burlap bagging, hopsacking is now used interchangeably with the term basket weave. See basket weave under entry for weaving.

horsehair (*hors*-hair) Horsehair is hair from the mane and tail of horses. It is occasionally used for upholstery but is more commonly used in interfacings for stiffening and strength. It is always combined with other fibers. True horsehair is rare now and fabrics loosely called horsehair are often actually made from other hairs (such as goat) or man-made fibers.

houndstooth (*howndz*-tooth) See check.

huck (huk) A type of toweling fabric used for drying dishes, glasses, and kitchen utensils. It is woven with a pattern, most often with a dobby attachment on the loom. Huck is traditionally made of cotton or linen although today other fibers may be used. Huck is also called huckaback. Embroidery enthusiasts often use huck as a ground for embroidery. See dobby.

huckaback (*huk*-uh-bak) See huck.

I

illusion (il-*oo*-zhun) Very fine net or mesh fabrics such as those used in bridal veils. Illusion is usually made of either silk or nylon. See mesh; see also, net.

Indian blanket (*inn*-dee-un *blang*-kit) A woolen blanket hand woven by American Indians in the western part of the United States. Indian blankets are usually made in bright colors or in earth colors. The term has come to be used for any blanket which resembles an authentic Indian blanket.

Indian muslin (*inn*-dee-un *muz*-lin) See muslin.

insertion (inn-*sur*-shun) A narrow fabric—lace is probably the most common—which is finished on both edges and can be sewn to another fabric for decoration.

intarsia (inn-*tar*-see-uh) A pattern which is knitted into a fabric. The term usually refers to a design on only one part of the fabric; knitted patterns that cover the entire fabric are usually called jacquards. See jacquard.

interfacing (*inn*-tur-fayss-ing) A stiffening fabric which may be made of horsehair (often goat hair, wool, man-made fibers, or combinations of these fibers). Interfacing is used to give additional body and strength to certain parts of garments. Areas which usually require interfacing include the front opening edges, collars, pocket flaps, and any place where stretching or a loss of crispness would be a disadvantage. See chart on interfacing fabrics in the appendix.

interlining (*inn*-tur-lyne-ing) A layer of fabric placed between the outer fabric and the lining of the garment to add warmth. It is most commonly found in coats and jackets. Interlinings are often made of reprocessed wool but other materials, such as polyester fiberfill, may be used. See fiberfill; see also, reprocessed wool. See chart on linings in the appendix.

114

interlock (*inn*-tur-lok) A fine gauge knit with a smooth surface on both front and back. The fabric was traditionally used for underwear, but today is being used for apparel. Despite the name of the fabric, poorly made interlock will develop runs at the edges and all interlock knits should be reinforced or finished in some way at these edges.

inverted pleats (inn-*vur*-tid pleetz) See entry under pleats.

iridescent (ir-ih-*dess*-ent) See changeable.

Irish lace (*eye*-rish layss) See lace.

Irish linen (*eye*-rish *lin*-'n) See linen.

Irish tweed (*eye*-rish tweed) See tweed.

J

jabot (zhah-*boh*) A decorative ruffle at the front of a neckline of a garment. Also, a ruffled drapery heading.

jacquard (*jak*-ard) A term used to describe fabrics with a woven or knitted pattern, whether or not they are made with a jacquard attachment on the loom. The jacquard attachment for weaving and knitting machines makes possible the manufacture of complicated, repeated geometrical designs in knits and wovens. See also dobby.

Jap silk (jap silk) Another name for China silk. See China silk under entry for silk.

jean (jeen) In theory, a sturdy twill weave fabric similar to drill and denim. In practice, the term denim is almost always used for the fabric, while the term jeans is used for pants made of denim. See also, dungaree.

jersey (*jur*-zee) A single knit fabric with plain stitches on the right side and purl stitches on the back. The word jersey is also occasionally used as a synonym for any knit. See entries for single knit and purl knit under knitting.

jute (joot) One of the natural fibers still used extensively for fabrics. It comes from jute plants grown primarily in India, Pakistan, and Bangladesh. Jute is used in many ways including the manufacture of burlap, twine and rope, trimmings, and backing for rugs.

K

kapok (*kay*-pahk) A fluffy fiber which comes from the seed pods of the kapok tree found in the tropics. Kapok at one time was extremely popular for stuffing pillows and was also used in life preservers as it is naturally buoyant. Today, man-made fibers have replaced kapok in many cases.

karakul (*kair*-uh-kul) See astrakhan.

kashmir (*kash*-meer) Another spelling for cashmere. Kashmir is also an alternate spelling for the name of the goat from which cashmere wool comes. See cashmere.

kersey (*kur*-zee) A woven fabric with a fine nap used for overcoats and uniforms. See nap.

khaki (*ka*-kee) A term used for both an earth color or an olive green color and for fabrics made in these colors whether of wool, cotton, or man-made fibers. Khaki is a classic uniform color and material.

kick pleat (kik pleet) See entry under pleats.

kid (kid) See leather.

knit terry cloth (nit *tair*-ee kloth) Terry cloth is a soft, absorbent fabric with loops on one or both sides. When this fabric is knit rather than woven, it is called knit terry. Knit terry is especially popular for bathrobes and beach wear because of its absorbency. Stretch knit terry (usually made stretchable by the addition of a synthetic elastic fiber) is popular for baby clothes for its absorbency and comfort.

knitting (*nit*-ing) A method of making fabrics by forming loops which are joined to loops in preceding and succeeding rows. Almost any textile item can be and has been knitted, including rugs. A warp knit is made on a machine in which parallel yarns run lengthwise and are locked into the series of loops. Warp knits have a good deal of crosswise stretch. Weft knits are made on a machine which forms loops in a circular direction and have one continuous thread running across the fabric. Following is a list of common knit terms. See also Chapter Two, From Fiber to Fabric.

double knit (*duh*-b'l nit) A weft knit fabric produced in two layers which cannot be separated. Its appearance is the same on either side with a characteristic fine vertical wale. See Chapter Two, From Fiber to Fabric. See also, wale.

jacquard knit (*jak*-ard nit) A knit with a design knit into the fabric in a regular all over pattern. Most jacquard patterns are closely knitted but it is possible to make some pattern knits with a jacquard machine. See pattern knits, below.

pattern knit (*pat*-urn nit) Knit made on a weft knit machine by dropping, adding, rearranging, and crossing various stitches to create intricate designs.

plain knit (playn nit) A flat-surfaced even knit made by hand or machine knitting. In hand knitting it is called stockinette stitch. The face of the fabric is smooth and the reverse is looped. See purl knit, below.

purl knit (purl nit) A term used to describe alternating rows of knit and purl stitches (purl is the reverse of a plain knit fabric with the loops showing) forming a pattern with considerable crosswise stretch.

raschel knit (ra-*shell* nit) A knit made on a raschel machine, a warp knitting machine which can use bulky yarns to form designs which imitate crochet or net.

rib knit (rib nit) A knit which consists of groups of alternate plain and purl stitches (the reverse of a plain knit with loops showing). Rib knit fabrics are stretchier and have a snugger fit than plain knits. Rib knit is frequently used at wrists, waists, and necklines of plain or patterned knit garments where it is called ribbing.

single knit (*sing*-'l nit) Single knit, made on a weft knitting machine, is another term for plain knit. See entry for plain knit above.

stable knit (*stay*-b'l nit) Any knit which is unlikely to stretch excessively. Double knits are usually stable knits.

stretchable knit (*strech*-uh-b'l nit) Any knit which has a good deal of give or "stretch." Most single knits would be considered stretchable knits.

L

lace (layss) A decorated fabric made either on a background fabric of net or without a background fabric. The pattern in lace is usually open and most often floral in design. Machine-made lace is the lace most commonly seen today and many patterns which were formerly only made by hand are imitated today by machine. Lace is the traditional bridal fabric but is also used for other non-formal clothing like sports clothes. Following is a listing of some of the major types of lace:

all over lace (awl-*oh*-ver layss) Lace in which the pattern covers the entire fabric, rather than being isolated on one section of background net.

ajour lace (ah-*zhur* layss) A very open lace design with the pattern scattered on the ground.

Alencon (ah-*len*-sun layss) Lace with a solid design which is outlined by cord. This lace is made on a sheer net fabric.

aloe lace (*al*-oh layss) Usually a bobbin or tatted lace made from aloe plant fibers, a group of plants which includes the agave. See bobbin lace and tatting, below.

antique lace (ann-*teek* layss) A heavy lace made on a square knotted net with designs darned onto the net. Machine made antique lace is often used for curtains. See darn under embroidery.

Argentan lace (*ahr*-jen-ten layss) Argentan lace is somewhat similar to Alencon but the designs are usually not outlined with cord and are often larger and bolder than those of Alencon.

Battenberg lace (*bat*-en-berg layss) A lace similar to Renaissance lace with a pattern formed by tape or braid joined by bars. See Renaissance lace, below.

beading (*beed*-ing) A type of lace made by the bobbin lace

119

method. Also, an openwork lace or embroidery which has holes designed for the insertion of decorative ribbon. See bobbin lace.

Belgian lace (*bel*-jin layss) Any lace made in Belgium. Originally, the term meant a bobbin lace worked on a machine-made net. See bobbin lace, below.

binche lace (beench layss) A lace in which hand-made lace motifs are appliquéd to a machine-made net ground. The name comes from Binche, a town in Belgium, where the lace is said to have originated.

bobbin lace (*bob*-in layss) Lace made using a pillow to hold pins around which thread is arranged. Bobbins are used to hold and feed the thread used. Bobbin lace is also called bobbinet lace and pillow lace.

bobbinet lace (bob-in-*et* layss) See bobbin lace, above.

bourdon lace (*boor*-dohn layss) Lace made by machine, usually in a scroll design, with the design usually outlined with a heavy thread.

Breton lace (bret-'n layss) Lace made on open net, usually embroidered with very heavy, often brightly colored, yarns. Breton is the area in France where the lace is said to have originated.

Brussels lace (*bruss*-lz layss) Brussels lace may be either a bobbin lace or a needlepoint lace. It is usually worked on a machine-made ground and sometimes the designs are appliquéd onto the ground. Because of the importance of Brussels, Belgium in the history of lace-making (many patterns developed there), several different laces are called Brussels lace. See bobbin lace, above; see also, needlepoint lace.

Chantilly (shan-*til*-ee [incorrect pronunciation, but the only one used]) One of the most popular of bridal laces often used for the trimming on bridal veils. It is made by the bobbin method and has designs outlined by thick cords. See bobbin lace, above.

Cluny lace (*kloo*-nee layss) A heavy lace, often made of thick cotton or man-made fibers using the bobbin method. It is the traditional lace for doillies and place mats but is also used in apparel. See bobbin lace, above.

crocheted lace (kroh-*shayd* layss) Lace made with a single yarn. A crochet hook is used to form loops which are joined to other loops to form the design.

hairpin lace (*hair*-pin layss) A delicate, narrow lace which is worked over a hairpin or a special hairpin-shaped, loom-like tool.

Irish lace (*eye*-rish layss) The term Irish lace can be used to refer to any lace made in Ireland, but crocheted laces are those most often given the name. Embroidered nets are another type of Irish lace. See crocheted lace, above.

needlepoint lace (*need*-'l-poynt layss) Lace made with a sewing or embroidery needle to form buttonhole stitches as the basis of the design.

Nottingham lace (*not*-ing-um layss) One of the first of the machine-made laces. It originated in Nottingham, England. Today, the term Nottingham lace is often used for any lace made by any machine.

pillow lace (*pill*-oh layss) See bobbin lace.

re-embroidered lace (ree-im-*broyd*-erd layss) Lace with designs outlined with embroidery stitching. See embroidery.

Renaissance lace (*rehn*-uh-sahns layss) A lace which is made of woven strips of fabric joined by flat stitches. See also Battenberg lace, above.

tatting (*tat*-ing) A method of lace-making worked with the fingers and a shuttle which holds the thread. Tatting forms a narrow, knotted lace, often used for edging.

Val lace (val layss) See Valenciennes lace.

Valenciennes lace (vel-en-see-*enz* layss) A flat bobbin lace worked with one thread forming both the background and the design for the lace.

Venetian lace (veh-*nee*-shun layss) See Venise lace.

Venice lace (*veh*-niss layss) See Venise lace.

Venise lace (veh-*neess* layss) A needlepoint lace usually having a floral pattern connected by picot edgings. It is also called Venice lace and Venetian lace. See picot.

lambrequin (*lam*-ber-kin) A structure at the top and sides of a window which frames the window and is usually part of the window decoration. Lambrequins are often covered with fabric and trimmed. They are usually made of wood and may be simply painted.

lambskin (*lam*-skin) See leather.

lamb's wool (lams wuhl) Wool from a lamb (up to age seven months). It is extremely soft.

lamé (lah-*may*) The name for any fabric woven or knitted with all metallic yarns or with a combination of metallic and other fiber yarns. Today, most lamé is made from one of the nontarnishable metallic fibers, a great improvement over lamé of the past which tended to darken with age. Glitter is sometimes used to describe this type of fabric instead of lamé.

laminating (*lam*-ih-nayt-ing) A method of joining one fabric to another by means of an adhesive. Polyurethane is often laminated to the back of an outerwear coating fabric for warmth. The term laminating is occasionally used as a synonym for bonding, but this is incorrect. See bonding.

lansdowne (*lans*-down) A lightweight twill fabric made from natural or man-made fibers and usually used for dresses.

lastrile (*las*-treel) Generic name for a man-made elastic fiber. There is not now and has never been any commercial production of this fiber in the United States. See generic name.

latex (*lay*-teks) The name for the liquid form of natural or man-made rubber. It can be formed into thread for use as an elastic yarn. Latex is also used extensively as part of the backing in the manufacture of rugs. At one time, latex was used extensively in corsets and brassieres. Now, however, although some latex foundation garments are still made, it has been largely replaced by spandex. Solid rubber is sometimes referred to as rubber. See spandex.

lawn (lawn) A fairly sheer, lightweight, plain weave fabric made originally from linen but today usually made from combed cotton or blends of cotton and man-made fibers. Lawn is slightly stiffer than batiste, but can be used for similar purposes. See batiste.

leather (*leth*-er) The hide of an animal with the fur removed. It has been used throughout history for clothing and other purposes. Today, man-made fabrics which imitate leather are widely available. Descriptions of various leathers will be found in the leather chart in this book. Common leather names include alligator, buckskin, calfskin, chamois, cordovan, cowhide, crocodile, doeskin, grain leather, kid, lambskin, morocco, nappa, patent, peccary, pigskin, pin seal, reptile, reversed leather, Russian, shearling, skiver, snakeskin, and suede.

leatherette (leth-uh-*ret*) A term used for imitation leathers. More correctly, these should be described by their actual construction, such as vinyl-coated fabric.

Leaver's lace (*lee*-verz layss) Machine-made lace named for the inventor of the machine on which it is made. Many hand-made lace patterns can be copied on this machine. The term is sometimes used in preference to machine-made lace to imply quality.

Leghorn straw (*leg*-horn straw) See straw.

leno (*lee*-noh) An open, lacy woven fabric made with a special loom attachment. In a leno weave a pair of filling yarns twist around the warp yarns in various patterns to achieve the lacy effect. Leno fabrics are popular for curtains and summer dresses.

Liberty prints (*lih*-ber-tee prints) Liberty, a shop founded in London in 1875, has been noted almost since its beginning for the unusual printed fabrics it sells. The prints are also available to other stores. These prints are often in muted colors and feature floral and other patterns, often on dark grounds. Liberty prints have traditionally been printed on lawn and on a blend of wool and cotton. The type of print Liberty has come to stand for over the years moves in and out of fashion; when these prints are popular the term "Liberty

prints" is often used incorrectly for prints that resemble those
made by this company.

linen (*lin-*'n) Linen, made from flax which comes from the flax
plant, is one of the oldest fabrics known. It is strong and today
man-made fibers are often blended with it to improve its wrinkle
resistance and give the fabric other desirable qualities. Linen is
woven in various weights for different purposes and is occasionally
used in knit blends. See fabric chart for linen characterists. Common linen names include:

   art linen (art *lin-*'n) A plain weave medium-weight linen or blended fabric, bleached or left its natural color, used for embroidery.
   It can be found in art needlework (embroidery) departments
   and stores.

   Belgian linen (*bel*-jin *lin-*'n) Any linen which has been produced
   in Belgium.

   embroidery linen (im-*broy*-der-ee *lin-*'n) See art linen.

   handkerchief linen (*han*-ker-chif *lin-*'n) A fine, sheer linen used
   for handkerchiefs, dresses, and blouses, and whenever a lightweight cloth is desired.

   Irish linen (*eye*-rish *lin-*'n) Irish linen refers to linen items from
   Ireland, both Northern Ireland and Eire.

linen straw (*lin-*'n straw) See straw.

linens and **domestics** (*lin'*-ns and doh-*mess*-tiks) The term used in
stores to describe various household items which, at one time, were
made of linen. Today, most linens and domestics are made of
cotton and man-made fibers. Following is a listing of some of the
items which can be found in the linens and domestics sections of
stores. See also entries for blankets, towels, and Chapter Seven,
Bedding and Towels.

   antimacassar (ann-tih-me-*kass*-er) A piece of cloth which was
   originally pinned to the back of a chair to protect the upholstery from hair oil (macassar). Today, although antimacassars
   are still available, changes in hair grooming and the development
   of fairly easy-to-clean upholstery fabrics have made their purpose primarily decorative.

   batting (*bat*-ing) Batting is usually stocked in linens and domestics departments although it is used today primarily for crafts.
   Batting is a filling material which can be used to stuff pillows,
   toys, and quilts. At one time, batting was made of cotton; today,
   it is usually polyester fiberfill. Batting may be sold in bulk form,
   ideal for stuffing toys and pillows, or in true batting form, in
   which case it is a long flat sheet. Correctly, only the sheets should
   be called batting but the term has come to be used for this type
   of stuffing in all forms.

   doily (*doy*-lee) A piece of fabric, round or square or rectangular in shape, which is used under plants and decorative objects partly to protect furniture surfaces and partly as decoration. Doillies are often crocheted. See crocheted lace under entry for lace.

mattress cover (*mat*-ress *kuv*-er) A quilted, fairly thick pad placed on top of a bed mattress and beneath a bottom sheet to protect the mattress and to make the bed more comfortable. A mattress cover often has elastic at all corners to hold it on the bed and it should completely cover the top of the mattress.

napkin (*nap*-kin) A rectangular piece of fabric or paper used to wipe the mouth and hands in the course of eating. Napkins are often matched to the tablecloth or placemats.

pillowcase (*pill*-oh-kayss) Pillowcases are washable covers for bed pillows which usually match the sheets and protect the pillow from soil. Most American pillowcases are made in a rectangular form with one open, hemmed edge. They are occasionally decorated on one of the narrower ends.

pillow cover (*pill*-oh *kuv*-er) A fabric cover which is placed over the bed pillow before the pillowcase. Pillow covers are designed to give more protection to pillows than is provided by pillowcases. See pillowcase, above.

placemat (*playss*-mat) A piece of cloth or other material (often foam-backed plastic) which is placed on a table between the table and the place setting to protect the table and to decorate it during meals. Placemats are available in a variety of sizes, shapes and colors.

rubber sheets (*rub*-er sheet) A sheet used on a bed to protect the mattress more than a mattress pad alone does. Although relatively few rubber sheets today are actually made of rubber, the term is still used. These sheets, because they are impervious to water, tend to hold perspiration. They are more comfortable for sleeping if covered by a mattress cover and sheet. See mattress cover. See also, sheet.

runner (*run*-er) A rectangular piece of fabric which is usually used with placemats to decorate and protect the dining table. It is placed in the center of the table under condiments (salt, pepper, mustard) and any decorations such as flowers or candles. Runners frequently match the placemats and are also used on chests of drawers to protect the top from spills.

sheeting (sheet) A rectangular piece of fabric used to cover and protect the top and sides of a mattress. This is usually referred to as a bottom sheet. A top sheet is placed on top of a bottom sheet to protect the skin from a sometimes scratchy blanket and to protect the blanket from soil. Traditionally, sheets were made of linen or cotton; today they are more likely to be made of cotton and polyester blends for easy care qualities. At one time, sheets were white; today they are available in many colors and patterns. See Chapter Seven, Bedding and Towels.

silence cloth (*sy*-lenss kloth) A cloth put on a dining table to protect it and (as the name suggests) to prevent the clatter of dishes against the table. A silence cloth is usually a napped, fairly heavy fabric. Silence cloths are placed beneath tablecloths and are also called silencers.

silencer (*sy*-lenss-er) See silence cloth. See also, table pad.

table pad (*tay*-b'l pad) A table covering used to protect the table and prevent clatter. Table pads are usually heavier and stiffer than silence cloths and are usually made with a felt back and a plastic top. See silence cloth, above.

tablecloth (*tay*-b'l-kloth) The traditional table covering for protection and decoration. Tablecloths range from very informal ones made, for instance, of checked fabrics, to very formal, such as double damask. See double damask. Napkins are usually matched to the tablecloth. See napkin.

lingerie (*lahn*-jeh-ree) Another term for women's underwear and nightwear. Lingerie implies delicate fabric, often lace-trimmed. The term lingerie fabrics is occasionally used for very delicate fabrics. Formerly, the finest lingerie was made of muslin, lawn, or silk; today, fabrics of man-made fibers, especially nylon tricot, are dominant.

lining (*lyne*-ing) Fabric made in the same shape as the outer fabric, a lining supports and protects the outer fabric and hides seams as well. Linings are found not only in apparel but also in draperies and occasionally curtains and bedspreads. Items which are lined tend to wear better and last longer than unlined items. The appearance of a lined item is usually better than that of an unlined one. Special lining fabrics include those sold under the trademarks like Si Bonne and Earl-Glo. Linings should be of the same construction as the outer fabric; wovens should be lined with wovens and knits with knits. See chart of linings and underlinings in the appendix.

linsey-woolsey (*lin*-zee-*wuhl*-zee) When linen and wool were woven together in the 18th century the resulting fabric which was coarse, loosely woven, and rather scratchy, was called linsey-woolsey. Although linen and wool blends are occasionally made today, the use of finer finishing techniques means they are extremely comfortable and the name linsey-woolsey is limited to historical references.

Linton tweed (*lin*-ton tweed) See tweed.

lisle (lyle) A hard, two-ply, usually cotton or wool yarn made into such items as socks.

llama (*yah*-ma [correct pronunciation]; *lah*-muh [common pronunciation]) An animal found in parts of Latin America. It is believed to be a member of the camel family. Llama wool is used in making some expensive coating fabric.

loden cloth (*loh*-den kloth) A thick, heavy, napped coating fabric similar to duffel cloth made of wool or occasionally man-made fibers. It is usually a light forest green color called loden from which it gets its name. Loden cloth moves in and out of fashion everywhere except in parts of Germany and Austria where loden jackets, suits, and coats are considered basic dress. Loden cloth is sometimes gray in color. See duffel cloth.

loom figured fabrics (loom *fig*-yerd *fab*-riks) Fabrics which have the design or pattern woven or knitted in as opposed to those which, for instance, have patterns printed on finished cloth.

loom finished (loom *fin*-isht) A term referring to certain fabric which is sold without most of the steps mentioned in the entry under finishing. Loom finished fabrics are relatively rare because the consumer has grown accustomed to finished fabrics. See finishing.

loop rug (loop rug) See entry for rugs and carpets.

loose cover (looss *kuv*-er) Another term for slipcover. See slipcover.

Lurex (*loor*-eks) Trademark of Dow Badische Company for metallic fiber.

Lycra (*lye*-kra) Trademark of DuPont for spandex fiber.

Lyons velvet (*lee*-ohn *vel*-vit [correct pronunciation]; *lye*-onz *vel*-vit [common pronunciation]) See velvet.

ᴹM

Macclesfield silk (*mak*-les-feeld silk) See silk.

macintosh (*mak*-en-tosh) Fabric named for its inventor, Charles Macintosh. It is coated with rubber to make it water-repellent. As a result, the name has come down not only for the fabric but also to refer to raincoats made from it. Today, although the process has been almost replaced by other methods of making fabrics water-repellent, the name macintosh is still used occasionally for a raincoat. See water-repellent.

mackinac (*mak*-en-naw) See mackinaw, below.

mackinaw (*mak*-eh-naw) A thick, heavy, usually coarse fabric with a certain degree of natural water repellency. It was originally made of wool but other fibers such as acrylics are being used today. It was named for the blankets made by the Mackinaw Indians in Michigan. Mackinaw and similar fabrics are extremely popular for hunting jackets and are usually plaid or checked. Mackinaw is also spelled mackinac.

mackintosh (*mak*-en-tosh) See macintosh.

macramé (*mak*-rah-may) An ancient method of forming open fabrics by knotting string, yarn, or other forms of thread. Macramé can be used to make anything from delicate trimmings to such sturdy items as hammocks. Recently, wall hangings of macramé have also become popular.

Madras (*mad*-rehss) A fine, hand-loomed cotton imported from Madras, India. The Federal Trade Commission has ruled that it is deceptive to apply this term to a fabric which does not meet this description. In addition, the FTC definition requires that any dyes used on this fabric must be vegetable dyes which will bleed (the colors will run into each other). The fact that the FTC felt called upon to make such a definition is some indication of the popularity of Madras and imitation Madras fabrics in recent years. The authentic Madras and its imitations usually have checked or plaid designs; with time, as the colors bleed into each other with washing, true Madras develops extremely soft colorings. It should, of course, be washed by hand separately from other fabrics.

maline (mah-*leen*) A gauze-like veiling of net used to trim hats. See also, net.

man-made fibers (*man*-mayd *fy*-berz) An over-all term referring to all fibers not found naturally. This includes rayon and acetate which are made from cellulose, a natural product. The term synthetic fibers also applies only to man-made fibers made entirely in the laboratory from such things as petroleum (polyester, for instance).

marabou (*mair*-ah-boo) See feathers.

marl (marl) A technical term which refers to a yarn made of different colored fibers. The word is used descriptively for fabrics to indicate randomly or uniformly colored slubs which appear on the surface giving added textural and design interest to the fabric.

marquisette (mahr-kwi-*zet*) A term used for a group of lightweight, open fabrics, extremely popular for curtains and mosquito netting. Marquisette is made of many different fibers, including cotton and nylon.

Marseilles (mahr-*say*) A firmly woven reversible fabric with raised geometric designs. Marseilles was originally made of cotton but is now usually made from man-made fibers or blends.

Marvess (mahr-*vess*) Trademark of Phillips Fibers for olefin fiber. See olefin.

mat (mat) See matte.

matelassé (mat-leh-*say*) One of the fabrics which, like cloqué, has a blistered or quilted look to the design. Officially, the word matelassé implies the use of two different yarns which, when finished, react differently to the finishing resulting in a puckered effect in the fabric. In practice, the term matelassé is usually applied to luxury fabrics for evening wear, while a word such as cloqué will be used for a similar fabric made from cotton. Matelassé is also popular for upholstery.

material (muh-*teer*-ee-ul) See fabric.

matte (mat) A dull surface on a fabric. Since one of the characteristics of fabrics made from man-made fibers is a shiny surface, matte-finished fabrics have become popular and matte looks for man-made fabrics are achieved in yarn processing or finishing. See finishing.

mattress cover (*mat*-ress *kuv*-er) See linens and domestics.

melamine resins (*mell*-uh-meen *reh*-zins) Finishes which are used to give wrinkle resistance and other desirable qualities (including a degree of shrinkage resistance) to fabrics, primarily those made from natural fibers. Melamine resins are chlorine retentive which means that if fabrics with these finishes are bleached with a chlorine bleach, they will keep both the color and the odor of the chlorine.

melton (*mell*-tun) Melton, usually called melton cloth, is a very closely woven fabric with a slight nap used extensively for coats. The close weave means that the fabric appears to be completely smooth. Melton was originally made of all wool or cotton and wool but today is made of other fibers. It is also used for uniforms. See nap.

mercerization (mur-ser-eh-*zay*-shun) A finish applied to cotton yarn or fabric or to a blend of cotton and other fibers to give the fabric additional luster and increased ability to take dye. Mercerization can be done at the yarn stage or the fabric stage. In common with several other textile processes, mercerization involves the use of caustic soda (sodium hydroxide or lye).

merino (meh-*ree*-noh) Wool from the merino sheep which produces a short staple fiber of extremely high quality. Merino wool is raised in the United States and in Australia. Occasionally, the term merino is used as a synonym for Botany. See Botany.

mesh (mesh) A term for a large class of open fabrics which may be made by almost all methods except felting. Mesh fabrics are used for everything from bags to shirts. Mesh hosiery is hosiery which has been knitted in such a pattern that, when one yarn is snagged, the stocking will not develop a long, vertical run but rather a hole. Mesh stockings and panty hose are believed to wear better than other constructions.

metallic (meh-*tal*-ik) A generic name for a manufactured fiber which may be metal, metal coated with a synthetic, or a man-made fiber core covered with metal. When the metal is coated with a man-made film, the metal does not tarnish.

middy twill (*mid*-ee twill) The term middy twill is used for many fabrics which are sturdy and have a twill weave. Traditionally made of cotton, middy twill today is likely to include at least some man-made fiber in its construction. When middy blouses are in fashion (a loose-fitting, hip-length overblouse with a sailor collar) the most popular color for this twill is navy blue. It is also used for school uniforms.

Milan straw (*mee*-lahn straw) See straw.

mildew resistant (*mill*-doo ree-*zis*-tent) Among the many properties that can be given to fabrics in the finishing is resistance to traditional enemies. Such fabrics as canvas, which are exposed to the damp conditions which encourage the growth of mildew fungus, can be treated with finishes to resist this fungus, making them mildew resistant. See finishing.

military braid (*mil*-ih-tair-ee brayd) See trimming.

Milium (*mil*-ee-um) Trademark of Deering Milliken for a finish which involves the application of aluminum to a lining fabric, said to make it retain and reflect heat. It is often used as a lining in winter coats eliminating the need for an interlining. See interlining; see also, lining.

mirror velvet (*mihr*-er *vel*-vit) See velvet.

mixture (*miks*-tcher) Although the word mixture is often ignored in favor of the word blend, it should be used for fabrics made from a combination of two or more fibers in which one of the fibers is used for the filling thread. See blend; see also, biconstituent fiber.

mock crepe (mahk krayp) A term for fabrics which have the appearance of crepe but are not made from crepe yarns. See crepe.

modacrylic (mahd-uh-*krill*-ik) The generic name for a modified acrylic fiber. It differs from acrylic in its chemical structure. Modacrylic is used most commonly to make fake furs and wigs. Modacrylic fibers are naturally flame-retardant (slow-burning). See acrylic.

modified fibers (*mahd*-eh-fyed *fy*-berz) Fibers which have been treated to eliminate characteristics considered undesirable and to add characteristics considered desirable. These treatments range from ones which will improve a fiber's ability to take dye to ones which give a fiber stretch it does not naturally have.

modified yarns (*mahd*-eh-fyd yarns) See modified fibers.

mohair (*moh*-hair) The long, lustrous hair of the angora goat. It is used, mixed with other fibers, in making mohair fabrics.

moiré (mwa-*ray*) A wavy, rippling pattern somewhat like a watermark produced in the finishing on certain fabrics by calendering. On acetate, a moiré made this way is permanent; on most other fabrics it is not. Moiré fabrics go in and out of fashion and are usually popular when taffeta is popular. Moiré effects can also be made by printing and in the weaving of fabrics, but the finishing method is the most common one. See calendering under finishing.

moiré taffeta (mwa-*ray taff*-eh-tah) Taffeta with a moiré finish. See taffeta; see also, moiré, above.

molding (*mohl*-ding) The thermoplastic nature of most of the man-made fibers means that they change their shape under heat, opening up the possibility of molding items rather than knitting them or cutting and sewing them to the desired shape. Although this method of manufacture has great promise, so far it has been successful primarily in brassieres (most seamless brassieres have molded cups) and in upholstery applications.

momie cloth (*mahm*-ee kloth) A fabric made with a weave that produces a pebbled effect similar to crepe.

momme (*mahm*-ee) A Japanese unit of weight used for weighing silk.

A momme equals a little less than 4 grams (about .034 ounces).

monk's cloth (mungks kloth) A heavy, coarse, loosely woven basket weave fabric. Traditionally, this fabric is brownish beige and is made of cotton with, sometimes, the addition of flax or jute; today it may be made of man-made fibers, too. Monk's cloth is most popular for home furnishings such as draperies and slip covers, but it is occasionally used in clothing. See basket weave under weaving.

monofil (*mahn*-eh-fil) See monofilament.

monofilament (mahn-en-*fill*-eh-mint) A single, fine thread of continuous man-made fiber. See also multi-filament, staple, and tow.

morocco (m*eh*-*rock*-oh) See leather; chart of leather.

mosquito netting (mehs-*keet*-oh *net*-ing) A coarsely meshed, net fabric used to make mosquito nets which are placed over windows and beds to keep mosquitoes out. See also net.

moss crepe (mawss krayp) Officially, moss crepe is made in a plain or dobby weave with rayon yarns which produce the moss-like effect. In practice, however, the term refers to any crepe, including polyester, which can be considered to have a moss-like surface. See weaving.

moss fringe (mawss frinj) See trimming.

moth repellency (mawth ree-*pell*-en-see) An example of the desirable qualities which can be given to fabrics in the finishing process. Fabrics which attract moths, such as woolens, can be treated for repellency. The treatment will also repel other insects such as carpet beetles. Wool rugs are almost always treated for moth repellency today.

motif (moh-*teef*) A design or color which may be used alone or repeated on a fabric.

mousseline (mooss-eh-*leen*) The name for a broad category of fabrics, usually fairly sheer and lightweight and made in a variety of fibers, including man-mades, silk, cotton, and wool. Mousseline usually has a crisp hand. The word mousseline is often used today for a fabric resembling mousseline de soie. See mousseline de soie. See also, hand.

mousseline de soie (*mooss*-eh-leen deh *swah*) The words "de soie" mean "of silk" which may explain why the fabric similar to this made from man-made fibers is usually called mousseline. Mousseline de soie is a lightweight, sheer, plain weave, silk fabric somewhat similar to chiffon in its appearance and uses, but a little crisper.

multi-filament yarn (mul-tih-*fil*-eh-mint yarn) A yarn made of two or more filaments (long threads) of man-made fibers which are joined together, usually by twisting.

muslin (*muhz*-lin) The name for a very large group of plain weave fabrics, originally made of cotton. When muslin looks are popular they are usually made of blends of cotton and man-made fibers. Muslins range from sheer to very heavy weights, the heavier weight being more popular. When muslin sheets are made of cotton and man-made fiber blends they are said to approach the softness of percale sheets after a few washings. Muslin is also used for inter-facings in ready-to-wear coats and suits and is extremely popular in dressmaking for testing garment appearance and fit before cutting into an expensive fabric. It is used as a furniture covering on expensive furniture which is subsequently covered with upholstery fabric or with sets of slipcovers selected by the customer. Muslin sheets are bleached; most muslin used for other purposes is un-bleached, which means that bits of trash, usually appearing as brown flecks, add color to the fabric. Occasionally, unbleached muslin becomes popular in fashion even for such uses as wedding gowns. Indian muslin is a very fine muslin from India, often printed with gold and silver. It is an expensive luxury fabric. See trash; see also, flecks.

N

nacré velvet (na-*kray vel*-vit) See velvet.

nainsook (*nayn*-sook) A plain weave, cotton fabric made from combed or carded yarns. Nainsook is usually white or pastel and has been used primarily for baby clothes, blouses, and lingerie. It has either a soft or a crisp finish. With the increasing importance of man-made fibers, nainsook has declined in significance.

naked wool (*nay*-kid wool) A relatively new term, much promoted by the International Wool Secretariat, the advertising and promotion organization for wool producers, as a description for sheer, lightweight woolen fabrics which can be worn throughout the year.

nap (nap) Officially, a fuzzy or soft, down-like surface which is produced by brushing the fabric, usually with wire brushes. However, the term nap has come also to mean any hair-like surface including ones which, more correctly, should be termed pile including velvet. The term nap is also occasionally used to describe the surface of a fabric which reflects light differently from different angles, even though the fabric has no true nap. The word nap is used in homesewing to describe all fabrics which must be cut with the pattern pieces facing in the same direction whether or not these fabrics have a true nap.

napkin (*nap*-kin) See linens and domestics.

nappa (*nap*-ah) See leather.

napping (*nap*-ing) The finishing process used to produce a true napped surface in which the fabric is passed over fine wires, brushes, or burrs which raise some of the fibers to the top, producing the characteristic soft or fuzzy napped surface. Shearing may be a part of the napping process; it cuts the raised nap to a uniform height, very much in the way a lawn mower cuts grass. This process is used primarily for fabrics in which a striped nap effect is considered desirable.

133

narrow carpet (*nair*-oh *kar*-pit) Narrow carpet is used as the opposite of broadloom carpet. Narrow carpet is woven in narrow widths like 36 inches and is popular for stair coverings. See rugs and carpets.

narrow fabrics (*nair*-oh *fab*-riks) The term narrow fabrics refers to items such as braids and tapes which are woven on a very narrow loom and have a selvage at each side. Officially, ribbons are not considered narrow fabrics but in practice they are often included.

natural fibers (*nat*-cher-'l *fy*-bers) Fibers found in nature which can be made into yarn with relatively few steps. The most commonly known fibers include cotton, silk, wool, linen, hemp, jute, ramie, and nettle. The term natural fibers has only come into use since the development of man-made fibers to distinguish between them. See separate entries for the fibers listed above.

natural color (*nat*-cher-'l *kul*-er) A term used very loosely, to describe the color of a natural fiber fabric as it comes from the loom before bleaching or dyeing. Natural also is used for many colors from off-white to a pale brown. See also neutral color.

Navajo rug (*nah*-vuh-hoh rug) See rugs and carpets.

needlepoint (*need*-'l-poynt) A form of embroidery worked on a very open fabric (called needlepoint canvas) which is unusable until the embroidery covers the openings. Although many different stitches can be worked on needlepoint canvas, the most commonly used are the basket weave, continental, and half-cross stitch. Needlepoint has several other names which depend on the size of the holes in the canvas. Petit point (pet-ee poynt), for instance, is done on a canvas with small holes extremely close together. Canvas with 20 holes per inch could be considered petit point canvas. Quick point (kwik-poynt) is the name for needlepoint worked with thick yarns on needlepoint canvas with large, widely-spaced holes (5 holes to the inch, for example). This work goes very fast as opposed to petit point which is very time-consuming. Gros point (grow poynt) is a synonym for regular needlepoint which is most commonly worked on canvas with 10, 12, or 14 holes to the inch. See needlepoint canvas, below.

needlepoint canvas (*need*-'l-poynt *kan*-vus) The fabric on which needlepoint is worked. It is a heavily sized (starched) mesh fabric. The open spaces in the mesh are filled with yarn and the yarns which form the mesh are covered with yarn as the needlepoint is worked. There are two kinds of needlepoint canvas. Penelope canvas has double threads used in the weave. These threads can be split so that certain areas can be worked in extremely small stitches (petit point) while other areas are worked in larger stitches. The other type of canvas is called mono canvas; it is woven with single threads. The color of needlepoint canvas is usually either white or a light beige and the sizes of the holes vary from those requiring as many as 200 stitches to the square inch up to those requiring only 16 stitches to the square inch. Rug canvas used in hooking rugs closely resembles needlepoint canvas but has even larger holes. See needlepoint, above.

needlepoint lace (*need-'l*-poynt layss) See lace.

net (net) An open fabric with geometrically shaped holes. Net and mesh are often used as synonyms and the fabrics themselves can be used for the same purposes. Net ranges from the delicacy of hair net, often made of human hair and used to hold hair in place, to mosquito nets, used for protection from insects, to fish nets, used for catching fish and draining the water from the catch. Net is either made by machine or knotted by hand and often forms the ground on which lace is made. Tulle, a favorite for bridal veils, made from silk or nylon, is another form of net.

nettle (*net-'l*) A plant found primarily in Europe sometimes used to produce a fiber by much the same method as that used in making linen from flax. The word nettle is sometimes used for fibers which are actually ramie. See ramie; see also, linen.

neutral color (*noo*-trul *kul*-er) A color which can be used with many other colors as an accessory color. Black, brown, gray, beige, and white are the most common neutral colors, but navy blue, burgundy, and red are often used as neutral colors for accessories.

ninon (*nee*-nohn) A transparent, open mesh fabric usually made of a synthetic fiber such as nylon. It is a lightweight, plain weave fabric originally made of silk.

noil (noyl) Short fibers, often those taken out by combing or carding. They may be used with other, longer fibers, to form yarn, producing a fabric with textural interest. Occasionally the noils are colored differently from the other fiber in the fabric. See combing; see also, carding.

non-woven (non-*woh*-ven) A way of describing a fabric which is neither knit nor woven. The category of non-woven fabrics usually includes fabrics which are felted as well as those in which fibers are joined by glue or heat. Occasionally, a distinction is made between felted fabrics, paper, and other non-wovens. See Chapter Two, From Fiber to Fabric. See also, felt.

notions (*no*-shens) See findings.

Nottingham lace (*not*-ing-um layss) See lace.

novelty (*nahv*-el-tee) Anything which is a little different from the usual. Novelty yarns, for instance, are often those with slubs. Novelty fabrics often have textural interest while novelty prints are just about anything except such classics as florals. In natural fibers, novelty yarns are formed when natural lumps form from uneven spinning. In man-made yarns, similar effects are produced by deliberately manufacturing filaments of varying thicknesses.

no-wale (*no*-wayl) See wale.

nub (nub) A synonym for slub. See slub.

nun's veiling (nunz-*vay*-ling) A plain weave, lightweight, quite sheer fabric traditionally used by nuns for veils as part of their habits and made of woolen, worsted, or man-made fibers in black or white. It is also used as a dress fabric.

nylon (*ny*-lon) Nylon, the first of the synthetic fibers, is very strong, resists abrasion and resists wrinkles. It has a natural luster, holds body heat, and resists moths. Nylon dyes well but fades in the sunlight, may pill and melts under high heat. Nylon is naturally mildew resistant, which has led to its popularity for such things as mosquito netting used in the tropics. Nylon is a thermoplastic man-made fiber synthesized from petroleum. See thermoplastic; see man-made fibers. See Chapter One, Fiber—The Start of It All.

nytril (*ny*-tril) The generic name for a man-made fiber containing at least 85% vinylidene dinitrile derived from ammonia and natural gas. Nytril is no longer produced in the United States. It was used with other fibers to form soft fabrics for such things as sweaters. See generic name; see also, man-made fiber.

O

off-grain (*off*-grayn) See grain.

oil repellency (oil ree-*pel*-ent-zee) The ability of a fabric to prevent or retard the penetration of oil. This ability is the result of a finish added to the fabric. The finish is used on some man-made fibers (notably polyester) which tend to hold oil-based stains once the stains penetrate the cloth.

oilcloth (oil-kloth) Any fabric treated with oil to make it waterproof. Oilcloth was used extensively at one time for such purposes as covering kitchen tables. Oiled silk was used for shower curtains and other areas requiring a waterproof fabric. Oilskin, also an oilcloth, was a term usually used to describe oilcloth used for making raincoats. Today, the name oilskin is used for a variety of waterproof coating fabrics, most commonly those with a thick synthetic coating on the right side of the fabric.

olefin (*oh*-leh-fin) The generic name for fibers derived from polyethylene or polypropylene. Olefin is primarily used in home furnishings for inexpensive rugs and upholstery as it has good bulk and coverage and resists chemicals, mildew, and weather. Its sensitivity to heat has limited its use in clothing as special care has to be taken in cleaning it. Olefin is occasionally, and incorrectly, called polypropylene. See also, generic name. See Chart on Fiber Properties.

ombré (*ohm*-bray [common pronunciation]; *ahm*-bra [correct pronunciation]) The word ombré is used to describe a design which changes, usually in rainbow-like gradations, from one color to another. Ombré patterns can be shades of one color or several colors.

ondulé (ohn-dyou-*lay*) The wavy appearance which certain fabrics, and especially sheer fabrics hung as curtains, have when looked at from a distance.

opacity (oh-*pass*-eh-tee) The opposite of transparency. This quality has become increasingly important as a fabric consideration with the development of man-made fibers. For their weight, most man-made fibers, unlike most natural fibers, have little opacity. (They are more transparent than natural fibers.) This is not objectionable in most cases but in such things as a pair of white slacks, it can prove a problem. Opacity can be increased at many different points in the manufacture of a fabric or a garment, from the way the fiber is produced to the processing of the yarn to the way the fabric is dyed and finished to the way the garment is made (with or without a lining). Opacity in hosiery is more a fashion matter. At a time when very sheer stockings are fashionable, opacity is relatively undesirable. When, on the other hand, it is fashionable for legs to be colored, opaque hosiery becomes important. See opaque.

opaque (oh-*payk*) Something is opaque when what is behind or under it cannot be seen. See opacity.

open fabric (*oh*-pen *fab*-rik) A fabric in which the yarns are spaced fairly far apart. Most curtain fabrics, for instance, are open fabrics to allow light to filter through the fabric.

optical brightener (*ahp*-tee-k'l *bryt*'-'n-er) Optical brighteners convert invisible ultraviolet light to visible light in the blue region making fabrics appear to reflect more light than they really do. This makes them appear brighter and, perhaps, cleaner. Optical brighteners are used in the manufacture of fabrics and are included in the formulas of some synthetic detergents sold for use by the consumer. See detergent.

optical dye (*ahp*-tee-k'l dy) Dye used to produce fluorescent fabrics. See fluorescent fabric.

optical whitener (*ahp*-tee-k'l *whyt*-ner) See optical brightener.

organdie (*oar*-gan-dee) See organdy.

organdy (*oar*-gan-dee) At one time, organdy was a sheer, lightweight, open cotton fabric with a stiff finish; organza was the same fabric made of silk. Today, those former distinctions have almost disappeared and the names organdy and organza are used almost as synonyms. The natural fibers have been replaced by man-made fibers for their manufacture. Permanent finishes on natural fiber organdy and man-made fiber organdy have eliminated the largest objection to this fabric—its tendency to wrinkle easily and its loss of crispness. Organdy is always popular for curtains and is often used in clothing, especially for blouses and evening wear.

organza (oar-*gan*-zah) See organdy.

Oriental rug (oar-ee-*en*-t'l rug) See rugs and carpets.

Orlon (*oar*-lon) Trademark of DuPont for their acrylic and moda-crylic fibers.

osnaburg (*oz*-neh-berg) Osnaburg is a coarse, plain weave cotton fabric. It is quite strong and is used extensively for bags and other industrial purposes. Osnaburg is also occasionally used for draperies and upholstery.

osprey (*oss*-pree) See feathers.

ostrich (*oss*-trich) See feathers.

ottoman (*ot*-teh-man) A fabric with wide horizontal ribs similar to faille. Ottoman is usually made in wool, silk or man-made fibers and is primarily used for evening clothes. It also appears in upholstery and draperies. See faille.

outing flannel (*owt*-ing *flan*-el) A soft, lightweight, cotton fabric, usually napped on both sides and traditionally used for sleepwear, diapers, underwear, and underlinings. See flannel.

overplaid (*oh*-ver-plad) See plaid.

overprinting (*oh*-ver-print-ing) Printing new colors or designs on a fabric already printed. See printing.

Oxford cloth (*oks*-ford kloth) Oxford cloth is most often used to describe a basket weave fabric made of cotton or a cotton blend. It often has a colored warp and a white filling. This fabric is given a smooth finish and is a popular fabric for men's shirts.

Oxford gray (*oks*-ford gray) A popular color which is very dark but not quite black. It is especially common in wool flannel and is often used for men's suits and slacks and occasionally for women's clothing.

oxidation (ock-seh-*day*-shun) The joining of oxygen and another substance. In the case of fabrics, the term is usually used in reference to fibers or dyes which weaken or change when they come in contact with oxygen.

oxygen-type bleach (*ocks*-eh-jen-typ bleech) Oxygen-type bleaches, which are milder and less effective than chlorine bleaches, are frequently recommended for laundering where bleaching is desirable but chlorine bleaches would cause fabric deterioration. Perborate bleaches are oxygen-type bleaches. See bleach.

℘

padding (*pad*-ing) Any item which provides a degree of support to a fabric. It usually describes the layer of fabric placed underneath a carpet or rug to provide it with longer life and to give it a more luxurious appearance and feeling. Carpet padding is made of cattle hair, rubberized hair, rubber, and combinations of jute and cattle hair as well as some of the man-made fibers. Some rugs and carpets have a bonded foam, sponge rubber, or man-made backing, in which case no separate padding is needed. Padding is also called cushion and underlay. See also rugs and carpets.

pailette (pie-*yet*) See sequins.

Paisley (*payz*-lee) Paisley is usually used to describe a design which was developed for use on fine wool shawls made in Paisley, Scotland. The shawls were originally woven to imitate the woven shawls of Kashmir which had a cone design. The woven shawls proved too expensive to produce and the design was adapted for printing. The Paisley design itself changed to the scroll-like form it now has. Paisleys, both large and small, are almost never out of fashion and may be knitted into fabrics, woven in, or, more usually, printed on fabrics.

panama (*pan*-uh-mah) A fairly lightweight summer suit fabric usually made of wool worsted. Before man-made fibers were available, it was used extensively for men's suits for its coolness and wrinkle resistance. See also, tropical suiting.

panne velvet (pan *vel*-vit, correct pronunciation; pan-*ay vel*-vit, incorrect but common pronunciation) See velvet.

paper fabric (*pay*-per *fab*-rik) Most paper fabrics are not, strictly speaking, paper at all, but non-woven fabrics. This is an area which holds great promise for the future because of anticipated savings in cost in the manufacture of these fabrics and because of the devel-

140

opment of varied applications any new fabric brings with it. This promise is, as yet, largely unrealized. Paper clothing had a brief vogue but now is rarely seen. However, such items as disposable underwear, baby diapers, industrial clothing, and hospital gowns and napkins are being made of these fabrics today.

paper taffeta (*pay*-per *taff*-eh-tah) See taffeta.

patchwork (*pach*-wurk) A fabric which results from joining small pieces of fabric together in a pattern or in random fashion to make one large piece. It was important in Colonial America when fabric was scarce as a means of utilizing fabric scraps and remnants. Patchwork was originally sewn by hand and often a completed piece of patchwork became the top of a quilt. Patchwork has become an art form in and of itself. Patchwork quilts are a traditional American folk craft and are collectors' items. Today, patchwork can be made by machine and is available by the yard for clothing and home furnishing items. Patchwork printed fabric is made to imitate the real thing. See also quilt.

patent (*pat*-'nt) See leather.

pattern (*pat*-urn) Any design which is repeated. A pattern on fabric is the design which is usually repeated several times in every yard of fabric. The word pattern is used as a synonym for design and motif. Pattern also refers to a printed paper guide which shows how a particular garment style is to be cut from fabric. A step-by-step instruction sheet is included which shows how to sew the garment together. See motif.

pattern knit (*pat*-urn nit) See knitting.

pearl cotton (purl *kot*-'n) A mercerized cotton thread with a loose twist used primarily in embroidery, crochet, knitting and weaving.

peau de soie (*poh* deh swah) Originally, a luxurious fabric made of silk (soie is the French word for silk). It is a rather heavy, smooth fabric usually woven in a satin weave and especially popular for formal uses including wedding gowns. Peau de soie has a dull sheen. Today, most of this fabric is made of polyester or other man-made fibers and it is referred to simply as peau. See satin weave under entry for weaving.

pebble (*peb*-'l) Pebble is used to describe a fabric with a somewhat bumpy, grainy appearance. It is most commonly used to describe crepes. See crepe.

peccary (*peck*-er-ee) See leather.

Pellon (*pell*-on) Trademark of the Pellon Corporation for a group of non-woven fabrics used primarily for interfacings.

pepper and salt (*pep*-er and salt) See salt and pepper; see tweed.

perborate bleach (per-*bohr*-ate bleech) An oxygen-type bleach. See bleach; see also, oxygen-type bleach.

percale (per-*kayl*) Originally, a plain weave cotton fabric with a smooth finish. Most percale today is a blend of cotton and man-made fibers. Calico prints are often printed on percale rather than on calico. Percale sheets are smoother and softer than muslin sheets as the yarns are combed as well as carded. See section on bedding and towels. See calico; see also, combing and carding.

perle cotton (purl *kot*-'n) See pearl cotton.

permanent finish (*pur*-me-nent *fin*-ish) A substance applied to fabric during the final, or finishing step in manufacture that will last throughout the life of the fabric. See finishing.

permanent press (*pur*-me-nent press) Another term for durable press although it is used more loosely than durable press. It is a misnomer because almost all fabrics so treated tend to need a minimal amount of pressing, so the press is not "permanent." See durable press and easy care.

Persian rug (*pur*-zhen rug) See rugs and carpets.

perspiration resistant (pur-speh-*ray*-shun ree-*sis*-t'nt) The ability of a fabric to resist the effects of perspiration which causes some fabrics and dyes to deteriorate. Perspiration resistant finishes are occasionally applied as part of the finishing process. See finishing.

petersham (*pee*-ter-shem) Petersham is a ribbon-like fabric similar to grosgrain. See grosgrain.

petit point (pet-ee poynt) See needlepoint.

photographic printing (*foh*-toh-graf-ik *print*-ing) Printing in which either rollers or silk screens are made from photographs. In the case of roller photographic printing, the photograph is engraved on the rollers. In the silk screen process, the photograph is transferred to the screens. Very exact reproductions of pictures are possible with photographic printing. See entries for roller printing and screen printing under printing.

pick (pik) See pilling.

picot (*pee*-koh) A series of small decorative loops which is placed along the edge of a fabric either in the manufacturing or by hand crochet or embroidery. Picot trimming is also available by the yard. See trimming.

piece dyed (peess dyd) See dyeing.

piece goods (peess goodz) Fabrics which are sold to the consumer by the yard. Piece goods are also called yard goods, yardage and fashion fabrics.

pigskin (pig-skin) See leather.

pile (pyl) A fabric surface formed by yarns which are brought to the right side of the fabric in the course of making the fabric. Some fabrics have pile surfaces on both sides. Looped fabrics such as terry cloth, tufted fabrics including candlewick and many rugs, and fabrics such as velvet made by the double cloth construction method in which the heavy joining yarns are subsequently split to make two fabrics are all pile constructions. In certain specialized areas, notably home sewing, pile fabrics are considered to have a nap. See nap; see also, terry cloth, candlewick and velvet.

pilling (*pil*-ing) The formation of small balls of fiber which appear on the surface of certain fabrics. Pills develop on woolen fabrics but tend to disappear when the fabrics are cleaned; man-made fiber pills remain on the fabric. Man-made fibers also tend to develop picks (small loose threads which can snag). The tendency of man-made fibers to pill and pick can be reduced by steps taken in the processing of the yarn or the finishing of the fabric.

pillow case (*pill*-oh kayss) See linens and domestics.

pillow lace (*pill*-oh layss) See entry for bobbin lace under lace.

pillow (*pill*-oh) A cloth bag (often made of ticking) which has been stuffed with feathers, down, kapok, rubber, synthetic foam, fiberfill, or a similar substance and is used to support some part of the body and to make furniture comfortable. See separate entries for stuffing materials listed. There are various kinds of pillows, including:

> **bolster** (*bohl*-ster) A long, narrow pillow of round or rectangular shape used for decoration and support.

> **box-edged** (boks-edjd) A pillow which has three dimensions rather than being two-sided as are most bed pillows. In other words, the pillow fabric covering is shaped like a round or rectangular box and has a fabric band (boxing) which covers the edges of the pillow and joins the top and bottom sides.

> **flange** (flanj) A flat border. On pillows, it is an unstuffed decorative edging surrounding a stuffed pillow. It differs from a ruffle in that it is flat rather than shirred. See shirring.

pin check (pin chek) See checks.

Pima cotton (*pee*-mah kot-'n) See cotton.

pin tuck (pin tuk) See tuck.

pinwale (*pin*-wayl) See wale.

pin seal (pin seel) See leather.

pinstripe (*pin*-stryp) See stripe.

piping (*pyp*-ing) See trimming.

piqué (pee-*kay*) A fabric woven with small, raised geometric patterns on a loom with a dobby attachment. It is usually made of cotton or a blend of cotton and synthetic and is usually a crisp fabric of medium or heavy weight. It is often printed with colorful designs. White piqué is a classic fabric for tennis clothes and for collars and cuffs on dresses and blouses. The look of woven piqué can be duplicated with embossing and heat setting. See dobby; see also embossing and heat setting.

placemat (playss-mat) See linens and domestics.

plaid (plad) Any pattern of multiple stripes which cross each other at right angles forming rectangles. Orginally, the word plaid was used for a length of fabric in a tartan design, a plaid design associated with a specific Scottish clan. See tartan for a listing of the names of some of the major authentic tartan plaids. Following is a list of the most common plaids.

argyle plaid (*ahr*-gyl plad) A plaid pattern of diamonds, often with thin stripes running over the diamond patterns in the same direction as the sides of the diamonds. Originally argyle designs appeared only in knits but today they are also found woven and printed.

balanced plaid (*bal*-'nst plad) A plaid in which the arrangement of stripes is the same both on the cross and on the length of the grain. Also called even plaid.

bias plaid (*by*-us plad) A plaid design which actually forms a diamond pattern with the intersection of its lines. An argyle plaid is a bias plaid.

blanket plaid (*blang*-ket plad) A very vividly colored plaid design usually on a napped fabric like those used for blankets.

even plaid (*ee*-ven plad) See balanced plaid.

overplaid (*oh*-ver-plad) A plaid design made of two or more plaids woven or printed so that one appears to be on top of the other.

unbalanced plaid (un-*bal*-'nst plad) An unbalanced plaid is one in which the arrangement of the stripes is different on the crosswise and lengthwise grain of the fabric. In constructing a garment of this type of plaid, special care must be taken in matching the plaid design.

uneven plaid (un-*ee*-ven plad) See unbalanced plaid.

plain knit (playn nit) See knitting.

plain weaving (playn *weev*-ing) See weaving.

plaiting (*playt*-ing) See braid.

plastic (*plas*-tik) A plastic substance is one which can be molded into another shape. The materials from which man-made fibers are made are "plastic," meaning that the same substance can, depending on how it is molded, be made into fiber, buttons, or zippers.

pleating (*plee*-ting) A way of folding cloth. Pleats differ from tucks in that tucks are usually stitched on the foldline while pleats usually are not. See pleats; see also, tucks.

pleats (pleetz) Folds of cloth arranged in a certain way. Pleats can be made as the fabric is produced (usually through heat setting) or as the garment is made. Pleats are used to control fullness or for decorative purposes. The thermoplastic nature of man-made fibers (they change their shape under heat) means that permanent pleating which does not have to be renewed when a pleated item is cleaned is now available. Following is a list of common types of pleats:

accordion pleats (uh-*kor*-dee-un pleetz) Very narrow, straight pleats, similar to knife pleats but facing in any direction desired for effect. See knife pleats, below.

box pleats (boks pleetz) Box pleats are made by folding fabric so that the edges of two pleats face in opposite directions on the right side of the fabric.

cartridge pleats (*kar*-trij pleetz) Unpressed, very narrow pleats. They are usually used more as decoration than to control fullness.

inverted pleats (inn-*vur*-ted pleetz) Pleats formed in the same way as box pleats, but the edges meet on the right side of the garment. See box pleats, above.

kick pleat (*kik*-pleet) A small pleat at the bottom of a straight, fairly long skirt to give room for walking.

knife pleats (*nyfe* pleetz) Narrow, straight pleats similar to accordion pleats with each pleat facing in the same direction.

sunburst pleats (*sun*-burst pleetz) Pleats which begin at a central point and move out to the edge of a fabric. They are often narrow at the top of the fabric and wider at the edge and are especially popular for skirts.

unpressed pleats (un-*prest* pleetz) Pleats whose edges (the folds) have not been set by pressing. The term unpressed pleats is usually used for wide unpressed pleats while cartridge pleats, which are also unpressed, is used to describe narrower, decorative pleats.

plissé (plih-*say*) A puckered fabric made by printing plain fabric, usually cotton, with a chemical (caustic soda). The area printed shrinks, causing the unprinted area of the fabric to pucker. The pucker is permanent. The same effect can be achieved in thermoplastic, man-made fiber fabrics by using heat to set the puckers. Plissé is used incorrectly as a synonym for seersucker. See seersucker.

plush (pluhsh) A thick, deep pile like that found in some coating fabrics and some rugs. It is usually a cut pile. See cut pile; see also, pile.

ply (ply) Ply describes two or more yarns twisted together to form one yarn. Two yarns twisted together form a two-ply yarn, four yarns, a four-ply yarn, and so forth.

pointillism (*pwan*-teh-liz-em, correct pronunciation; *point*-teh-liz-em, common pronunciation) A method of printing dots of color on a fabric to give an impression of being one color from a distance. This technique was first developed by French painters around the turn of the century.

polished cotton (*pol*-isht *kot*-'n) Cotton fabrics with a shiny surface, ranging from the slightest sheen to a definite glaze. Generally, the term polished cotton refers to fabrics which have a lower sheen than glazed chintz, for instance. The sheen is added to the fabric in finishing by the application of starch, wax, or synthetics. The finish is almost always permanent today. See chintz.

polka dots (*poh*-kah dotz) See dots.

polyester (pol-ee-*es*-ter) Probably the most versatile and widely used of the man-made fibers. It is extremely strong, has excellent wrinkle and abrasion resistance and resists mildew and moths. It may be warm and clammy when used as apparel as it holds body heat. It may pill and attracts lint. See chart on Fiber Properties.

polynosic (pol-ee-*nohs*-ik) See rayon.

polypropylene (pol-ee-*proh*-peh-leen) See olefin.

polyurethane (pol-ee-*yoor*-eh-thayn) A man-made material used for foam which is laminated to other fabrics to provide warmth. It is also used for mattresses and stuffing. Polyurethane foam tends to yellow upon exposure to air but, it is claimed, this does not affect its performance. It will not harden and is not affected by mildew, moisture, or strong sunlight. Spandex fibers are based on polyurethane. See foam. See also, laminating.

polyvinyl chloride (pol-ee-*vih*-nel *klor*-yde) See vinyon; see vinyl.

pompon (*pom*-pon) See trimming.

pongee (pon-*jee*) See silk.

poodle cloth (*poo*-d'l kloth) A heavy, looped fabric usually used for coats. Originally made of wool, today this fabric is often made of man-made fibers.

poplin (*pop*-lin) A fabric with a fine horizontal rib. It is usually made of cotton, a combination of cotton and man-made fibers, silk, or man-made fibers designed to imitate silk.

positive-negative (*pahz*-eh-tiv *neg*-eh-tiv) The name for two coordinated fabrics, one of which, for instance, would have white dots on a blue ground, the other of which would have blue dots on a white ground. Positive-negative effects can be made in an infinite number of designs but are usually only in two colors.

power net (*pow*-er net) An elastic net fabric which stretches in one or both directions. It is used primarily for support garments such as girdles.

preshrinking (pree-*shringk*-ing) A step in the finishing of fabrics in which they are treated so they will not shrink (become smaller) in later cleaning. Acceptable shrinkage is less than 1%; anything more will affect the fit of a garment. Unfortunately, shrinkage standards are extremely arbitrary. A term such as shrinkage controlled, quite commonly used in the textile industry, means only that a fabric won't shrink more than a certain amount—but that may be as much as 6% in some cotton knits. When a garment is sewn at home, it is wise to preshrink all fabrics and notions before making the garment.

press (press) A machine which flattens fabric. Press also refers to the act of flattening fabric. In the home, pressing is most often done with an iron but small home pressers or "ironers" are also available.

press cloth (press kloth) A piece of fabric placed between the press or iron and the fabric being pressed or ironed to prevent unwanted shine and other effects of excessive heat.

prêt à porter (pray ah por-tay [correct pronunciation]; pret ah por-ter [incorrect pronunciation, but occasionally used]) The French name for ready-to-wear clothing. Recently, the French ready-to-wear industry has developed tremendously. The designs which appear at showings of French ready-to-wear firms are imported to the United States and sold under the name prêt à porter.

printing (*print*-ing) A process for adding a colored pattern to fabric. Following are some of the most common printing methods:

    block printing (blok *print*-ing) In block printing, a block, usually of wood or linoleum, is cut so only the design to be printed is left on the surface. The block is inked and then placed on the fabric. This method of printing is almost entirely limited to the craft field today because it is very time-consuming.

    burn-out printing (burn-owt *print*-ing) In burn-out printing, a fabric made of two fibers with different characteristics is printed with a chemical which eats away (burns out) one of the fibers and not the other. This printing method is used to make some sculptured velvets (the pile of the velvet is eaten away) and to make fabrics with some sheer and some non-sheer areas. In making the sculptured velvets, the pile of the velvet reacts to the chemical; in making the sheer fabrics, the yarn is spun from two fibers one of which is sensitive to the chemical and one of which is not.

    calender printing (*kal*-en-der *print*-ing) See roller printing.

    cylinder printing (*sil*-en-der *print*-ing) See roller printing.

    direct printing (duh-*rekt print*-ing) See roller printing.

    discharge printing (*dis*-charj *print*-ing) A method of obtaining light designs on a very dark ground. The fabric is piece dyed (see dyeing) and the color is then bleached from the design areas in a pattern. An additional step is often the roller printing of these design areas with patterns and colors.

    duplex printing (*doo*-pleks *print*ing) A method of printing the same design on both sides of the fabric to give the design additional definition and clarity of color. Also called register printing.

    extract printing (*eks*-trakt *print*-ing) Another name for discharge printing. See discharge printing.

    heat transfer printing (heet *trans*-fer *print*-ing) In heat transfer printing, elaborate colors and designs are printed onto a special type of paper. The paper is placed over the fabric and the designs and colors are transferred to the fabric through the application of heat.

register printing (*rej*-iss-ter *print*-ing) See duplex printing.

resist printing (ree-*zist print*-ing) Printing similar to resist dyeing. See dyeing. In resist printing, the fabric is coated with a paste which protects it from the printing colors in certain areas; when the printing is completed, the paste is removed. See resist dyeing under entry for dyeing.

roller printing (*rohl*-er *print*-ing) Roller printing may be the most important method of printing used today. The design is etched onto a roller through which the fabric is passed. For each color in the design a different roller is used. High speed can be obtained in roller printing.

screen printing (skreen *print*-ing) In screen printing, a sheer fabric such as silk or nylon gauze is stretched over a wood or metal frame to form a screen. The entire screen, except for the design area to be printed, is coated with a substance which closes the pores of the fabric screen. The dye is poured onto the screen and forced through the uncoated design areas onto the fabric below. A different screen must be used for each color in the print.

sublistatic print (sub-lih-*sta*-tik *print*-ing) A form of heat transfer printing. See heat transfer printing.

print-on-print *(print*-on-print) See separate entry for overprinting.

warp printing (worp *print*-ing) A printing method in which only the warp yarns are printed with a design before the fabric is woven. The resulting fabric has a wavy, shadowy effect. It is also called shadow printing.

pucker (*puhk*-er) A bump or wrinkle in a fabric such as that found in crinkle crepe. See crinkle crepe.

purl (purl) See knitting.

Q

Qiana (kee-*ah*-nah) Trademark of DuPont for nylon.

quality control (*kwahl*-ih-tee kon-*trohl*) A term used to imply inspection of an item throughout the manufacturing process to ensure that the finished product meets high standards. Unfortunately, the term is inexact and can mean everything or nothing.

quilt (kwihlt) A fabric construction most often used as a bed covering for added warmth. It consists of a layer of fabric, known as the quilt top, and backing fabric with a layer of cotton, wool, or synthetic batting between. All three layers are held together with stitching (quilting) that usually creates a design of its own. Quilted bed coverings filled with down feathers are called eiderdowns or comforters. A patchwork quilt has a patchwork quilt top. See also, quilting, patchwork, and batting.

quilting (*kwihlt*-ing) Stitching through two or more layers of fabric to form a design or pattern. The most common quilting design today is a diamond pattern but quilting stitches (usually a short running stitch) may also be done in other geometric or floral patterns. Quilting stitches are often used to outline patchwork or appliqué designs on a quilt. See appliqué; see also, quilt and patchwork.

R

rabbit (*rab*-it) See furs.

rabbit hair (*rab*-it hair) The hair of rabbits is often added to other fibers to give softness or an interesting texture to the surface of the finished fabric. Rabbit hair is used in both woven and knit fabrics.

raffia straw (*raf*-ee-uh straw) See straw.

rag rug (rag rug) See rugs and carpets.

ramie (*ray*-mee) A strong, lustrous, natural fiber from the ramie plant grown in Asia.

ramie straw (*ray*-mee straw) See straw.

raschel (ra-*shel*) See knitting.

rat-tail (rat-tayl) See trimming.

rat-tail fringe (rat-tayl frinj) See trimming.

ravel (*rav*-'l) The tendency of fabric to come unwoven or unknitted at unfinished edges. The term unravel means the same as ravel. Loosely woven fabrics tend to ravel more than those made of tight weaves. Occasionally the tendency to ravel is desirable in order to create a fringed edge.

raw silk (raw silk) See silk.

rayon (*ray*-on) The first successful man-made fiber. Rayon was originally called artificial silk. It is made from cellulose and is weak when it is wet. Rayon is soft and comfortable and dyes well, but is weakened by exposure to sunlight. Because of its low wet strength, rayon may shrink or stretch unless treated. Several different types of rayon are being made and are listed below. See also, cellulose.

    cuprammonium rayon (kyou-pre-*moh*-nee-um *ray*-on) Rayon made by a process that allows very fine filament fibers to be formed. The fineness of its filaments is its best known characteristic.

    high wet modulus rayon (hy wet *mahd*-you-les *ray*-on) Rayon made by a modified "viscose" process. The resulting rayon is much stronger when wet than ordinary rayon is. Zantrel and Avril are examples of high wet modulus rayon. See viscose rayon, below.

polynosic rayon (pol-ee-*nah*-sik *ray*-on) Rayon which is less likely to shrink or stretch when wet because of the way in which it is made. Regular rayon shrinks and stretches when wet and is said to have poor wet-strength.

saponified rayon (sah-*pahn*-eh-fyd *ray*-on) A type of rayon which is made from cellulose acetate filaments, the same kind used in making acetate. These fibers are treated in a special way to produce a rayon which is very strong. Fortisan is an example of saponified rayon.

viscose rayon (*viss*-koss *ray*-on) Rayon made by the viscose process, the process used to make the majority of rayon on the market, today. True viscose rayon is not strong, especially when wet. This has led to modifications of the viscose process to produce high wet modulus rayon. See high wet modulus rayon, above.

ready-to-wear (*red*-ee-to-wayr) A term used in the fashion industry. It was developed to distinguish between manufactured items of clothing and those made from fabric sold by the yard to the consumer. The term is sometimes shortened to r-t-w. See also, pret a porter.

reclaimed textile fibers (ree-*klaymd teks*-til *fy*-berz) Fibers which have been made into fabric (whether sold commercially or not) and then converted back into fiber. Most reclaimed textile fibers are wool and other natural fibers as it is extremely difficult to reclaim man-made fibers. See also reprocessed fibers and reused fibers.

recovery (reh-*kuv*-er-ee) The ability of a fabric to return to its original shape after being stretched. This term is used most often in reference to stretch fabrics. A quality stretch fabric will recover promptly. Recovery may also be used in reference to knit fabrics since they have varying amounts of stretchability.

recycled fiber (ree-*sy*-keld *fy*-ber) See reclaimed textile fibers, reprocessed fiber, and reused fiber.

re-embroidered lace (ree-im-*broyd*-erd layss) See lace.

regimental stripe (rej-eh-*men*-t'l stryp) See stripe.

register printing (*rej*-iss-ter *print*-ing) See printing.

remnants (*rem*-nents) Left-over pieces of fabric including fabric originally sold by the yard and rug and carpeting material. Usually, because remnants are of odd sizes, the price is reduced and they can be true bargains. Care labelling is not required on remnants under ten yards in size so it is important to note fiber content if it is available in order to determine care requirements.

repeat (ree-*peet*) Repeat refers to a design which appears over and over again on a fabric. It also refers to the amount of space the design takes before it starts over again. Since it is desirable to center the design in a fabric on such things as sofas, the size of the repeat must be known in order to determine the yardage needed. The larger the pattern, the larger the repeat and the more fabric needed. The size of the repeat in a plaid, for instance, is also important in buying fabric for home-sewn garments.

reprocessed fibers (ree-*pross*-est *fy*-berz) Fibers obtained from scraps of new fabrics (never used) which have been shredded back into fiber form and then remade into new yarns. Reprocessed fibers are usually wool fibers and must be relabelled as "reprocessed wool" according to Federal Trade Commission standards. Reprocessed fibers are less desirable than new or virgin fibers. See virgin fiber.

reptile (*rep*-tihl) See leather and the chart on leather in Chapter Three.

residual shrinkage (reh-*zij*-you-el *shring*-kij) The amount of shrinkage remaining in a fabric or garment after all manufacturing processes are completed. More than 1% residual shrinkage is undesirable but common since in many fabrics the removal of residual shrinkage is not always included as part of the finishing process. Because fabrics often have residual shrinkage, it is important to preshrink before cutting fabrics used in home sewing. See preshrink.

resin finish (*rez*-'n *fin*-ish) A finish made of synthetic resins applied to fabrics to impart certain characteristics such as wrinkle and crease resistance. See finishing.

resist dyeing (ree-*zist dy*-ing) See dyeing.

resist printing (ree-*zist print*-ing) See printing.

reused fibers (ree-*youzd fy*-berz) Fibers obtained from rags and used clothing which, after sorting and cleaning, have been shredded into fiber. Products made from reused fiber must be labelled as such. Reused fibers, like reprocessed fibers, are less desirable than new fibers. See virgin fiber. See also, reprocessed fibers.

reversed leather (ree-*verst leth*-er) See leather.

reversible fabric (ree-*vers*-eh-b'l *fab*-rik) A fabric which can be used on either side. Generally, the term reversible is applied to two quite different fabrics which have been joined together by such methods as laminating or double cloth construction. Reversible fabrics are frequently used for coats, less frequently for other garments. See laminating; see also, double cloth.

rhinestone (*ryne*-stohn) A faceted piece of glass (the glass is cut with faces which reflect light). Rhinestones are used in costume jewelry or as decoration on clothing or trimming. Rhinestones are also called diamante.

rib (rib) A straight, ridged or corded effect which usually moves vertically or horizontally on a fabric.

ribbing (*rib*-ing) See entry for rib knit under knitting.

rib knit (rib nit) See entry under knitting.

rib weave (rib weev) A plain weave which forms ridges in a fabric either through the way in which it is woven or by the use of thicker yarns for the filling than those used for the warp. See weaving. See also, filling and warp.

ribbon (*rib*-en) See trimming.

rick-rack (rik-rak) See trimming.

roller blinds (*rohl*-er blindz) See shades.

roller printing (*rohl*-er *print*-ing) See printing.

roller shades (*rohl*-er shaydz) See shades.

Roman shades (*roh*-men shaydz) See shades.

Roman stripe (*roh*-men stryp) See stripe.

rubber sheet (*rub*-er sheet) See linens and domestics.

ruche, ruching (roosh, *roosh*-ing) See trimming.

rugs and carpets (rugs and *kar*-pits) Usually the most expensive fabrics most people ever buy. The words rug and carpet are often used interchangeably. Rug usually refers to a floor covering which does not cover the entire floor and is not fastened to it, while carpet is used for fabric which does cover the entire floor and is fastened to it. Following are common rug and carpet terms. See also Chapter Six, A Guide to Rugs and Carpets.

> **area rug** (*air*-ee-ah rug) A small, usually decorative rug often placed on a carpet as an accent in a room or to define an area such as a dining section in a living room.

> **Aubusson** (oh-boo-*sohn*) A woven rug with little or no rib and a low pile.

> **Axminster** (*aks*-min-ster) A rug woven on a loom which makes fairly complicated designs possible.

> **braid rug** (brayd rug) A rug made of strips of fabric which are braided together and then stitched together to form a rug. See braid.

> **broadloom carpet** (*brawd*-loom *kar*-pit) A carpet woven on a loom at least nine feet wide or wider. It is incorrectly used to suggest carpet quality. The term is also used to describe wide, tufted carpeting in which tufts of yarn are pulled through a backing to form the rug surface. See the chapter on rugs and carpets for a further discussion of tufted rugs.

> **brocade** (broh-*kayd*) A rug in which a pattern is formed by using yarns of the same color with different twists. The light strikes the yarns differently, giving a shaded design effect. See twist.

> **drugget** (*drug*-it) A coarse, felted floor covering made from mix-

tures of such fibers as cotton, jute, and wool. Drugget is usually napped on one side and is a traditionally inexpensive floor covering used by institutions.

hand-knotted rug (*hand*-not-id rug) Hand-knotted rugs, including Oriental and Persian rugs, are among the most expensive made. Intricate designs are possible. The higher the number of knots to the inch, the finer the rug.

hooked rug (hookt rug) A rug made by hand or machine using a hook to pull loops of yarn or fabric through a coarse backing or canvas to form a pile.

indoor-outdoor carpeting (*in*-door-*out*-door *kar*-pit-ing) Carpeting which can be used outdoors where it will be exposed to weather conditions, as well as indoors. Most of this type of carpeting is made of olefin. See olefin.

loop rug (loop rug) Usually, a rug with an uncut loop pile. Types of loops include high-low loop (a rug in which some loops are higher than others giving a sculptured effect), one-level loop, and random-sheared loop (a rug with some loops cut and others uncut to create a sculptured effect). See pile.

narrow carpet (*nair*-oh *kar*-pit) Carpet made on a loom about three feet wide. The term is used to distinguish this carpeting from broadloom carpeting. Narrow carpet is often used on stairways. See broadloom, above.

Navajo rug (*nah*-vuh-hoh rug) A rug woven in a tapestry weave in a geometric pattern by Navajo Indians in the western part of the United States. Navajo rugs are usually brightly colored and have become true collectors' items. See tapestry.

Oriental rugs (oar-ee-*en*-t'l rugs) Hand-made rugs produced in both the Middle and Far East. They are either hand-woven, in the tapestry method, or they are hand-knotted. True Oriental rugs are extremely expensive and are collectors' items. Machine-made imitations are available. See tapestry. See also, entry for hand-knotted rug, above.

Persian rug (*pur*-zhen rug) An Oriental rug made in Iran (formerly called Persia). See Oriental rug, above.

rag rug (rag rug) A rug woven with strips of cotton or wool or synthetic fabrics used as the filling on a cotton or synthetic yarn warp. Rag rugs are made both by hand and machine and, with the exception of some hand-made antique rag rugs, they are usually the most inexpensive rugs.

random-sheared rug (*ran*-dum-sheerd rug) A pile rug in which some sections of the pile are cut and other sections are not. See pile. See also, shearing.

rya rug (*rye*-ah rug) A Scandinavian shag rug. Rya rugs are popular in the United States as area rugs largely because of their dramatic color combinations. The highest quality rya rugs, which are also quite expensive, are hand-knotted.

sculptured carpet (*skulp*-cherd *kar*-pit) Carpet (or rugs) in which the pile is cut in different lengths to form a pattern or design.

shag rug or carpet (shag rug/*kar*-pit) A rug or carpet with an extremely long pile.

tufted rug (*tuf*-tid rug) The most common type of rug construction. Tufted rugs are formed by needles rapidly punching yarn into the rug backing to form a pile which can be left looped as it is, cut, or sheared. See pile. See also, cut pile fabric and shearing.

twist rug (twist rug) A rug or carpet made of twist, a strong, long-wearing yarn which has been tightly twisted in its manufacture. Twist rugs and carpets are recommended for high traffic areas. They have a corkscrew-like, cut pile which forms a pebbled look. See cut pile fabrics.

Wilton rug (*wil*-ten rug) A woven, cut pile rug with a velvety texture. The designs in Wilton rugs often show an Oriental influence. Wilton rugs are quite expensive. See cut pile fabric. See pile.

rug or carpet pad (rug/*kar*-pit pad) See padding.

Russian leather (*rush*-en *leth*-er) See leather.

rustle (*russ*-el) See scroop.

rya (*rye*-ah) See rugs and carpets.

S

sailcloth (*sayl*-kloth) Originally, a firmly woven, cotton canvas used for making sails. Today, sailcloth is made of man-made fibers as well as cotton. In common usage, the terms duck, sailcloth and canvas are often used interchangeably. See canvas; see also, duck.

salt and papper (salt and *pep*-per) A fabric made of a combination of white and black yarns. The term is most usually used to describe tweed fabrics. See tweed.

Sanforize (*san*-for-eyez) Trademark of Cluett Peabody and Company Incorporated for a process of pre-shrinking fabric leaving a residual shrinkage of less than 1%, a desirable characteristic. See residual shrinkage.

saran (*se*-ran) The generic name for a man-made fiber derived from vinylidene chloride. Saran is strong, resists common chemicals, sunlight, and weather. It is used primarily in the fabric field for upholstery on public transportation vehicles and for garden furniture.

sari (*sah*-ree) A piece of fabric twelve to sixteen feet long used by Hindu women to drape and cover the body. The fabric is often silk with silver or gold threads forming a border design; other fabrics are also used. A sari is wrapped around the waist and then over the torso. Fabrics used for this type of dress are referred to as sari cloth.

sateen (sa-*teen*) A strong, lustrous, satin weave fabric made of cotton. Sateen is also used to distinguish between the cotton satin weave fabric and satin weave fabrics made of silk or man-made fibers. See satin weave under entry for weaving.

satin (*sat*-'n) One of the basic weaves. Satin weave has proved so popular that various types of satin weave fabrics have developed. Following is a listing of many of the types of satin fabrics. See also, weaving. See sateen, above.

156

antique satin (ann-*teek sat-*'n) A satin weave fabric primarily used for draperies. It can be used on either side. The face is a classic lustrous satin, the reverse has a slubbed look similar to shantung. See shantung.

crepe-backed satin (*crayp*-bakt *sat-*'n) A satin which can be used on either side. The face is satin, the back is crepe. It is often used as a jacket or coat lining. See crepe.

double-faced satin (*dub*-b'l-fayst *sat-*'n) A satin fabric which has the satin appearance on both sides unlike ordinary satin which has a definite right and wrong side.

duchesse satin (doo-*shess sat-*'n) One of the heaviest and richest looking satins. It is important for such formal clothing as wedding gowns.

slipper satin (*slip*-er *sat-*'n) A tightly woven satin fabric, usually lighter in weight than duchess satin, and used for many purposes including evening shoes or slippers

Saxony (*saks*-seh-nee) Saxony is a heavyweight, napped coating fabric, traditionally made from merino wool. Saxony originated in Saxony, Germany. See merino.

scallops (*skal*-ups) Decorative semi-circular curves usually used as edge-trimming. They are popular clothing accents and are often used on café curtains. See café curtains under curtains and draperies.

Schiffli (*shif*-lee) See embroidery.

Scotchgard (*skoch*-gard) Trademark of 3M Company for an oil and water-repellent finish. See finishing.

Scottish tweed (skot-ish tweed) See tweed.

screen printing (skreen *print*-ing) See printing.

scrim (skrim) An open, plain weave, mesh fabric used for curtains, bunting, and as a supporting fabric for some laminated fabrics. Scrim was traditionally made of cotton but today is usually made of nylon or other man-made fibers. See bunting.

scroop (skroop) The rustle that certain fabrics such as silk taffeta have. Scroop is considered a desirable characteristic in luxury fabrics.

scrubbed (skrubd) See scrubbing.

scrubbing (*skrub*-ing) Another name for the brushing method of raising a nap. Scrubbed denim, for example, means napped denim. See napping.

sculptured rug (*skulp*-cherd rug) See rugs and carpets.

Sea Island cotton (see *eye*-land *kot-*'n) A cotton with a long, lustrous, staple fiber. See cotton.

seal (seel) See leather.

seam binding (seem *bynd*-ing) Usually a narrow strip of twill weave fabric finished at each edge. It is stitched to a raw edge of fabric to cover it and prevent it from raveling. Strips of bias fabric can be used in the same way, and when they are, they are also called seam binding. See trimming.

seamless (*seem*-less) A self-explanatory term. A seamless garment has either no seams or fewer seams than the ordinary cut-and-sewn garment of its type. The word seamless is used primarily for garments which are given their final shape either by heat setting (called boarding in the case of hosiery) or molding. See cut-and-sewn. See also, heat setting, boarding, and molding.

seersucker (*seer*-suk-er) A puckered fabric. A puckered look appears in the alternating stripes and is achieved in the actual weaving process. Groups of tight warp yarns alternate with groups of slack or loose warp yarns so that when the filling thread is woven in, the loose yarns pucker. Seersucker is used incorrectly as a synonym for plissé. Seersucker is available in plain colors and stripes and is also popular in plaids and prints. Seersucker effects can be imitated in knits. See crinkle crepe; see plissé. See Chapter Two, From Fiber to Fabric.

selvage (*sehl*-vij) The edge of a woven fabric which does not ravel because the filling yarns wrap around the warp yarns. It may also be self-edge or selvedge.

semi-fashioned (*seh*-mee *fash*-end) A hosiery term for seamless hosiery which has had a fake seam added so that it will resemble full-fashioned hosiery. See full-fashioned.

sequin (*see*-kwin) A shiny, usually metallic, decoration or spangle. Sequins are sewn to clothing, especially evening dresses. They shimmer and sparkle in the light. Sequins usually have a single, central hole for fastening to the garment or fabric. Sequins are also known as paillettes (pie-*yet*). Fabric covered with sequins is available by the yard.

serge (surj) A smooth fabric made in a twill weave. Traditionally, a basic, hard-wearing woolen suiting, today, serge is made from the man-made fibers and the natural fibers. See entry for twill weave under weaving.

sewing-knitting machine (*soh*-ing-*nit*-ing meh-*sheen*) The latest machine for making fabrics. In the best known of these, the malimo machine, the warp thread is placed on top of the filling thread and then the two are stitched together with a third thread.

shade cloth (shayd kloth) The name for any fabric used for window shades.

shades (shaydz) A window covering that plays a double role. Shades provide both light control and privacy and can also lend a decorative accent. Shades range from the traditional roller blinds, available in versions which exclude light completely and in versions that permit some light to come in, to some with a more decorative purpose like Austrian shades. Below is a listing of some of the popular types of shades. The term blind is more or less a synonym for shade.

accordion shades (uh-*kor*-dee-un shaydz) Shades made of accordion pleats sharply creased at regular intervals horizontally across their width. Accordion shades take up relatively little room when drawn up to bare the window. See accordion pleats under entry for pleats.

Austrian shades (*aws*-tree-uhn shaydz) Shades made of fabric which is shirred across the width of the shade. When drawn up, Austrian shades hang in graceful loops of fabric. See shirring.

roller blinds (*rohl*-er blindz) Roller blinds are shades which are wound around a roller or dowel when the window is exposed. Originally made only in neutral colors, today these shades are often made in colors or matched and coordinated with the draperies in a room.

roller shades (*rohl*-er shaydz) See roller blinds, above.

Roman shades (*roh*-men shaydz) Shades similar to Austrian shades. When the window is exposed, the fabric of Roman shades hangs in graceful folds at the top of the window. However, Austrian shades are shirred throughout when they cover the window, but Roman shades hang straight and only form folds when drawn up to bare the window.

sky line shades (*sky* lyne shaydz) Another name for Roman shades. See Roman shades, above.

Venetian blinds (veh-*nee*-shen blindz) One of the most popular window coverings for controlling light and privacy. Venetian blinds are made of strips of fabric, metal, or plastic. These strips can be tipped to shut out light completely or opened to varying degrees to filter light to the desired intensity. They can also be raised to the top of the window to bare it completely. Conventional Venetians hang with the slats or strips horizontal to the windowsill but vertical Venetians are also available and are often used as room dividers as well as window covering. Venetians are available in various colors and widths.

shadow printing (*shad*-oh *print*-ing) See printing.

shadow stripes (*shad*-oh strypes) Faint impressions of stripes achieved by using yarns of the same color but different twists in weaving a fabric. The shadow effect comes from the way in which the light strikes the yarns of varying twists. See twist.

shag (shag) See rugs and carpet.

shantung (*shan*-tung) Originally, a rough, plain weave, silk fabric in which slubs in the yarn provided a textural effect. Today, shantung is usually made of man-made fibers or combinations of man-made and natural fibers. See silk. See slub.

sharkskin (*shark*-skin) A heavyweight, fairly lustrous fabric which, today, is almost always made of acetate or triacetate. Sharkskin is best known in a stark white color especially popular for tennis outfits, and for permanently pleated white skirts when they are in fashion.

shearing (*sheer*-ing) A method of removing the hair from an animal (the wool from sheep, for instance) without injuring the animal. Shearing also refers to trimming the pile on a fabric to a desired height.

sheer (sheer) The opposite of opaque. Sheer fabrics are usually made in an open weave which creates fabrics with varying degrees of transparency. Batiste, organdy, and voile are examples of sheer fabrics. See separate entries for these fabrics.

sheet (sheet) See linens and domestics.

shetland yarn (*shet*-land yarn) Officially, only yarn from sheep raised on the Shetland Islands off the coast of Scotland. However, the term is often used to describe very soft, fluffy, two-ply woolen yarns popular in hand-knitting. It is also used to describe fabrics which look as if they were made from such yarns.

shirring (*sher*-ing) A method of gathering fabric to create decorative fullness. Shirring consists of parallel rows of stitching which are drawn up (gathered) together to form bands of controlled gathers. Shirring is used in clothing and in items of home furnishings.

shirting (*shurt*-ing) Any lightweight fabric appropriate for shirts or blouses. The term top-weight (its opposite is bottom-weight) is often used for this type of fabric rather than the word shirting. Some crepes and satins as well as voile and Oxford cloth are examples of shirting fabrics. There are many others.

shoddy (*shod*-ee) Originally, a fabric made from reprocessed wool. Today, the word is used for a fabric—or anything else, for that matter—which is poorly made or made of inferior materials. See reprocessed fibers.

shoot (shoot) See filling.

shot (shot) See changeable.

shoulder pad (*shohl*-der pad) A support placed in the shoulder area of a garment to give a wider look to the shoulder when this look is in style. A thinner version known as a shoulder shape is used in coats and suits to maintain shape and give support in the shoulder area. Shoulder pads and shoulder shapes are available in notions departments and in fabric stores. See findings.

shower curtain (*shou*-er *kur*-ten) A shower curtain is a length of fabric hung around a bathroom shower or shower-tub combination to keep water from splashing onto the floor. Shower curtains should be waterproof. When decorative, non-waterproof shower curtains are used, a waterproof liner, usually made of plastic, should be placed inside them.

showerproof (*shou*-er-proof) One of the many terms used to describe varying degrees of imperviousness to water. A showerproof fabric will repel water to a limited extent, but is not waterproof. See waterproof.

shrinkage-controlled fabric (*shringk*-ij-kon-*trold fab*-rik) Fabric which has been treated in some way to prevent it from shrinking more than a specified amount. Unfortunately, the term shrinkage-controlled is an arbitrary standard which varies from manufacturer to manufacturer and gives the consumer no true measure of quality. Shrinkage-control is usually achieved by shrinking the fabric in the finishing steps or by the addition of finishing agents to the fabric.

shute (shoot) See filling.

shuttle (*shut*-'l) The part of the weaving machine (loom) which carries the filling yarn over and under the warp yarns.

silence cloth (*sy*-lenss kloth) See linens and domestics.

silencer (*sy*-lenss-er) See linens and domestics.

silhouette (sil-oo-*et*) Literally, shadow or outline. Silhouette refers to the shape of a garment. When the silhouette is soft, soft drapeable fabrics are popular; when the silhouette is stiff, crisper fabrics with lots of body come into demand. See crisp fabric; see also, soft fabric.

silicone (*sil*-eh-kohn) Generic name for certain compounds obtained from silicon, a component of sand. Silicones are used in fabric finishing to impart stain and wrinkle resistance. See finishing.

silk (silk) The product of the silk worm and the only natural filament fiber (it is produced in a long thread). Silk was the leading luxury fiber for thousands of years. There were many types of silk and many ways of making it into cloth. Today, man-made fibers have to a very large extent replaced silk, but the traditional names for certain silk fabrics are still used including the following:

    China silk (*chy*-nuh silk) A lightweight, inexpensive silk fabric used primarily for linings. It is available today but often difficult to find. It is also referred to as Jap silk.

    Honan silk (*hoh*-nan silk) Silk similar to pongee. See pongee, below.

    Macclesfield silk (*mak*-les-feeld silk) Macclesfield silk was originally woven in Macclesfield, England. The name has come to apply to small, yarn dyed, dobby designs used in men's neckties.

    pongee (pon-*jee*) A plain weave, fairly lightweight silk fabric with a slight slub to the yarns. The terms Honan and pongee are today used interchangeably for fabrics with this texture but made from man-made fabrics.

    raw silk (raw silk) A term used incorrectly for wild silk. Raw silk is the silk fiber before it has been processed in any way. Raw silk is coated with a glue-like substance called sericin. The sericin is removed in later processing and is not silk.

shantung (*shan*-tung) A silk somewhat similar to pongee in that it, too, is made with slubbed yarns, but in shantung the unevenness of the yarns is even greater. Shantung is one of the fabrics which originated in silk and has been imitated extensively in the man-made fibers.

surah (*soor*-ah) A silk which can be recognized by its sheen and its fine twill weave. Surah is popular for dresses and neckties and is also imitated in man-made fibers.

Thai silk (tye silk) Silk made in Thailand. Most Thai silk is fairly heavyweight, often slubbed, and made in vivid colors which are usually iridescent or changeable. See changeable.

tie silk (tye silk) Any silk used for men's neckties. Surah is one of these silks. Small, colorful patterns are often featured in this type of silk. See surah, above.

tussah (*tuss*-ah) Silk fabric woven from silk made by wild, uncultivated silkworms. Tussah is naturally tan in color, cannot be bleached and has a rougher texture than cultivated silk. Wild silkworms eat leaves other than mulberry leaves which cultivated silkworms eat exclusively. The difference in diet accounts for the different fiber and fabric characteristics. Tussah is also used to describe fabrics designed to imitate this kind of silk. See wild silk.

tussore (*too*-sorh) See tussah.

wild silk (wyld silk) The silk from uncultivated silkworms which eat leaves other than mulberry leaves. Wild silk is less smooth and is more uneven than cultivated silk. The resulting fabric is usually duller in finish and rougher in texture than other types of silk. Tussah is a silk fabric made from wild silk.

single knit (*sing*-'l nit) See knitting.

sisal straw (*sis*-'l straw) See straw.

sizing (*syz*-ing) Starch or gelatine which is added to fabrics in the finishing stages to give fabric additional body and a smoother appearance. Cotton fabrics are those most commonly treated in this manner. At one time, sizing had to be replaced after each cleaning. Today, with more advanced finishing techniques, sizing is rarely used and fabrics usually retain their initial appearance through cleaning. A few fabrics such as needlepoint canvas are still sized so that they can be handled more easily. This in no way affects their final performance. Sizing also refers to the starch which is applied to the warp yarns to help prevent abrasion on them during the weaving process. This sizing is usually removed from the fabric in one of the finishing steps.

skein (skayn) A coil of yarn, which, unlike a spool of thread, has no center supporting object. The term skein and hank are sometimes considered synonyms. See hank.

skiver (*sky*-ver) See leather.

sky line shade (sky lyne shayd) See Roman shades under the entry for shades.

slipcover (slip-*kuv*-er) An unattached covering for a sofa or chair. Slipcovers are made with openings so they can be removed for cleaning. They are also called loose covers.

slipper satin (*slip*-er *sat*-'n) See satin.

slub (slub) An uneven area in a yarn which gives the fabric made from it a degree of texture. Slubs can be produced naturally (as in hand spinning which often has slubs) or artificially, by deliberately making them in spinning. Slubs in man-made fibers are usually produced by making parts of the fiber thicker than other parts. Short, staple fibers mixed with other fibers in the yarn will produce slubs. Nub is another word for slub.

smallwares (smawl wayrz) See findings.

smocking (*smahk*-ing) Rows of shirring done in a pattern to add some give (stretch) to a garment and for decoration. It is often done with colored embroidery thread, and gives an effect similar to shirring. See shirring.

snakeskin (*snayk*-skin) See leather.

soft fabrics (soft *fab*-riks) Fabrics which tend to drape in soft folds and to cling rather than stand away from the figure or item being covered with them. Soft fabrics as a term is usually used as the opposite of crisp fabrics. Single knits are usually considered soft fabrics, for example.

soil release (soyl ree-*leess*) A finish applied to some man-made fiber fabrics in an attempt to overcome one of their disadvantages—a tendency to retain dirt, especially oil-based stains, once it has penetrated the fibers. Polyester is one of the fibers that retains oil-based stains.

solution dyeing (suh-*loo*-shun *dye*-ing) See dope dyeing under entry for dyeing.

space dyeing (spayss *dye*-ing) A method of dyeing yarn so that different sections of the yarn are different colors. The resulting fabric often has unusual, rainbow-like effects.

spandex (*span*-deks) The generic name for man-made elastic fiber which has a good deal of stretch and recovery for its weight. Spandex is used extensively in foundation garments and is much more comfortable than rubber because it is lighter in weight. Spandex is also found in some fabrics where stretch is considered desirable such as in ski clothes. Spandex is made of polyurethane. See polyurethane. See chart on fiber properties.

spinneret (spin-er-*et*) A spinneret, which looks very much like a shower head, is used in the manufacture of man-made fibers. The material from which the fibers are formed is forced through holes in the spinneret while it is in a syrupy or melted state. The resulting long strands harden into filament fibers. See Chapter One, Fiber—The Start Of It All. See also, filament.

spinning (*spin*-ing) A method of drawing out and twisting together fibers to make a continuous thread or yarn. Spinning also refers to the manufacture of man-made fibers as they are formed by forcing the material from which they are made through a spinneret. In conventional spinning, the tighter the twist, the stronger the yarn, but too tight a twist can weaken the final yarn. Crepe yarns have an extremely high twist, so high that the yarn actually turns back on itself (kinks) producing the characteristic crepe or corkscrew look. Fabrics can be given shadow effects by the use of two yarns which have been twisted in opposite directions in spinning. The light will strike each of these yarns in a different way producing this effect. See spinneret, above.

sponging (*spunj*-ing) A method of shrinking wool fabrics involving the application of water to the fabric followed by drying it, usually with some heat, in order to shrink it. Some wool fabrics sold by the yard are labeled "sponge shrunk, ready for the needle," and they should not shrink again when cleaned.

spread (spred) Any kind of covering. A bedspread is usually a decorative covering which covers the blanket and pillows on a bed during the day. Bedspreads are available in many styles from simple throws arranged casually over the bed to tailored box spreads. A box spread is a shaped and fitted bedspread with a tailored appearance. The corners are square, giving the spread its name. See throw. See also, Chapter Seven, Bedding and Towels.

spun dyeing (spun *dye*-ing) See dope dyeing under the entry for dyeing.

spun fiber yarn (spun *fy*-ber yarn) Yarn made from staple lengths of man-made fibers rather than the long filaments in which man-made fibers are formed. To accomplish this, long, filament fibers are chopped into staple lengths and then spun to imitate natural fiber yarns. See filament; see staple.

spun polyester (spun pol-ee-*es*-ter) See spun fiber yarn.

spun rayon (spun *ray*-on) See spun fiber yarn.

stain and spot resistant (stayn and spot ree-*zis*-tent) The ability to prevent stains and spots from remaining in a fabric. Stain and spot resistance is achieved by applying a finishing agent, silicone for example, to fabric in the final stages of manufacturing. See also, soil release.

stable knit (*stay*-b'l nit) See knitting.

staple (*stay*-p'l) Short lengths of fiber like those naturally found in cotton and wool. These short lengths must be spun to obtain a length sufficient for weaving or knitting. Silk is the only natural fiber that does not come in staple lengths, but instead in filament lengths. Man-made fibers are often cut into staple lengths for spinning to imitate natural fibers. See spinning and see spun fiber yarn. See also, filament.

stencil printing (*sten*-sil *print*-ing) See printing.

stitch (stich) A single passage of a threaded needle through fabric and back again, as in sewing or embroidery. Stitches may be taken by hand or done on a sewing machine to hold layers of fabric together or to decorate fabric as in embroidery, stitchery and needlepoint. The most commonly used hand stitches are listed below. See also embroidery, needlepoint, and stitchery.

> **back stitch** (bak stich) One stitch taken backwards on top of another to lock the stitch in place or for extra strength. The back stitch is often used to end a row of running stitches but can also be used in a continuous row in the same way as a running stitch. See running stitch, below.

> **hemming stitch** (*hem*-ing stitch) A stitch used to finish the raw edge of a fabric, usually by turning up and catching the edge to another point on the fabric. The needle is inserted in a slanting direction into the edge being hemmed and then into the fabric to which it is being caught. Many other types of stitches can also be used for hemming. See hem.

> **running stitch** (*run*-ing stich) The basic hand stitch. The needle is inserted into the fabric and then moves in and out of it, usually joining two sections of fabric together. The stitches formed are, ideally, of the same length on both the top and the bottom layer of the fabric.

stitchery (*stich*-er-ee) The contemporary approach to traditional embroidery in which the same basic stitches are used but in a freer, less restricted manner to create its own form and shapes. The yarns used in stitchery go beyond traditional wool and silk embroidery floss—anything can be used to make the stitches from ribbon and cord to narrow strips of fabric or even fish-line. Stitchery may be used to decorate clothing and home furnishings items and for wall hangings. See embroidery.

straw (straw) A fairly stiff material made from the stems, leaves, bark, or stalks of various plants. It is usually braided or woven to form a fabric. Straw is used in large quantities for hats when they are in style. Most straw today is used for baskets and handbags of various kinds. Chip straw is used almost exclusively for baskets. It is a by-product of the lumber industry and is made from chips and other pieces of wood including shavings. Leghorn straw is a braided straw popular for hats and is made from wheat grown in Italy.

Panama, another braided hat straw, is made from the screw pine. Other types of straw include Bangkok, linen (straw made to resemble woven linen), Milan, ramie, sisal (used for rugs and ropes), toyo, and Tuscan.

stretch fibers (strech *fy*-berz) Rubber or man-made elastic fibers (such as spandex and anidex) which are naturally elastic or man-made fibers which have been highly twisted, heat set, and then untwisted, leaving a strong crimp. Polyester has a certain degree of natural stretch and more can be given to the yarn in the processing or in the finishing of the fabric, so that occasionally polyester woven fabrics are described as stretch fabrics. Usually, stretch implies a degree of visible "give" in a fiber or fabric which stretches and then returns quickly to its original shape. Stretch fabrics are sometimes described as elastic. See elastic, crimp, and recovery. See spandex and anidex in chart on fiber properties.

stretchable knit (*strech*-eh-b'l nit) See knitting.

stripe (stryp) A band of color, usually on a plain ground. Stripes are usually used in multiples. They can be very narrow or wide, in all one color, in patterns of alternating colors, or in multi-colored patterns. Common types of stripes include:

> **awning stripes** (*awn*-ing stryps) Stripes seen on awnings which are designed to protect windows from sun. Awning stripes are sometimes used on fabric for apparel and are usually brightly colored and at least 1½" wide. Awning stripe patterns may also have a narrow stripe about ¼" wide on each side of the main stripe.

> **balanced stripes** (*bal*-'nst stryps) A pattern of stripes in which the same colors and widths are used on both sides of the center. A blue stripe on a white ground with a narrow red stripe on each side is an example of a balanced stripe; a blue stripe on a white ground with a narrow red stripe on the right side and a narrow yellow stripe on the left side is an example of an unbalanced stripe.

> **blazer stripes** (*blay*-zer stryps) A type of stripe originally used on jackets ultimately called blazers because of the bright blazing colors used in the stripes. Blazer stripes are usually at least 1½" wide and are very vividly colored.

> **chalk stripes** (chawk stryps) Narrow white stripes usually on a dark-colored ground fabric. See pin stripes.

> **pin stripes** (pin stryps) Very narrow stripes in any color. When pin stripes are white, they are often called chalk stripes.

> **Roman stripes** (*roh*-men stryps) Narrow, multi-colored stripes which cover an entire fabric. The colors may be as vivid as those of blazer stripes or as subtle as soft ombre shadings. See blazer stripes, above. See also, ombré.

unbalanced stripes (un-*bal*-'nst stryps) See balanced stripe, above.

studs (studz) Small, decorative objects added to fabric. They are usually round and metallic and are occasionally jewelled. Studs have teeth on the bottom which are pushed through the fabric by hand or with a tool called a stud setter. The teeth are then bent against the fabric to hold the stud in place.

stuff (stuf) See fabric.

suiting (*soot*-ing) Fabric heavy enough to tailor well and take a sharp crease. Suiting fabrics should be durable and wrinkle resistant. Custom and climate determine what is considered a suiting weight in different places. Typical suiting fabrics include tropical suiting, panama, flannel, butcher rayon, tweed, and crash. See separate listings for these fabrics.

suede (swayd) See leather.

summer-weight suiting (*sum*-er-wayt *soot*-ing) See tropical suiting.

sunburst pleats (*sun*-burst pleetz) See pleat.

supported vinyl (suh-*por*-tid *vy*-nel) Vinyl which is backed with fabric. Supported vinyl wears better than unsupported vinyl when used in upholstery. See vinyl.

surah (*soor*-ah) See silk.

swag (swag) A decorative, draped fabric section placed over a window. Swags are usually used in conjunction with draperies or curtains.

swatch (swoch) A small piece of fabric, usually large enough to show color and pattern. It is given to a potential buyer as a sample.

sweater knit (*swet*-er nit) See knitting.

sweat shirt fabric (swet shurt *fab*-rik) A knitted fabric with a smooth face and a fleecy, pile back. Sweat shirts were originally designed for exercise during which perspiration was encouraged, but they are also worn for warmth in cold weather and are available in several styles. They were made of cotton for its absorbency but acrylic versions are also available.

Swiss dot (swis dot) See dotted Swiss.

Swiss (swis) A sheer, lightweight, crisp fabric. See dotted Swiss.

synthetic fiber (sin-*thet*-ik *fy*-ber) See man-made fibers.

𝕋

table pad (*tay*-b'l pad) See linens and domestics.

taffeta (*taf*-eh-tah) A plain weave fabric with a crisp, somewhat shiny surface. Taffeta was originally made of silk but is also made of rayon or acetate. Taffeta usually has a good deal of scroop—it rustles. A list of the most common types of taffeta follows. See also, scroop.

    antique taffeta (ann-*teek taf*-eh-tah) A stiff taffeta designed to resemble fabrics from the 18th century. It is often made with iridescent or changeable effects. See changeable fabric.

    changeable taffeta (*chayn*-juh-b'l *taf*-eh-tah) See changeable fabric.

    faille taffeta (fyle *taf*-eh-tah) Taffeta made with a prominent crosswise rib, as in faille. See faille.

    moiré taffeta (mwa-*ray taf*-eh-tah) The most common moiré fabric. A moiré is a watermark design produced by passing the fabric through heated rollers engraved with the designs.

    paper taffeta (*pay*-per *taf*-eh-tah) A very lightweight, very crisp taffeta used for evening clothes.

tapa cloth (*ta*-pah kloth) A papery cloth made by pounding and flattening the inner bark of certain trees found in the Pacific Islands. It is often used in America for decorative wall hangings. See bark cloth.

tapestry (*tap*-es-tree) Usually, a decorative wall hanging, traditionally woven to depict a scene. The filling threads are changed in color to fit the design. Some rugs are made in tapestry weaves. The word is also used for needlepoint, but this use is generally considered incorrect. Machine-made fabrics, also called tapestry, have regular designs on the surface and a slightly looped pile. They are used for such things as coats and handbags.

tarlatan (*tar*-le-ten) A thin, open fabric which is used extensively for theatrical costumes and hangings. It is transparent, but layers of it are usually used to provide a degree of opacity. Tarlatan usually has a very stiff glazed finish. See opacity.

tarnish resistant fabric (*tar*-nish ree-*ziss*-tent *fab*-rik) A fabric used for wrapping silver to keep it from becoming darkened by atmospheric pollution. The cloth itself is made to absorb sulphur from the atmosphere, a major cause of tarnish.

tartan (*tart*-'n) A pattern made of intersecting stripes. Each tartan pattern is associated with a certain specific family or area group, called a clan. Plaid, a term used generally for tartan, is actually the name of a shawl made of tartan fabric. However, the use of plaid has become so general that tartan is almost always limited to authentic clan designs. Some of the most common tartans are listed below, but there are many others.

> **Barclay** (*bar*-klee) Wide stripes of black on a yellow ground crossed at intervals by narrower white stripes.
>
> **Black Watch** (blak woch) A regimental tartan, that of the 42nd Royal Highland Regiment. It consists of green stripes on a light blue ground.
>
> **Campbell** (*kam*-bell) A tartan made of green stripes on a blue ground, crossed with darker blue, narrower stripes. The blue ground is also crossed with darker blue, narrow stripes.
>
> **Cumming** (*kum*-ing) Stripes of dark and light green combined with red and blue stripes to form a plaid. In faded or antique colors, this tartan is especially attractive.
>
> **Linsay** (*lin*-zee) A pattern of crossed stripes of green and bright pink.
>
> **Mackay** (meh-*kay*) A checked pattern of stripes of blue on light green.
>
> **Ogilvie** (*oh*-gel-vee) One of the more complicated tartans. It combines stripes of red, yellow, greenish blue, and dark blue in an intricate pattern.
>
> **Rob Roy** (rob roy) A classic hunting jacket pattern of red and black checks.
>
> **Stewart** (*stoo*-ert) The tartan of the royal family of Great Britain. Stewart tartan has narrow stripes of yellow, blue, and white widely spaced on a red or white ground.

tassel (*tass*-el) See trimming.

tattersall check (*tat*-er-sol chek) See check.

tatting (*tat*-ing) See lace.

teasel (*tee*-zel) A plant with a prickly flower head. It is used for raising a nap on fabrics. See napping.

tentering (*ten*-ter-ing) A fabric finishing step in which the fabric is stretched on a frame to its finished width and final shape and then dried to maintain these dimensions.

terry cloth (*tair*-ee kloth) A fabric made of cotton or blends of cotton and other fibers which has uncut loops on one or both sides and is noted for its ability to absorb moisture. Terry cloth is used primarily for towels, but it is also used in wearing apparel. It is also called Turkish toweling. See velour, towels, and knit terry cloth.

textiles (*teks*-tylz) An extremely broad term referring to any materials which can be made into fabric by any method. It also refers to the resulting fibers themselves.

Texturalized (*teks*-trah-lyzd) Trademark of Bancroft Licensing for a method of adding texture to otherwise smooth yarns. See textured yarn.

texture (*teks*-chur) One of the elements which determines the way in which a finished fabric looks—smooth, rough or nubby for example. Texture can be altered by the processing of yarn, by blending the yarn, or in the finishing of the fabric. Texture also influences the hand of a fabric. See hand.

textured yarn (*teks*-churd yarn) Man-made yarn which has been treated in some way, such as crimping, coiling, or curling, so that the naturally smooth nature of the man-made filament is changed. Texturing may also alter certain undesirable characteristics of these fibers, such as their tendency to be transparent and to pill.

Thai silk (tye silk) See silk.

thermal (*thur*-mel) An adjective used to describe fabrics which are warmer for their weight than other fabrics. It is usually limited to those fabrics which have been woven in a honeycomb pattern leaving small paces in which air can be trapped. Thermal fabrics are popular for underwear and blankets. See honeycomb.

thermoplastic (thurm-oh-*plas*-tik) A word used to describe fibers which are heat-sensitive. (Most man-made fibers are thermoplastic.) A thermoplastic fiber is one whose shape can be changed when heat is applied. This can be both an advantage and a disadvantage. It is advantageous because in fabrics made of thermoplastic fibers, certain features like pleats can be made permanent through heat setting. However, care must be taken in drying and ironing fabrics made of thermoplastic fibers because of their sensitivity to heat. See man-made fibers; see also, heat setting.

thermosetting (thurm-oh-*set*-ing) A process for giving thermoplastic fibers or fabrics certain characteristics such as crimp or permanent pleats through the application of heat. Thermosetting is also used to develop certain finishes in a fabric to produce desirable characteristics like durable press. See heat setting. See also, thermoplastic and durable press.

thread (thred) A thin continuous length of twisted fibers. Thread is used primarily in sewing. The term thread is occasionally used instead of yarn, as in the terms "warp thread" and "filling thread."

The most common types of thread are listed below.

buttonhole twist (*but*-n-hohl twist) A thick, twisted silk cord. Buttonhole twist is lustrous and is used for topstitching (decorative, straight stitching, usually along seams or garment edges). It is also used for sewing buttons on a garment as well as for making buttonholes. It may be used for embroidery.

carpet thread (*kar*-pit thred) A heavy thread used for repairing carpets and for sewing on buttons. Carpet thread was originally made of cotton but is usually made of polyester today.

cotton thread (*kot*-'n thred) Formerly, the most common thread but difficult to find today. It is usually made in two types. A plain thread with a dull surface is called basting thread. Mercerized cotton thread has a shiny surface which enables it to slide smoothly through fabric. It is suggested for general purpose sewing. Polyester thread has replaced cotton thread to a large extent. See mercerization.

cotton-wrapped polyester thread (*kot*-'n-rapt pol-ee-*es*-ter thred) A type of polyester thread made with a polyester core wrapped with cotton, theoretically giving the thread characteristics of both fibers.

nylon thread (*ny*-lon thred) The thread introduced as an alternative to silk thread which has more "give" than most natural fiber threads and is used extensively for sewing man-made fiber fabrics, especially knits. It can be used on almost any fabric. Polyester thread is strong but tends to knot easily.

polyester thread (pol-ee-*es*-ter thred) Thread made of 100% polyester. Polyester thread has more "give" than most natural fiber threads and is used extensively for sewing man-made fiber fabrics, especially knits. It can be used on almost any fabric. Polyester thread is strong but tends to knot easily.

silk thread (silk thred) A classic sewing thread for fine work and for sewing silks and woolens. It has more "give" than other natural fiber threads but less than polyester or nylon. It is used primarily for sewing on silk fabrics.

throw (throh) Any piece of fabric—such as an afghan or bedspread—that does not fit closely to the item it is covering but is instead arranged on or over it casually. See afghan or spread.

ticking (*tik*-ing) A broad term for extremely strong woven fabrics which are used as a covering for pillows, mattresses, and box springs. Ticking is made so that the stuffing (originally feathers or down but often man-made filling today) will not sift out through the fabric. Ticking usually has a pattern of woven stripes, jacquard or dobby designs, or printed patterns. When ticking is used in clothing, striped ticking with narrow woven stripes is usually most popular. Red and white, black and white, and navy and white are the most popular ticking color combinations.

tie-back (tye-bak) See curtains and draperies.

tie dye (tye dye) A form of resist dyeing. See dyeing.

tie silk (tye silk) See silk.

toile (twahl) The French word for cloth. Toile is also a woven fabric which has been printed, usually in one color only, with a scenic design. This is occasionally called toile de Jouy. It is most commonly found in home furnishings fabrics. Toile is also used in the field of expensive designer clothing where the word is used to describe a fabric pattern for a garment.

toile de Jouy (twahl deh *Joo*-ee) See toile.

toweling (*tow*-ling) The name given to any fabric which is meant for use as a towel, that is, for drying purposes. See towel, below.

towel (towl) A rectangular piece of fabric which is used for drying (people, glasses, dishes). Following is a list of common types of towels:

> **dish towel** (dish towl) One of the few textile products which is still made of linen. (Occasionally they are made of cotton or even paper.) Dish towels are used for hand-drying dishes after washing. Many linen dish towels are made in Ireland and printed with colorful pictures. Dish towels can also be made of terry cloth and huck toweling. See terry cloth; see huck.

> **face cloth** (fayss kloth) A piece of terry toweling, usually square in shape. It is used for washing the face and body and may also be called a wash cloth.

> **glass cloth** (glass kloth) A towel used to dry drinking glasses, glass plates and silver. It is made from linen as are dish towels. Glass towels are often checked red and white and may have the word "Glass" woven into the fabric.

> **turkish toweling** (*turk*-ish *towl*-ing) See terry cloth.

> **terry cloth** (*tair*-ee kloth) A cotton or cotton and man-made fiber fabric with a looped pile on one or both sides. It is made into towels for drying after a bath. It may also be used for dish towels. See pile.

> **velour** (veh-*loor*) A knit or woven fabric with a thick, short pile. Terry velour cloth has cut loops to produce the velour effect. It also has a rich look but is not as effective in drying as conventional terry cloth. May also be spelled velours.

toyo straw (*toy*-oh straw) See straw.

tracing cloth (*trays*-ing kloth) A non-woven, transparent fabric which can be used for tracing designs and especially patterns. Since tracing cloth is fabric, it can be marked and altered more easily than paper used for the same purpose.

trademark (*trayd*-mark) A word or symbol which has been legally registered and serves to distinguish the merchandise of one manufacturer from another. For example, Dacron is a trademark of DuPont for their polyester fiber.

traditional (truh-*dish*-'n-el) A word used for fabrics or methods of making fabrics which have been in use for a number of years.

trapunto (trah-*pun*-toh) A form of quilting in which fabric is quilted only in certain areas. The design to be quilted, a monogram for instance, is first worked through two layers of fabric. Then the backing fabric is slit so that the quilted areas can be padded with yarn or cord or with a filling like fiberfill. See fiberfill.

trash (trash) Bits of fiber, dirt, and plants which may be left in a fabric. During certain fashion periods, when a natural look is important, trash is considered desirable. It shows as tiny specks of darker coloring in a lighter fabric and is usually found in cotton and wool fabrics.

Trevira (trah-*veer*-ah) The trademark of Hoechst Fibers Incorporated for their polyester fiber.

triacetate (try-*ass*-eh-tayt) A modification of acetate. Triacetate fabrics resist shrinkage, wrinkles, and fading. They can be washed and ironed at higher temperatures than those made of acetate. See acetate. See also chart on fiber properties in Chapter One.

tricot (*tree*-koh) See knitting.

trimming (*trim*-ing) Anything used to decorate clothing or home furnishings. Below is a list of some of the more common types of trimmings.

ball fringe (bawl frinj) A trimming consisting of round fluffy balls (pompons) attached by threads to a band of fabric by which the trimming is sewn to fabric. It is often used on curtains and upholstery.

banding (*band*-ing) A narrow, flat fabric which may be woven, knitted, or braided and is used as it is to trim an edge or folded over to bind an edge.

bias tape (*by*-us tayp) A strip of fabric cut on the diagonal between the lengthwise and crosswise grain of the fabric. Because bias tape has considerable stretch, it is used to bind edges where a certain degree of stretch is necessary for a smooth finish. Curved areas are often finished with bias tape. Bias tape can also be used for purely decorative trimming. It is available pre-cut and packaged in a wide range of colors.

binding (*bynd*-ing) Any narrow fabric which is used to enclose (bind) edges, usually raw edges. It can also be used for purely decorative purposes. Bias tape is often used as binding. See bias tape, above.

braid (brayd) A term usually used to describe narrow trimmings which have multi-colored designs woven into them. Various types of braid such as peasant braid are popular during certain fashion periods.

bullion (*bool*-yun) A twisted, shiny, cord-like fringe used primarily in upholstery.

chainette fringe (*chayn*-et frinj) A yarn fringe which is designed to resemble chain. It is used as a trimming for window shades.

cord (kord) A heavy, round string consisting of several strands of thread or yarn twisted or braided together. See cording, below.

cord gimp (kord gimp) Cord gimp combines cord with gimp. See cording and gimp.

cording (*kord*-ing) A round decorative edging. The term is also used to describe white cord which can be covered with bias strips of fabric to form welting or piping. See welting, below.

festoon (fes-*toon*) A decorative cord which usually is accented by tassels. It forms a decoration for the edge of such items as table cloths.

fringe (frinj) A trimming made of hanging yarns, cords, or tassels. It may be made in loop form or with the loops cut.

frog (frog) A decorative fastening for clothing which consists of twisted cord wound into a design which looks somewhat like three petals joined to a similar design on the opposite edge of an opening with a loop of the cord.

galloon (ga-*loon*) A closely woven, flat braid used for accenting draperies and furniture and also called braid. The term galloon is also used for any narrow fabric with decorative edges such as scallops which are finished the same on each side. Lace made in this way is called galloon lace.

gimp (gimp) An edging which often has small scallops of fine cord along its edges. Gimp was originally designed to hide such things as upholstery tacks on chairs and sofas, but is now used for other decorative purposes.

knotted fringe (*not*-id frinj) Fringe in which the hanging sections are knotted to form a pattern and then the ends are allowed to hang like regular fringe. See fringe.

military braid (*mil*-eh-tair-ee brayd) A flat, ribbed braid used for decorating military and other uniforms. It is also used as a trimming on clothing when the military look is popular.

moss fringe (mawss frinj) A short, thick fringe usually made of fluffy yarns of wool or acrylic.

picot trimming (*pee*-koh *trim*-ing) A narrow band edged with a series of delicate loops.

piping (*pype*-ing) See welting.

pompon (pom-pon) A fluffy ball, usually made from yarn, and used as a decorative accent.

rat-tail (rat-tayl) A narrow, round cord used for trimming and for macramé. See macramé.

rat-tail fringe (rat-tayl frinj) A decorative edging made of rat-tail in which the rat-tail forms loops across the edging. See rat-tail above.

ribbon (*rib*-en) A narrow, woven fabric with two finished edges. Both natural and man-made fibers are used in making ribbon. It is available in many patterns and colors and in such fabric constructions as velvet, satin and grosgrain. See velvet, satin, and grosgrain.

rick-rack (rik-rak) A flat braid woven in a zig-zag, serpentine shape. It is available in several widths and is an extremely popular and inexpensive trimming.

ruche (roosh) A ruche is a ruffle. See ruffle, below.

ruffle (*ruhf*-f'l) A piece of fabric which has been gathered along one edge. Ruffles are usually narrow and are used to trim necklines, sleeves, hems, and the edges of home furnishings items like pillows and slipcovers.

seam binding (seem *bynd*-ing) A flat, narrow twilled ribbon, used to cover raw edges of seams to protect them from ravelling.

tassel (*tass*-el) Several strands of yarn loops joined together shortly below the top and cut at the end. Tassels are used in rows as home furnishings trimmings and singly for such uses as zipper pulls or on the corners of pillows.

twill tape (twil taype) A narrow, twill weave ribbon, fairly heavy in weight. It is stitched into garment areas such as collar lapels, shoulders, and facing edges for strength and to prevent stretching. It is also used in the seams of slip covers and other home furnishings items for added strength. Twill tape is usually available only in white and black. See twill under entry for weaving.

welting (*welt*-ing) A decorative edging which lends a certain degree of strength to the area in which it is sewn. Welting is made by covering cord with bias strips of matching or contrasting fabric. It is a popular finish for seams on upholstery and slipcovers and is occasionally used on clothing. Welting and piping are synonyms. When used on clothing, it is usually called piping. See cord and bias.

tropical suiting (*trahp*-ih-kel *soot*-ing) A general term for many fabrics which have the characteristics of suiting fabrics—they are crisp, take sharp creases well, and are lightweight for wear in hot weather. A typical tropical suiting is linen.

tuck (tuk) A small, narrow section of fabric which is folded and then stitched, either down the fold of the tuck or across each end. Pin tucks are the narrowest of tucks. Tucks usually have a decorative function and are narrow, while pleats made in much the same way are usually used to control fullness as well. However, horizontal tucks are taken in children's clothing for a functional purpose—so that the garment can be lengthened when the child grows. See also pleats.

tuft (tuft) A bunch of yarns or threads forced through a quilt, mattress, or upholstery to secure the stuffing. See quilt.

tufting (*tuft*-ing) The most common method for making rugs. Groups of yarns are forced through a backing fabric. The yarns are held in place permanently when the underside of the rug is coated, often with liquid latex. See Chapter Six, A Guide to Rugs and Carpets.

tulle (tool) A very fine net. Formerly made only of silk, tulle is now also made of nylon and is a favorite for bridal veils. See net.

Turkish toweling (*turk*-ish *towl*-ing) See terry cloth and towel.

Tuscan straw (*tuss*-kan straw) See straw.

tussah (*tuss*-ah) See silk.

tussore (too-*sohr*) See silk.

tweed (tweed) A woven fabric characterized by colored slubs of yarn on a somewhat hairy surface. Tweed may be made of any fiber or fiber combination although wool tweed is probably the most common. Knots are sometimes used to resemble tweed slubs. Included below is a listing of the common types of tweeds. See also, slub.

Donegal (*don*-eh-gahl) Originally, a fabric woven by hand in County Donegal, Ireland. Today the word is used to refer to any tweed with thick, usually colored slubs as part of the fabric.

Harris (*hair*-iss) Tweed hand-woven from yarns spun by hand or machine on the islands of the Outer Hebrides off the coast of Scotland. Harris is one of these islands.

Irish (*eye*-rish) Tweed made in Ireland, Northern Ireland, or Eire. These tweeds generally can be distinguished by a white warp and colored filling threads. Donegal is a type of Irish tweed.

Linton (*lin*-ton) The trademark of Linton Tweed, Ltd., Carlisle, England. These tweeds are noted for their softness and subtle or vivid colorings.

Scottish (*skot*-ish) Originally made in Scotland, Scottish tweed is a term often used today for tweed woven with very nubby yarns, often with white warp and colored filling. See also, Irish tweed.

twill (twill) See weaving. See also trimming.

twist (twist) A technical term referring to the way in which yarn is turned during the course of its manufacture. In carpeting, twist is a corkscrew-like, cut pile which has a pebbly appearance. It resists footmarks and is good for high traffic areas.

U

Ulster (*uhl*-ster) Originally, the name for a frieze overcoating fabric made in Ulster, Ireland. Today, the word is usually used as a synonym for overcoat. See frieze.

unbalanced stripe (un-*bal*-'nst stryp) See stripe.

unbalanced plaid (un-*bal*-'nst plad) See plaid.

uncut velvet (un-*kut vel*-vit) See velvet.

underlay (*un*-der-lay) A synonym for padding. See padding.

uneven plaid (un-*ee*-ven plad) See plaid.

union cloth (*yoon*-yen kloth) A traditional name for fabric made from two or more different fibers, such as a fabric woven with a wool worsted warp and a cotton filling. The term "union cloth" was used primarily when this fabric was used for underwear, perhaps because a "union suit" was another name for shoulder-to-ankle, one-piece underwear.

union dyeing (*yoon*-yen *dy*-ing) Dyeing different fibers in the same cloth one shade. See dyeing.

unpressed pleat (*un*-prest pleet) See pleat.

unravel (un-*ra*-vel) See ravel.

V

valance (*val*-enss) A decorative top for curtains or draperies. It is usually hung from a rod and made of fabric or fabric over a stiffening material such as buckram. A valance differs from a ruffle in that it is absolutely flat. See buckram. See ruffle under entry for trimming.

Valenciennes lace (vel-en-see-*enz* layss) See lace.

vat dyeing (vat *dy*-ing) See dyeing.

Velcro (*vel*-kroh) The trademark for a patented fastening device which is a burr-like fastener with one side made of a velvet-like material and the other of small stiff hooks. This fastening can be used for clothing and home furnishings items; it also has many industrial applications. Velcro is available to the consumer for use in home sewing and decorating.

velour (veh-*loor*) A knit or woven fabric with a thick, short pile. Terry velour cloth has cut loops to produce the velour effect and it is often used for bath towels. Terry velour has a rich look like velvet or velveteen but is not as effective in drying as conventional terry cloth. See pile, velvet and velveteen. See also, terry cloth.

velvet (*vel*-vit) A fabric with a short, closely woven pile. There are two methods of making velvet. One method uses double cloth construction in which two layers of fabric are woven with long threads joining them. After the double fabric is woven, the center threads which join them are cut, producing two pieces of velvet. The other method of making velvet utilizes wires. In the weaving process the yarn is lifted over the wires to form the pile. When the wires are removed, the yarn is cut to form the velvet surface. Velvet was originally made of silk but today it is made of many other fibers. Nylon is one of the most popular. Some knit fabrics with a pile are called velvets but this is actually incorrect. Following is a listing of some important types of velvet.

beaded velvet (*beed*-id *vel*-vit) Another name for cut velvet. See cut velvet.

cisele velvet (*sis*-eh-lay *vel*-vit) A satin weave fabric with a velvet pattern woven in. Similar fabrics are made by flocking. See flock.

cisele velvet (*sis*-eh-lay *vel*-vit) A satin weave fabric with a velvet a pattern of velvet on a sheer ground. It is occasionally imitated by the burn-out method of printing. See jacquard. See also, burn-out printing under entry for printing.

faconne velvet (*fass*-oh-nay *vel*-vit) A cut velvet made by the burn-out method of printing. See cut velvet, above. See also, burn-out printing under entry for printing.

Lyons velvet (*lee*-ohn *vel*-vit [correct pronunciation]; *lye*-onz *vel*-vit [common pronunciation]) Velvet originally made of silk in Lyons, France. Lyons is a thick, rather stiff velvet with a very short pile. Today, this type of velvet (often called Lyons-type) is made of man-made fibers. It is used for home furnishings as well as for evening wear.

mirror velvet (*mir*-er *vel*-vit) Velvet with the pile pressed flat in one or several directions to impart a shimmering appearance.

nacré velvet (na-*kray vel*-vit) A velvet with a changeable appearance created by using one color for the pile and another for the backing.

panne velvet (pan *vel*-vit [correct pronunciation]; pan-*ay* [incorrect but common pronunciation]) Velvet which has had the pile flattened in one direction. See also mirror velvet, above.

uncut velvet (un-*kut vel*-vit) A velvet in which the pile is left in loop form. It is made by the wire method and is also occasionally called terry velvet. See velvet, above, for a description of the wire method.

velveteen (vel-veh-*teen*) Strictly speaking, a cotton, cut pile fabric. It differs from corduroy in that the pile on velveteen covers the surface and is thicker than the pile on corduroy. It differs from velvet in that the pile in velvet is made with the warp threads while the pile in velveteen is made with the filling threads. The distinction between velvet and velveteen originated when velvet was made only from silk. Today, man-made fibers are being used for both velvet and velveteen. See velvet.

Venetian blinds (veh-*nee*-shun blindz) See shade.

Venetian lace (veh-*nee*-shun layss) See lace.

Venice lace (*veh*-niss layss) See lace.

Venise lace (veh-*neess* layss) See lace.

Verel (veh-*rel*) Trademark of Eastman Kodak for their modacrylic fiber.

vicuna (vy-*koon*-ah) Vicuna, one of the most expensive of all wools, comes from the vicuna, a type of llama found in Latin America.

The wool is used to make vicuna cloth. See llama.

vinal (*vy*-nel) The generic name for a man-made fiber made from units of vinyl alcohol. Vinal fibers soften at low temperatures but resist chemicals. Although vinal is not now made in the United States, it is made in Japan and is found in tires, some home furnishings, and industrial products.

vinal-vinyon (*vy*-n'l *vin*-yon) A recent combination of two molecules which has resulted in a new fiber somewhat similar to acrylic with excellent flame retardancy. This fabric will be found primarily in garments like children's sleepwear which must meet high flammability standards. It is soft to the touch. See flame retardant fabric.

vinyl (*vy*-n'l) Any fabric made with a base of vinyl, including those listed as vinal and vinyon, above. The term is usually used to refer to thick fabrics coated with a vinyl-based coating used for such purposes as upholstery and raincoats.

vinyon (vin-*yon*) The generic name for a man-made fiber made from units of vinyl chloride. Vinyon fibers soften at low temperatures but resist chemicals. Vinyon is often referred to as polyvinyl chloride. Its primary use is in commercial products.

virgin fibers (*vur*-jun *fy*-berz) By Federal Trade Commission standards, fibers which have never been made into fabric before. The term is used primarily for wool fibers to differentiate between these and reclaimed, reprocessed, and reused fibers. See reprocessed fibers, reclaimed fibers, and reused fibers.

viscose rayon (*vis*-kohss *ray*-on) See rayon.

voile (vwal [correct pronunciation, used very rarely]; voyl [common pronunciation]) A lightweight, crisp, sheer fabric of a plain weave. Voile is especially popular when made of cotton or blends for summer wear and is often printed to match heavier fabrics. Voile is used for clothing, especially blouses, and also for curtains.

W

waffle weave (*wahf-*'l weev) See honeycomb.

wale (wayl) In knitted fabrics, a row of loops lying lengthwise on the fabric. In woven fabrics, a series of ribs or ridges which usually runs lengthwise on the fabric. Wale describes the pile ribs found on corduroy fabrics. The terms narrow wale, pin wale, and wide wale describe different types of ribs in corduroy. No-wale corduroy has an all over pile shorter than the pile on velveteen. See corduroy and velveteen. See also, pile.

warp (worp) The group of yarns which is placed on a loom first in weaving. Warp runs parallel to the selvage forming the length of the fabric. The filling threads are interlaced over and under the warp threads in a pattern or weave. See weaving. See also, selvage.

warp knit (worp nit) See knitting.

warp print (worp print) See printing.

wash and wear (wosh and wair) A term used to describe fabrics and garments which can be washed and then worn with little or no ironing. There are no standards governing its use. See easy care. See also, durable press.

washable (*wosh-*eh-b'l) A very inexact term, meaning only that an item can be washed and does not have to be dry cleaned. The term is unsatisfactory, however, since it doesn't say how the item should or can be washed—whether by machine or by hand, with hot or cold water. The care labeling law should lead to elimination of this term from labels. See Chapter Four, Basic Fabric Care Techniques.

waterproof fabric (*waw-*ter-proof *fab-*rik) A fabric which will not permit water to penetrate it. Among methods of waterproofing are coating the fabric with rubber or plastic. True waterproof fabrics are warm and clammy to wear as the waterproof nature also prevents the evaporation of perspiration and blocks the circulation of air.

water repellent fabric (*waw*-ter ree-*pell*-ent fab-rik) A fabric which resists water but does not prevent its penetration entirely. A water repellent fabric will give protection in a shower but not in a heavy rain. Water repellency is often created with wax or silicone resin finishes which enable the pores of the fabric to stay open so that it is more comfortable to wear than waterproof fabrics. Another name for water repellent is water resistant. See waterproof fabric, above.

weaving (*weev*-ing) Weaving is a method of making fabric in which threads called filling threads pass over and under threads called warp threads which are at right angles to the filling threads. Different weaves are determined by the number of warp threads over which the filling threads pass before going under. See also Chapter Two, From Fiber to Fabric. Following is a listing of the most common weaves:

> **basket weave** (*bas*-kit weev) Basket weave is made with two or more filling threads passing over and under an equal number of warp threads on alternate rows.

> **plain weave** (playn weev) Plain weave, the best known and most basic form of weaving, is made by passing the filling thread over and under one warp thread in alternating rows.

> **satin weave** (*sat*-'n weev) A weave which produces a very smooth surfaced fabric. It is made by passing the filling threads under several warp threads before passing over one warp thread. Satin weave is used to make sateens in which cotton filling thread goes over several cotton warp, then under one warp.

> **twill weave** (twill weev) A weave with a diagonal rib (twill line) which runs from the upper left to the lower right, or from upper right to lower left. In a twill weave, each filling thread passes over or under at least two warp threads, with the point where the filling thread goes under moving up and over by at least one thread in each row. Herringbone weave is a broken twill weave which forms "v"'s in the weave pattern.

webbing (*web*-ing) A strong, narrow fabric made from jute or man-made fibers. It is used for belts and straps that must resist strain. Webbing is usually woven and is used on the underside of uphol-stered chairs and sofas.

weft (weft) See filling.

welt (welt) The final edge on certain knitted items such as women's stockings. The welt on stockings is usually thicker than the rest of the stocking and is usually made of a different, stronger stitch so that garters can be fastened to it.

welting (*welt*-ing) See trimming.

wet look (wet look) A descriptive term for extremely shiny fabrics. Fabrics such as vinyl and ciré are often described as wet look fabrics.

whipcord (*whip*-kord) An extremely strong, often twilled fabric made in farily heavy weights in cotton, wool worsted, and fabrics of man-made fibers and blends. Whipcord is heavier than gabardine which it resembles. It is used for uniforms, riding clothes, and other wearing apparel where a strong fabric is required. See twill under entry for weaving.

wide wale (wyd wayl) See wale.

wild silk (wyld silk) See silk.

Wilton (*wil*-ten) See rugs and carpets.

windbreaker (*wind*-bray-ker) A jacket made of a closely woven fabric or a fabric treated with a finish designed to prevent the passage of air. The fabric used in windbreakers often has a degree of water repellency because of its tight construction. Windbreaker cloth describes a fabric with these characteristics.

woof (woof) See filling.

wool (wuhl) The term wool is used, usually for the fleece of sheep, but also applies to similar fibers from such animals as the angora and cashmere goats and the llama. Wool differs from hair and fur in that it has a natural felting ability. See felt. See also, woolen, and worsted.

woolen (*wuhl*-en) A fabric made from wool fibers. Woolens usually have somewhat fuzzy surface, do not shine from wear and may hold a crease well. Woolens may have a nap. See worsted.

worsted (*woos*-tid [correct pronunciation]; *wur*-stid [common pronunciation]) A type of wool fabric or yarn. Worsted fabrics are made from yarns which have been combed as well as carded (woolen yarns have only been carded). Combing eliminates short fibers and impurities so the resulting yarn is compact and sturdy. Worsted yarns are smoother than woolen yarns and when woven into fabric result in a fabric with a clean, smooth surface as opposed to the fuzzy, soft surface of woolens. Worsted fabrics wear better than woolen fabrics, resist felting at points of wear, and have a harder surface than woolens. See carding. See also, combing.

Y

yard goods (yard goodz) See piece goods.

yardage (*yard*-ij) See piece goods.

yarn (yarn) A continuous strand spun from staple fibers (short lengths of fibers), filaments (long lengths), or other materials which can be used in the manufacture of textiles and especially woven and knit fabrics.

yarn dyed (yarn dyed) See dyeing.

Z

Zantrel (zan-*trel*) Trademark of American Enka for their high wet modulus rayon fiber. See high wet modulus under entry for rayon.

Zefran (*zef*-ran) Trademark of Dow Badische for their acrylic, nylon, and polyester fibers.

zephyr yarn (*zef*-er yarn) A fine, soft yarn with a low twist popular for hand knitting. Originally made from wool, zephyr is usually made of acrylic and often has other fibers such as silk added to it.

zibeline (*zib*-eh-leen) A heavily napped coating fabric with the nap pressed in one direction. Zibeline is usually made of a combination of such fibers as camel hair or mohair with wool or a man-made fiber in the largest percentage.

zipper (*zip*-er) A garment closure made of interlocking teeth attached to strips of fabric known as the zipper tape. Zippers were originally made of metal but are now available with polyester or nylon molded teeth on a woven or knit polyester tape. Most zippers are attached to garments by stitching the zipper tape to the garment seam. Invisible zippers do not show once they are attached to the garment because the teeth of an invisible zipper are covered by the zipper tape and are hidden in the seam of the garment.

Appendix

FABRIC WIDTH CONVERSION CHART

The back of your pattern envelope usually provides the information you need to make fabric and notions purchases. Sometimes the fabric you've chosen is not available in the standard widths listed on the pattern envelope. As an example, suppose you have decided on a cotton blouse fabric which is 36" wide but the pattern envelope shows yardage requirements for fabric 45" wide. The chart below will help you convert and *estimate* the yardage you will need for the particular width of fabric you've chosen. In the above case, simply locate the yardage shown for 45" fabric and then move across the chart on the same line until you reach the column for 36" fabric. If the pattern requires 2-1/2 yards of 45" fabric, you would buy 3-1/8 yards of 36" fabric.

The chart makes no allowances for changes in fabric requirements caused by pattern alterations, large-scale fabric designs, directional and napped fabrics, and pattern designs with unusually shaped or large pieces. In these instances, use the chart only as a guide and exercise your own judgement about how much fabric you will need.

Fabric Width	32"	35"-36"	39"	41"	44"-45"	50"	52"-54"	58"-60"
	1-7/8	1-3/4	1-1/2	1-1/2	1-3/8	1-1/4	1-1/8	1
	2-1/4	2	1-3/4	1-3/4	1-5/8	1-1/2	1-3/8	1-1/4
	2-1/2	2-1/4	2	2	1-3/4	1-5/8	1-1/2	1-3/8
	2-3/4	2-1/2	2-1/4	2-1/4	2-1/8	1-3/4	1-3/4	1-5/8
	3-1/8	2-7/8	2-1/2	2-1/2	2-1/4	2	1-7/8	1-3/4
	3-3/8	3-1/8	2-3/4	2-3/4	2-1/2	2-1/4	2	1-7/8
	3-3/4	3-3/8	3	2-7/8	2-3/4	2-3/8	2-1/4	2
	4	3-3/4	3-1/4	3-1/8	2-7/8	2-5/8	2-3/8	2-1/4
	4-3/8	4-1/4	3-1/2	3-3/8	3-1/8	2-3/4	2-5/8	2-3/8
	4-5/8	4-1/2	3-3/4	3-5/8	3-3/8	3	2-3/4	2-5/8
	5	4-3/4	4	3-7/8	3-5/8	3-1/4	2-7/8	2-3/4
	5-1/4	5	4-1/4	4-1/8	3-7/8	3-3/8	3-1/8	2-7/8

(Yardage — left vertical label)

Reprinted courtesy of New Jersey Cooperative Extension Service, Rutgers, The State University.

DETERMINING FABRIC STRETCHABILITY

Knowing just how stretchable a knit fabric is will aid you in selecting the right combination of pattern and fabric. Most pattern envelopes will indicate whether the pattern is suitable for knits with slight stretch (also called stable knits), knits with a moderate amount of stretch, or knits with super stretch (stretchable knits). The Butterick Select-A-Knit™ Gauge printed below will enable you to select the knit fabric with the needed stretch for your pattern requirements.

SLIGHT STRETCH

| Gently Stretch 4" of Crosswise Folded Knit Fabric from Here | to at Least Here ▲ |

4" (10 cm) of knit fabric, stretching to 4-3/4" (12 cm) (approximately 18% of stretch) fall into this category. This minimal amount of stretch is utilized only to acquire a slightly closer fitting garment and for wearing ease.

MODERATE STRETCH

| Gently Stretch 4" of Crosswise Folded Knit Fabric From Here | to at Least Here ▲ |

4" (10 cm) of knit fabric, stretching to 5" (12.5 cm) (approximately 25% stretch) fall into this category. You have an intermediate knit. Styles will be more closely fitted to the body.

SUPER STRETCH

| Gently Stretch 4" (10cm) of Crosswise Folded Knit Fabric from Here | to at Least Here ▲ |

4" (10 cm) of knit fabric, stretching to 6" (15 cm) (approximately 50%) fall into this category. This is considered a very stretchy knit. Stretchability is utilized for garments that are body fitting.

HOW TO USE BUTTERICK'S SELECT-A-KNIT™ STRETCH GAUGE

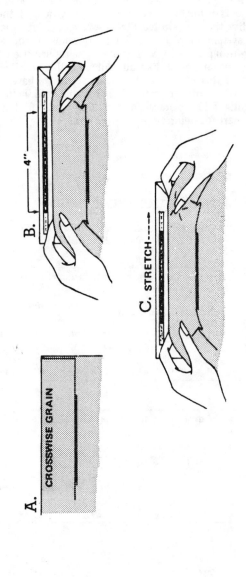

A. To determine stretchability, make a crosswise fold in fabric about 2″ (5 cm) from the edge.
B. Place fold of fabric over SELECT-A-KNIT™ Stretch Gauge, holding fabric in place at each end of 4″ (10 cm) area.
C. Gently stretch fabric to the right. Knit fabric is suitable for pattern if it stretches to at least the amount indicated on the SELECT-A-KNIT™ Gauge or slightly beyond.

A WORD ABOUT METRICS

If you're a home sewer, the thought of buying three and a half yards of fabric is probably second nature to you. But there is a strong possibility that the United States will soon adopt the metric measurement system in place of the measurements you are now accustomed to using. It really will be easier to use because it's based on the decimal system much like our dollars and cents. Because of the possibility of this change taking place soon, we have included here a group of metric conversion charts that will help you in purchasing fabric and notions. In addition, you'll find a metric measurement chart for determining pattern sizes.

METRIC MEASUREMENT CHART

APPROVED BY THE MEASUREMENT STANDARD COMMITTEE OF THE PATTERN INDUSTRY

MISSES'

Misses' patterns are designed for a well-proportioned, and developed figure; about 1.65m to 1.68m without shoes.

Size	6	8	10	12	14	16	18	20	
Bust	78	80	83	87	92	97	102	107	cm
Waist	58	61	64	67	71	76	81	87	cm
Hip	83	85	88	92	97	102	107	112	cm
Back Waist Length	39.5	40	40.5	41.5	42	42.5	43	44	cm

MISS PETITE

This new size range is designed for the shorter Miss figure; about 1.57m to 1.60m without shoes.

Size	6mp	8mp	10mp	12mp	14mp	16mp	
Bust	78	80	83	87	92	97	cm
Waist	60	62	65	69	73	78	cm
Hip	83	85	88	92	97	102	cm
Back Waist Length	37	37.5	38	39	39.5	40	cm

JUNIOR

Junior patterns are designed for a well-proportioned, shorter-waisted figure; about 1.63m to 1.65m without shoes.

Size	5	7	9	11	13	15	
Bust	76	79	81	85	89	94	cm
Waist	57	60	62	65	69	74	cm
Hip	81	84	87	90	94	99	cm
Back Waist Length	38	39	39.5	40	40.5	41.5	cm

JUNIOR PETITE

Junior Petite patterns are designed for a well-proportioned, petite figure; about 1.52m to 1.55m without shoes.

Size	3jp	5jp	7jp	9jp	11jp	13jp	
Bust	78	79	81	84	87	89	cm
Waist	57	58	61	64	66	69	cm
Hip	80	81	84	87	89	92	cm
Back Waist Length	35.5	36	37	37.5	38	39	cm

YOUNG JUNIOR/TEEN

This size range is designed for the developing pre-teen and teen figures; about 1.55m to 1.60m without shoes.

Size	5/6	7/8	9/10	11/12	13/14	15/16	
Bust	71	74	78	81	85	89	cm
Waist	56	58	61	64	66	69	cm
Hip	79	81	85	89	93	97	cm
Back Waist Length	34.5	35.5	37	38	39	40	cm

WOMEN'S

Women's patterns are designed for the larger, more fully mature figure; about 1.65m to 1.68m without shoes.

Size	38	40	42	44	46	48	50	
Bust	107	112	117	122	127	132	137	cm
Waist	89	94	99	105	112	118	124	cm
Hip	112	117	122	127	132	137	142	cm
Back Waist Length	44	44	44.5	45	45	45.5	46	cm

HALF SIZE

Half Size patterns are for a fully developed figure with a short backwaist length. Waist and hip are larger in proportion to bust than other figure types; about 1.57m to 1.60m without shoes.

Size	10½	12½	14½	16½	18½	20½	22½	24½	
Bust	84	89	94	99	104	109	114	119	cm
Waist	69	74	79	84	89	96	102	108	cm
Hip	89	94	99	104	109	116	122	128	cm
Back Waist Length	38	39	39.5	40	40.5	40.5	41	41.5	cm

CHILDREN'S MEASUREMENTS

Measure around the breast, but not too snugly. Toddler patterns are designed for a figure between that of a baby and child.

TODDLERS'

Size	½	1	2	3	4	
Breast	48	51	53	56	58	cm
Waist	48	50	51	52	53	cm
Approx. Height	71	79	87	94	102	cm
Finished Dress Length	35.5	38	40.5	43	46	cm

CHILDREN'S

Size	1	2	3	4	5	6	6x	
Breast	51	53	56	58	61	64	65	cm
Waist	50	51	52	53	55	56	57	cm
Hip				61	64	66	67	cm
Back Waist Length	21	22	23	24	25.5	27	27.5	cm
Approx. Height	79	87	94	102	109	117	122	cm
Finished Dress Length	43	46	48	51	56	61	64	cm

GIRLS'

Girls' patterns are designed for the girl who has not yet begun to mature. See chart below for approximate heights without shoes.

Size	7	8	10	12	14	
Bust	66	69	73	76	81	cm
Waist	58	60	62	65	67	cm
Hip	69	71	76	81	87	cm
Back Waist Length	29.5	31	32.5	34.5	36	cm
Approx. Height	127	132	142	149	155	cm
Finished Dress Length	66	69	74	79	84	cm

BOYS' AND TEEN-BOYS'

These size ranges are for growing boys and young men who have not yet reached full adult stature.

BOYS'				TEEN BOYS'					
Size	7	8	10	12	14	16	18	20	
Chest	66	69	71	76	81	85	89	93	cm
Waist	58	61	64	66	69	71	74	76	cm
Hip (Seat)	69	71	75	79	83	87	90	94	cm
Neckband	30	31	32	33	34.5	35.5	37	38	cm
Approx. Height	122	127	137	147	155	163	168	173	cm

NOTE: For Toddlers' and Little Boys (1 to 6)—See Toddlers' and Children's cnarts.

MEN'S

Men's patterns are sized for men of average build about 1.78m without shoes.

Size	34	36	38	40	42	44	46	48	
Chest	87	92	97	102	107	112	117	122	cm
Waist	71	76	81	87	92	99	107	112	cm
Hip (Seat)	89	94	99	104	109	114	119	124	cm
Neckband	35.5	37	38	39.5	40.5	42	43	44.5	cm
Shirt Sleeve	81	81	84	84	87	87	89	89	cm

METRIC EQUIVALENCY CHART

CONVERTING INCHES TO CENTIMETERS
AND YARDS TO METERS

This chart gives the standard equivalents
as approved by the Pattern Fashion Industry.

mm—millimeters   cm—centimeters   m—meters

CHANGING INCHES TO MILLIMETERS AND CENTIMETERS
(Slightly rounded for your convenience.)

inches	mm	cm	inches	cm	inches	cm
1/8	3mm		7	18	29	73.5
1/4	6mm		8	20.5	30	76
3/8	10mm or	1cm	9	23	31	79
1/2	13mm or	1.3cm	10	25.5	32	81.5
5/8	15mm or	1.5cm	11	28	33	84
3/4	20mm or	2cm	12	30.5	34	86.5
7/8	22mm or	2.2cm	13	33	35	89
1	25mm or	2.5cm	14	35.5	36	91.5
1-1/4	32mm or	3.2cm	15	38	37	94
1-1/2	38mm or	3.8cm	16	40.5	38	96.5
1-3/4	45mm or	4.5cm	17	43	39	99
2	50mm or	5cm	18	46	40	101.5
2-1/2	65mm or	6.5cm	19	48.5	41	104
3	75mm or	7.5cm	20	51	42	106.5
3-1/2	90mm or	9cm	21	53.5	43	109
4	100mm or	10cm	22	56	44	112
4-1/2	115mm or	11.5cm	23	58.5	45	114.5
5	125mm or	12.5cm	24	61	46	117
5-1/2	140mm or	14cm	25	63.5	47	119.5
6	150mm or	15cm	26	66	48	122
			27	68.5	49	124.5
			28	71	50	127

YARDS TO METERS

(Slightly rounded for your convenience.)

Yardage

Yd	m	Yd	m	Yd	m	Yd	m	Yd	m	Yd	m	Yd	m	Yd	m
1/8	0.15	1/4	0.25	3/8	0.35	1/2	0.50	5/8	0.60	3/4	0.70	7/8	0.80	1	0.95
1-1/8	1.05	1-1/4	1.15	1-3/8	1.30	1-1/2	1.40	1-5/8	1.50	1-3/4	1.60	1-7/8	1.75	2	1.85
2-1/8	1.95	2-1/4	2.10	2-3/8	2.20	2-1/2	2.30	2-5/8	2.40	2-3/4	2.55	2-7/8	2.65	3	2.75
3-1/8	2.90	3-1/4	3.00	3-3/8	3.10	3-1/2	3.20	3-5/8	3.35	3-3/4	3.45	3-7/8	3.55	4	3.70
4-1/8	3.80	4-1/4	3.90	4-3/8	4.00	4-1/2	4.15	4-5/8	4.25	4-3/4	4.35	4-7/8	4.50	5	4.60
5-1/8	4.70	5-1/4	4.80	5-3/8	4.95	5-1/2	5.05	5-5/8	5.15	5-3/4	5.30	5-7/8	5.40	6	5.50
6-1/8	5.60	6-1/4	5.75	6-3/8	5.85	6-1/2	5.95	6-5/8	6.10	6-3/4	6.20	6-7/8	6.30	7	6.40
7-1/8	6.55	7-1/4	6.65	7-3/8	6.75	7-1/2	6.90	7-5/8	7.00	7-3/4	7.10	7-7/8	7.20	8	7.35
8-1/8	7.45	8-1/4	7.55	8-3/8	7.70	8-1/2	7.80	8-5/8	7.90	8-3/4	8.00	8-7/8	8.15	9	8.25
9-1/8	8.35	9-1/4	8.50	9-3/8	8.60	9-1/2	8.70	9-5/8	8.80	9-3/4	8.95	9-7/8	9.05	10	9.15

AVAILABLE FABRIC WIDTHS

25"	65 cm	42"	107 cm	54"/56"	140 cm
27"	70 cm	44"/45"	115 cm	58"/60"	150 cm
35"	90 cm	48"	122 cm	68"/70"	175 cm
39"	100 cm	50"	127 cm	72"	180 cm

AVAILABLE ZIPPER LENGTHS

4"	10 cm	8"	20 cm	14"	35 cm	22"	55 cm
5"	12 cm	9"	22 cm	16"	40 cm	24"	60 cm
6"	15 cm	10"	25 cm	18"	45 cm	26"	65 cm
7"	18 cm	12"	30 cm	20"	50 cm	28"	70 cm

GUIDE TO INTERFACING FABRICS

The following chart provides information on interfacings available under trade names. It also includes the width, type of interfacing, fiber content, care instructions (following the triangle system of the Textile Distributors Association—see chart in Chapter Four) and the color in which each type is available.

FOR USE WITH LIGHT-TO-MEDIUM-WEIGHT FABRICS

Name	Company	Width	Type	Description	Fiber Content	Care	Color
Acro	Armo	25"	woven	lightweight washable hair canvas	70% rayon/ 21% polyester/ 9% goathair	4—Machine Wash Warm, Delicate Cycle, Tumble Dry Low, Use Cool Iron	natural
Armo-Press	Armo	22" 45"	woven	lightweight permanent press interfacing	50% polyester/ 50% rayon	3—Machine Wash Warm, Tumble Dry, Remove Promptly	white, black
Easy Shaper	Stacy	24"/25"	non-woven	lightweight & suit-weight stretchable fusible interfacing	70% nylon/ 20% polyester/ 10% rayon	1—Machine Wash Warm	white, charcoal
Featherweight All-Bias Polyester	Pellon	25"	non-woven	super soft all-purpose interfacing	100% polyester	1—Machine Wash Warm	white, grey
Finolight	Armo	25"	woven	lightweight quality hair canvas	46% wool/ 40% cotton/ 14% goathair	6—Hand Wash Separately, Use Cool Iron	natural
Formite	Armo	25"	woven	sheer canvas interfacing	50% rayon/ 50% cotton	7—Dry Clean Only	natural, black, white

196

Name	Brand	Width	Type	Use	Fiber Content	Care	Color
Fusible Formite	Armo	23"	woven fusible	lightweight interfacing applied with an iron	50% rayon/50% cotton	4—Machine Wash Warm, Delicate Cycle, Tumble Dry Low, Use Cool Iron	natural, white
Fusible P-91	Armo	19" 38"	woven fusible	sheer interfacing applied with an iron, for detail areas	100% cotton	4—Machine Wash Warm, Delicate Cycle, Tumble Dry Low	black, white
Interlon Bias Featherweight	Stacy	25" 37"	non-woven	for fabrics cut on the bias or those requiring give or stretch—lightweight fabrics	100% polyester	1—Machine Wash Warm	white
Interlon Bias Lightweight	Stacy	25"	non-woven	for fabrics cut on the bias or those requiring give or stretch—medium-weight fabrics	100% polyester	1—Machine Wash Warm	white, black
Interlon Durable Press	Stacy	25"	non-woven	for light and medium-weight durable press	100% polyester	1—Machine Wash Warm	white, black
Interlon (light)	Stacy	25" 37"	non-woven	for lightweight fabrics	75% rayon/25% nylon	1—Machine Wash Warm	white, black
Interlon (regular)	Stacy	25" 37"	non-woven	for medium-weight	75% rayon/25% nylon	1—Machine Wash Warm	white, black
Lightweight All-Bias Polyester	Pellon	25" 37"	non-woven	firmer support for jackets, coats,	100% polyester	1—Machine Wash Warm	white, grey

Name	Company	Width	Type	Uses	Fiber Content	Care	Color
Lightweight (regular)	Pellon	25" 37"	non-woven	light, crisp, stable interfacing	30% nylon/ 70% rayon	1—Machine Wash Warm	white, black
Shape-Flex Dual Purpose	Stacy	18"	fusible woven	for natural or synthetic fibers	100% cotton	1—Machine Wash Warm	white, black
Shape-Flex Non-woven	Stacy	18"	non-woven fusible	for small areas, where crispness is desired—home decorating	100% rayon	1—Machine Wash Warm	white, black
Siri	Armo	44" 45"	woven	soft or firm finish lightweight interfacing	100% spun viscose rayon	4—Machine Wash Warm, Delicate Cycle, Tumble Dry Low, Use Cool Iron	white, black
Sta-Shape #50	Stacy	25"	canvas woven	medium-weight fabrics	56% rayon/ 44% cotton	4—Machine Wash Warm,	white, black, natural
Sta-Shape Durable Press	Stacy	22" 23"	woven	all permanent press	50% polyester/ 50% rayon	3—Machine Wash Warm, Tumble Dry, Remove Promptly	white, black
Veriform Durable Press	Stacy	45"	woven	all durable press fabrics and polyester, as an underlining or interfacing	50% polyester/ 50% rayon	3—Machine Wash Warm, Tumble Dry, Remove Promptly	white, black
Worsted Canvas	Stacy	25"	canvas woven	for lightweight luxury fabrics	50% rayon/ 39% cotton/ 11% wool	7—Dry Clean Only	natural

198

FOR USE WITH MEDIUM-TO-HEAVY-WEIGHT FABRICS

Name	Company	Width	Type	Uses	Fiber Content	Care	Color
Bravo Canvas	Stacy	25"	woven	for tailoring medium-weight fabrics	20% wool/ 40% rayon/ 40% polyester	7—Dry Clean Only	natural, white
Bravo Set	Stacy	25"	woven	for tailoring medium-weight washables	52% polyester/ 40% viscose rayon/8% wool	1—Machine Wash Warm	eggshell
Fino	Armo	25"	woven	quality hair canvas	92% wool/ 8% goathair	6—Hand Wash Separately, Use Cool Iron	natural
Fino/white	Armo	25"	woven	quality hair canvas	54% cotton/ 46% wool	6—Hand Wash Separately, Use Cool Iron	white
Fusible Acro	Armo	25"	woven	washable hair canvas applied with an iron	70% rayon/ 21% polyester/ 9% goathair	4—Machine Wash Warm, Delicate Cycle, Tumble Dry Low, Use Cool Iron	natural
Hair Canvas #77	Stacy	25"	woven	for heavy suitings and coatings	66% cotton/ 21% rayon/ 13% goathair	7—Dry Clean Only	natural
Hair Canvas #88	Stacy	25"	canvas woven	heavy-weight suitings and coatings	59% cotton/ 23% rayon/ 18% goathair	7—Dry Clean Only	natural
Heavy-Weight (regular)	Pellon	25" 37"	non-woven	very stiff, firm support for craft and home decorating	40% rayon/ 60% nylon	1—Machine Wash Warm	white, black

FOR USE WITH MEDIUM-TO-HEAVY-WEIGHT FABRICS *(Continued)*

Name	Company	Width	Type	Uses	Fiber Content	Care	Color
Interlon (heavy)	Stacy	25"	non-woven fusible	heavyweight suitings and coatings	70% rayon/ 30% nylon	1–Machine Wash Warm	white, black
Medium-weight (regular)	Pellon	25" 37"	non-woven	firm shape for accessory and craft items	70% rayon/ 30% nylon	1–Machine Wash Warm	white, black
P-17	Armo	25"	woven	economical hair canvas	55% cotton/ 20% rayon/ 20% goathair/ 5% wool	7–Dry Clean Only	natural
P-26	Armo	25"	woven	economical hair canvas	60% cotton/ 30% rayon/ 10% goathair	7–Dry Clean Only	natural
P-27	Armo	25"	woven	economical crisp hair canvas	59% cotton/ 31% rayon/ 10% goathair	7–Dry Clean Only	natural
Polyester Fleece	Pellon	40"	non-woven	fluffy interfacing for warmth, padding and trapunto effects	100% polyester	1–Machine Wash Warm	white
Shape-Flex Suit Shape	Stacy	22"	woven fusible	for tailoring men's and women's garments in knits and wovens	60% cotton/ 40% rayon	1–Machine Wash Warm	white, black

Name	Brand	Width	Construction	Description	Fiber Content	Care	Color
Siri	Armo	44"/45"	woven	soft or firm finish lightweight interfacing	100% spun viscose rayon	4–Machine Wash Warm, Delicate Cycle, Tumble Dry Low, Use Cool Iron	white, black
Thermolan Multi-Purpose Fleece	Stacy	45"	non-woven fleece	for use as an interlining or fluffy interfacing	100% polyester	1–Machine Wash Warm	white
Ti-Rite	Armo	25"	woven	washable tie interfacing for warmth, padding	60% polyester/40% rayon	4–Machine Wash Warm, Delicate Cycle, Tumble Dry Low, Use Cool Iron	natural
Tie-Shape Multi-Purpose Canvas	Stacy	25"	woven	interfacing for polyester knits, fine wools, for shaping ties	50% polyester/50% rayon	1–Machine Wash Warm	eggshell
Worsted/Canvas	Stacy	25"	woven canvas	for tailoring luxury fabrics of medium weight	85% wool/15% hair	7–Dry Clean Only	natural
Worsted/Canvas	Stacy	25"	woven canvas	for tailoring luxury fabrics of medium weight	50% wool/50% rayon	7–Dry Clean Only	white

CHOOSING FABRICS FOR LINING AND UNDERLINING

Lining and underlining fabrics are an important purchase to consider when planning to construct a garment. A lining fabric is used to cover the raw edges and wrong sides of a garment or an item of home furnishings such as draperies. A lining supports the outer fabric and prevents unnecessary wear. In the case of curtains or draperies, a lining also prevents the fabric from fading due to sunlight.

Underlining performs a function similar to lining in that it adds extra body and supports the garment. Underlining is cut like the outer fabric and attached to each piece of the garment before any seams are sewn.

Interlining is a fabric added to a lining fabric for increased warmth and insulation.

Choosing the proper lining or underlining depends on coordinating it with the weight of the outer fabric and the effect desired. It is also important to consider the fiber content and choose a fabric that is compatible with the outer fabric where care is concerned. The following chart is designed to help you make these buying decisions.

Fabric Name (Trade Name Owner)	Fiber Content	Construction	Weight	Color	Use
Armo-Wool (Armo)	100% wool	basket weave	medium	black, white	Interlining for added warmth in tailored, dry cleanable garment.
batiste	100% cotton or blends of cotton and synthetic fibers	plain weave	light	range of colors	Usually as an underlining for soft, fluid garments.
brocade	silk or synthetic fibers	jacquard-patterned weave	medium to heavy	range of colors	Usually used as a lining for fur coats and evening coats.
Butterfly (Stacy)	100% polyester	plain weave	light	range of colors	Lining for light to medium-weight fabric. Underlining in lightweight fabrics.
Casino Plus (Skinner)	100% polyester	plain weave	light	range of colors	Underlining for most fabric weights. Lining for lightweight garments.
Ciao (Armo)	100% polyester	plain weave	medium	range of colors	Underlining and lining for all weights for a soft silhouette.

Fabric	Fiber content	Weave	Weight	Color	Use
crepe	usually acetate, rayon or polyester	plain weave	light to medium	range of colors	Lining and/or underlining in most fabric weights, especially when soft look is desired. Lining for suits, coats, and jackets.
crepe-back satin	rayon, acetate or other synthetic fibers	usually plain weave	heavy	range of colors	Lining for coats, suits, and dresses of medium-weight fabrics.
Dura Press (Stacy)	50% rayon/50% polyester	plain weave	light	white, black	Underlining for easycare fabrics.
Earl-Glo faille (Erlanger-Blumgart)	100% acetate	plain weave	medium	range of colors	Lining for medium-weight jackets, coats, and vests.
Earl-Glo quilted nylon (Erlanger-Blumgart)	100% nylon	plain weave, quilted	medium to heavy	range of colors	Lining for additional warmth.
Earl-Glo woven stretch nylon (Erlanger-Blumgart)	100% nylon	plain weave	medium	range of colors	Underlining or lining for knit or stretch fabrics.
Keynote Plus (Burlington)	65% polyester/35% cotton	plain weave	light	range of colors	Lining or underlining, especially for permanent press fabrics.
lawn	cotton or blends of cotton and synthetic fibers	plain weave	light	range of colors	Lining or underlining in lightweight fabrics.
Loomgold satin with Milium (Skinner)	100% acetate with lacquer on back for insulation	satin weave	medium	range of colors	Lining, especially when warmth is desired in a coat.
marquisette	synthetic fibers or blends; occasionally silk	netted	light	range of colors	Underlining to add body to chiffons and other sheer fabrics.
Marvelaire (Erlanger-Blumgart)	100% polyester	plain weave	light	range of colors	Lining or underlining for all fabric weights in dresses, suits, and coats.

Fabric Name (Trade Name Owner)	Fiber Content	Construction	Weight	Color	Use
Milium (Deering Milliken)	usually acetate with lacquer on back for insulation	usually satin weave	medium to heavy	range of colors	Combination of lining and inter-lining for coats and suits.
muslin	100% cotton; occasionally a blend of cotton and synthetic fibers	plain weave	medium	off-white, natural	Underlining for suits, coats, and dresses.
organdy	cotton, silk, or synthetic fabrics	plain weave	light	range of colors	Delicate stiff underlining for light-weight definition or silhouette.
Poly Si Bonne (Armo)	65% rayon/ 35% polyester	plain weave	light	range of colors	Lining or underlining garments of all weights.
Sheath Lining	synthetic fibers	plain weave	light	range of colors	Lining or underling for all fabric weights except sheers.
Siri (Armo)	100% rayon	plain weave	medium	range of colors	Underlining for all fabric weights.
Sunback Satin (Skinner)	60% acetate face, 28% rayon/ 12% acrylic	satin weave with napped back	heavy	range of colors	Combination lining and inter-lining for suits and coats.
taffeta	rayon or other man-made fibers or silk	plain weave	medium	range of colors	Lining for dresses, suits, and coats of medium to heavyweight fabrics.
Ultressa (Burlington)	100% polyester	twill weave	light	range of colors and prints	Lightweight lining for dresses, suits, and coats.
Veriform Basic Liner (Stacy)	53% cotton/ 47% rayon	plain weave	medium	black, white	All-purpose underlining.

Index

The index which follows is designed to guide you through the early chapters of this book and the appendices. The dictionary section which is, of course, in alphabetical order, is not indexed.